A Route for the Overland Stage

Colonel James H. Simpson shown during his Civil War service as an officer of the Fourth New Jersey infantry.

A ROUTE

FOR THE

OVERLAND STAGE

JAMES H. SIMPSON'S 1859 TRAIL
ACROSS THE GREAT BASIN

JESSE G. PETERSEN

Foreword by David L. Bigler

Utah State University Press
Logan, Utah

Utah State University Press
Logan, Utah 84322-7800
www.usu.edu/usupress

Manufactured in the United States of America
Printed on recycled, acid-free paper

ISBN: 978-0-87421-693-6 (paper)
ISBN: 978-0-87421-694-3 (e-book)

Library of Congress Cataloging-in-Publication Data

Petersen, Jesse G.
  A route for the overland stage : James H. Simpson's 1859 trail across the Great Basin / Jesse G. Petersen ; foreword by David L. Bigler.
      p. cm.
  Includes bibliographical references and index.
ISBN 978-0-87421-693-6 (pbk. : alk. paper)
  1. Simpson, J. H. (James Hervey), 1813-1883–Travel–Great Basin. 2. Great Basin–Discovery and exploration. 3. Great Basin–Surveys. 4. Great Basin–Geography. 5. Scientific expeditions–Great Basin–History–19th century. I. Title.
  F789.P47 2008
  917.904'4092–dc22

                              2007050285

Contents

Acknowledgments

THE RESEARCH FOR this work extended over a period of nearly ten years and was assisted by more people than can be mentioned. Nevertheless, I do feel compelled to acknowledge the contribution of several whose help and encouragement made it possible for me to turn my interest in Simpson's trail into a book.

First of all, and probably most important, is John Alley, the executive editor of the Utah State University Press, who decided to take a chance on a novice writer and publish this book.

Joe Nardone, the indefatigable researcher of the Pony Express Trail, let me pester him with questions about locations of the route and its stations.

James O'Neil Hall, who now lives in St. George, Utah, came to my house several years ago to discuss some aspects of the Lincoln Highway in Tooele County. Since that day, he has accompanied me on several field trips and has shared with me the contents of numerous emigrant journals, which show that Simpson's route was traveled by a surprisingly large number of emigrants.

Gregory Franzwa, the widely read author of more trails-related books than anyone that I know of, took pity on me and helped me with the proper use of the English language.

Marie Irvine, who answered my many questions about Howard Egan's explorations of western Utah and central Nevada, brought the invaluable journal of William Lee to my attention.

Mark Trotter, the manager of Camp Floyd State Park, provided me with information relating to the layout of the old army post.

Geno Oliver of Reno, who has spent many years researching and traveling the old trails and roads of Nevada, helped me by going over the Nevada portion of an early version of my manuscript.

Will Bagley brought to my attention the post-expedition letter from General Johnston to Simpson, which told him to go easy on promoting the new route as an emigrant trail.

Evelyn Eggenhofer Herman most generously allowed the use of the drawings of the army wagons that appeared in her father's book, *Wagons, Mules, and Men.*

The courteous and helpful staff at the Utah State Historical Society, provided me with copies of the William Lee journal and the H. V. A. Von Beckh and John J. Young watercolors.

My father-in-law, Louis Dunyon, showed me the trail across the western ridge of Keg Mountain, helped me find Brewer's Spring, and introduced me to GPS technology.

I need also to thank Bill Henroid, who lives in Pleasant Valley; Wes Parsons, whose ranch is in the mouth of Simpson Park Canyon; James and Vera Baumann of Eureka, Nevada; and David and Molly Stanley of the Stanley Horse Ranch in Mason Valley. All of them allowed me to spend some time exploring their private property.

Most of all, I need to say thanks to my wife and partner, Nancy Dunyon Petersen, who, although she has no real interest in old trails and army expeditions, nevertheless endured countless dusty and rocky miles, spent many long hours waiting for me to return from hikes along the trail, and never failed to encourage me to continue my research and travel. This book is dedicated to her.

Foreword by David L. Bigler

At the end of the Utah War in June 1858, General Albert S. Johnston selected Cedar Valley to establish a military post for some twenty-four hundred officers and men of the US Army's Utah Expedition. The location west of Utah Lake at present Fairfield, Utah, met the immediate needs of his command for grass for its animals and remoteness from population centers to avoid clashes between his soldiers and settlers of the territory ruled by Brigham Young.

At the same time, Johnston knew that the location for his new post, named Camp Floyd, was less than ideal when it came to its mission to support enforcement of federal law in the defiant territory. For one thing, it was some forty miles from the capital at Salt Lake City. For another, the same geographical formations that had allowed the territorial militia to block his advance the year before and force him to spend the winter of 1857–58 at Fort Bridger made his force vulnerable in the event of renewed hostilities. The winding Echo Canyon corridor through the Wasatch Mountains ruled his line of communications on the east. And the way to northern California from Camp Floyd led through Salt Lake Valley and around the north end of Great Salt Lake, two hundred miles out of the way.

To make his army effective in relation to its duties, Johnston had to open a supply line on the east that bypassed the Mormon Trail from Fort Bridger and the easily fortified Echo Canyon portal to Salt Lake Valley. In addition, he needed to make a wagon road to northern California that eliminated the northern loop around the Great Salt Lake. Instead, it should run due west from Camp Floyd on the south side of that briny body to meet the California Trail near Genoa in today's western Nevada.

Johnston had the right man to fill these requisites in Captain James H. Simpson of the US Army's elite Corps of Topographical Engineers, who arrived at Camp Floyd in July 1858. The forty-five-year-old engineer first surveyed a new line of supply to the east that ran up Provo Canyon to Parleys Park and down the Weber River to present Coalville. From there, it continued up Chalk Creek to bypass Echo Canyon on the south. During the 1857 conflict, Utah Militia General Hiram B. Clawson had inspected this avenue to find out if it offered a way for the US Army to flank Echo Canyon defenses. He reported that it did not, without extensive roadwork.

Also that fall, a preliminary reconnaissance of the proposed route west motivated the energetic engineer to expand the wagon road survey to Genoa. With the approval of Secretary of War John B. Floyd and Johnston, Simpson set his sights on a vast area of the American West from which no water flows to any ocean. He planned to conduct the first recorded exploration directly across the heart of the Great Basin, a region large enough to encompass New England, New York, Pennsylvania, and Ohio.

In width, the area of high-altitude desert and north-south running mountain ranges extends from central Utah's Wasatch Range to the crest of the Sierra Nevada. From north to south, it stretches more than eight hundred miles from Oregon to the Baja Peninsula in Mexico. In between, its triangular-shaped rim encloses most of Nevada and parts of Utah, California, Idaho, and Oregon. As a region of interior drainage, its waters flow into briny bodies, such as the Great Salt Lake and Pyramid Lake, and desert flats, never into the sea. Its longest perennial rivers are the Bear, which flows into Great Salt Lake, and the Humboldt, followed by the California Trail and today's Interstate 80.

On May 2, 1859, the topographical engineer headed into this virtually unknown region "to explore the country between [Camp Floyd] and Carson River, at the east foot of the Sierra Nevada, for a new and direct route to California." The sixty-four members of his expedition included an artist, geologist, wheelwright, blacksmith, teamsters, twenty soldiers, twelve six-mule wagons, scientific apparatus, and one of Nevada's first citizens. In 1851, John Reese had purchased Genoa, the state's earliest settlement, when it was still a trading post named Mormon Station on the Carson Trail's Carson River route. Now he served, but not always to the captain's satisfaction, as Simpson's guide.

Over the next three months, Simpson traveled over eleven hundred miles across part of central Utah and virtually all of Nevada. His westbound exploration covered 564 miles to Genoa, while his more southern return route to Camp Floyd added only eight more to this number. Either way would shorten travel from Salt Lake City to Genoa along the Humboldt River by more than two hundred miles. His report also estimated the cost to open a wagon road and included the geology, plant and animal life, and Native American tribes of the Great Basin, among other things.

As Simpson was the right one to complete this significant study and report, Jesse G. Petersen of Tooele, Utah, has proved the right man to locate his trails and evaluate his major contribution to western expansion. Since 1999, the retired police chief of Tooele, Utah, has traveled some thirty thousand miles by SUV and an estimated two hundred eighty miles on foot. In his personalized narrative and seventy-two maps he describes his search and pinpoints Simpson's routes and campsites to within a few yards.

Petersen brings to his book a lifelong interest in history and overland avenues of travel and transportation. A charter member of the Lincoln Highway Association's Utah Chapter, in 1997 he produced the first study of the first transcontinental highway across the state, *The Lincoln Highway in Utah*, now in its fourth edition. In 2003, he and Gregory M. Franzwa co-authored *Lincoln Highway: Utah*. When he heard it said that the coast-to-coast thoroughfare followed Simpson's path across the Great Basin, he looked into it and found there was little information on the topographical engineer's exact routes to back up that claim. Typically, Petersen decided to find out for himself.

The product of his search manifests his character and background on every page. The quality of his scholarship reflects his degrees from Brigham Young University and the University of Utah. His experience in law enforcement can be seen in his dedication to accuracy and attention to evidence on the ground. His narrative is richly detailed, and incorporates interesting and accurate information on the region's history as it goes along. His writing is clear, straightforward, and trustworthy. His work makes it possible for a novice to go with Simpson across what has been called the loneliest region in America without losing the trail more than a stone's throw on either side.

In normal times, Simpson's expedition would have won the acclaim Americans normally bestowed on western explorers, such as John C. Frémont, but as he prepared his detailed report, the nation was torn by the Civil War. General Johnston, who ordered the exploration, lost his life leading a Confederate army in 1862. Not until 1876 did the War Department carry out his instructions while he was serving as Utah Department commander, and order the publication of Simpson's report.

Meanwhile, if Washington looked the other way for over ten years, Simpson's exploit won the immediate attention of the nation's emigrants and entrepreneurs. Within a year, westering American families had worn a new wagon road across the central basin. In 1860, trim young men aboard fast horses began to carry mail between Sacramento and St. Joseph, Missouri, on Simpson's route across the vast expanses of the Great Basin. The short-lived Pony Express was followed by the Pacific telegraph, Overland Stage, Lincoln Highway, and US 50, known today as "the loneliest highway in America." All followed the corridor Simpson opened in 1859.

As further recognition of James Hervey Simpson's contribution to the history of the Great Basin and western exploration, Jesse Petersen's volume makes an excellent companion to the topographical engineer's report, which was reprinted in 1983 as *Report of Explorations Across The Great Basin In 1859*, with a foreword by Steven D. Zink.

One

Introduction

DURING THE SUMMER of 1859, Captain James Simpson of the US Army's Corps of Topographical Engineers led an expedition of exploration from Camp Floyd to Genoa. Camp Floyd was an army post in Cedar Valley, about forty miles southwest of Great Salt Lake City. Genoa was a small settlement located at the eastern foot of the Sierra Nevada mountains. The mission of the expedition was to find a practical route for wagons through the central part of Utah and Nevada. If such a route could be found, it was believed that it would shorten the distance between Salt Lake City and California by as much as two hundred miles. The members of the Simpson expedition were not the first to travel through this region of the American West. During the preceding three decades, a number of fur trappers, explorers, and emigrants had made their way across some sections of this area. Jedediah Smith, Joseph R. Walker, John Charles Frémont and Kit Carson, the Bidwell-Bartleson party, Lansford Hastings and James Clyman, the Donner-Reed party, Capt. E. G. Beckwith, O. B. Huntington, George Washington Bean, Orrin Porter Rockwell, and Howard Egan had all traveled through different sections of this territory. These travelers had cut across various portions of the region, traveling in various directions, but none of them had taken the shortest possible route from east-to-west or west-to-east, and it appears that Lansford Hastings was the only one who had taken any meaningful action toward the establishment of a wagon road through this central region.

Before the Simpson expedition, most of the travelers who intended to make the journey from Salt Lake City to California followed a route that went around the northern end of the Great Salt Lake and joined the California Trail near City of Rocks, near the Utah-Idaho border. A smaller number of California-bound travelers headed south by way of the Mormon Corridor, now the route of Interstate 15, and got onto the Old Spanish Trail near present-day Cedar City. It is true that the relatively few travelers who followed the Hastings Road did take a more central route, but about a quarter of the way across present-day Nevada, near the southern tip of the Ruby Mountains, this road turned to the north along Huntington Creek and the South Fork of the Humboldt River, and joined the California Trail not far from the city of Elko. None of these wagon routes traveled through the area that the Simpson expedition intended to explore.

It had always been apparent that a road through this central area could save many miles and perhaps a great deal of time, but until this time, no one had attempted to take wagons across the entire distance. In 1854, Col. Edward Steptoe of the US Army had given it some serious consideration. Steptoe was in the Salt Lake City area with a force of about three hundred soldiers, and wanted to find the best way to get them to California. In an effort to locate a new and shorter route, he engaged two different groups of men to make scouting trips into the desert. Oliver B. Huntington was in charge of the first group, which included himself, his nephew, an Indian named Natsab, John Reese (whose home at the time was in Carson Valley and who would later become Simpson's guide), and two of Reese's friends. Somewhere between Salt Lake City and the Great Salt Lake they were joined by eleven soldiers who had recently deserted from Steptoe's command. Huntington's party traveled all the way to Carson Valley, most of the time following a trail that had been made earlier that year by Captain E. G. Beckwith of the army's Topographical Corps, who was engaged in a railroad survey. When Huntington and his nephew returned to Salt Lake City, they reported to Steptoe, telling him they had found a practical route that would save about two hundred miles, and they would be willing to act as guides. However, when the time came to leave for California, Huntington became evasive and Steptoe decided he was not to be trusted.[1] After Steptoe became convinced that he could not depend on Huntington's help, he obtained the services of a second group, the leader of which was Orrin Porter Rockwell. Another member of this group was George Washington Bean, who later acted as Capt. Simpson's guide during a relatively short trip into Utah's West Desert in late 1858. The Rockwell-Bean group traveled about eighty miles into the desert and when they returned, they told Steptoe that the country was not fit for wagon travel. At this, Steptoe gave up on any further attempts to find a central route and marched his troops to California by way of the north-of-the-lake and Humboldt River route.[2]

In 1855, a noted Mormon explorer named Howard Egan, and a few companions mounted on mules, made a speedy trip across this central area. Leaving from Salt Lake City, they made it to Sacramento in ten days. But like the Huntington party, they followed the Beckwith Trail to the Humboldt River near Lassen Meadows, then followed the California Trail to Sacramento.[3]

Captain Simpson first became involved in the concept of a central route in the fall of 1858, when he received orders from his commanding officer, Gen. Albert Sidney Johnston, to lead an expedition of a few days' duration into Utah's western desert. As a result of this short trip, Simpson became interested in further exploration of this area, and in January 1859, he submitted a proposal to the War Department, requesting permission to make a much more extensive expedition. Johnston endorsed this proposal and

forwarded it up the chain of command. In April, orders came down from army headquarters, assigning Simpson to lead an expedition that would travel from Camp Floyd to Genoa. The expedition would turn around when it reached Genoa, because of the existence of serviceable roads between there and San Francisco.

Throughout the expedition that followed, Simpson kept a daily journal, and from this he compiled an extensive report to Congress. The title of this document was *Report of Explorations across the Great Basin of the Territory of Utah for a Direct Wagon Route from Camp Floyd to Genoa, in Carson Valley, in 1859*. Simpson completed his report within a couple of years after the expedition, but primarily due to the onset of the Civil War, it was not published until 1876. The report was much more than a simple recitation of the events of the expedition. The first major section was devoted to a history of previous explorations into the region of the Great Basin, including the journeys of Fathers Domínguez and Escalante, Father Garcés, Jim Bridger, Joseph Walker, John Charles Frémont, Capt. Howard Stansbury, and Capt. E. G. Beckwith. Taking up thirteen pages of the report, this section shows that Simpson had done his homework, and had familiarized himself with the available information relating to previous explorations of the country he was about to enter.

The next ninety-two pages of the report consist of Simpson's account of each day's journey, and a description of the country through which they traveled. Simpson did not limit himself to simply reporting the basic facts about where they went and when they got there. He described the country in some detail, talking about geographical features and the existence, or lack of, water and forage. Some of Simpson's entries reflected his enthusiasm and apparent enjoyment of what he was doing. An example of this was written on May 26 as the expedition left a campsite in Central Nevada's Monitor Valley.

The crack of the whip, the "gee! Get up!" of the teamsters, the merry laugh, the sudden shout from the exuberance of spirits, the clinking of armor, the long array of civil, military, and economic personnel, in due order, moving with hope to our destined end, coupled with the bright, bracing morning, and, at times, twittering of birds, make our morning departure from camp very pleasing.[4]

Following the description of the journey, the report contains 346 pages, which include twenty different subsections on such subjects as astronomical observations, tables of distances, geological information, descriptions and drawings of indigenous wildlife, and descriptions of the native inhabitants of the area.

My interest in the Simpson expedition was a result of my interest in the history of the Lincoln Highway. I was attending the Lincoln Highway Association's 1996 conference in Reno, Nevada, when one of the presenters mentioned that the historic highway had followed much of the route that James Simpson had opened through Nevada in 1859. I had been vaguely aware of the Simpson expedition for some time, but this comment stirred my interest. A short time later, I obtained a used copy of the Simpson report and started studying it. I soon found that a general concept of the location of the Simpson route could be gathered from the report, but it proved to be quite difficult to translate the exact details of the route onto modern maps. After reading the report, I started looking for other books that included information about the expedition. It did not take long to discover that although the general route of Simpson's expedition seemed to be fairly well known, specifics were vague. And the more I learned about it, the more I wanted to figure out exactly where the expedition had gone.

My next step was to obtain a number of United States Geological Survey (USGS) 30 × 60 minute series maps. Then, working from Simpson's descriptions of his travels, I started drawing lines on the map which showed where I thought the trail might have been. After doing this for a while, I decided that I would have to get into the field and travel the route wherever I could. Since that time, I have traveled the entire route, driving wherever possible, and hiking many sections that are not accessible by automobile. Eventually I came to the decision that I would have to write something that would document what I had learned about the route.

When I first began writing about the expedition, my inclination was to simply report on what I had learned about the location of the route. Later on, I began to realize that how I reached these conclusions, and what I had done in attempting to verify them, were also important parts of the story. As a result, this work is comprised of two separate but mutually dependent and interrelated components. First is the information that relates to the location of the route and the campsites. The second component is a description of how I came up with this information and some of the experiences that I had during my travels along the trail. Today, much of the route can be easily driven in an ordinary family vehicle, and I have said very little about my travels along these sections. What I have described are my experiences in traveling the more difficult, off-pavement sections of the expedition's route.

I feel a need to mention to the reader that I am not attempting to offer irrefutable proof of anything. I am only attempting to share what I believe to be reasonable and logical conclusions about the most likely route, and the most likely locations for the campsites. These conclusions have been reached after studying Simpson's description of the terrain, after plotting his mileage figures onto modern maps, and after making many on-site visits to the areas involved.

In developing my conclusions about the route, I did not always get it right the first time. In fact, in many instances I failed to get it right the second and the third times. Tentative locations were moved around on the map up to a dozen or more times before I was finally satisfied. On several occasions, after studying the maps and making my best guess about the location of the route, I traveled to the area in question and found that the terrain would not have allowed the wagons to follow the route that I had projected. When this happened, it was back to the maps to look for other possibilities.

When I first started on this project, I had a presumption that much of the route would travel through roadless areas, and I would be seeing very little evidence of the trail. It soon became clear that the exact opposite is true. I found that a high percentage of Simpson's route soon evolved into well-traveled roads, and many of these are still in use today. Some sections of the route have been paved and are now a part of major highways, such as US Highway 50 and US 95. Some are well-maintained and frequently traveled dirt and gravel roads. There are also a number of sections that are now abandoned, but can still be driven in high-clearance vehicles. Other abandoned sections are not drivable, but are still recognizable as traces in the sagebrush. There are only a very few sections where no visible evidence of a trail can be found today.

The methods that I used in attempting to determine the route evolved over time. In the beginning, my only tools were the USGS 30 × 60 minute maps and a pair of dividers. Before my research was finished, I had learned how to use global positioning satellite (GPS) technology, and was making use of mapping systems and aerial photography programs that are available on the Internet. Microsoft Terraserver and Google Earth are the programs that I have used most extensively.

As briefly mentioned above, my first steps in looking for the trail were to open my copy of Simpson's report, spread a map on the table, carefully study the description of the route that had been traveled during a particular day, and attempt to plot that route on the map. I would look for features that might correspond with Simpson's descriptions, and would use dividers to measure the distances between tentatively identified points. I would repeat this process a number of times, all the while looking for alternate possibilities. By using this process, I was able to develop a general theory about the approximate location of the route, but was still a long way from determining its exact alignment.

Then I began taking trips to areas that contained sections of what I felt was the most likely route. My first long-distance trip was in the summer of 1999. This journey took me from Camp Floyd to Middlegate Station in central Nevada. As this was just a familiarization trip, I intentionally bypassed many of the hard-to-get-to places, including several mountain passes. I later returned to these places and found my way across them, either in my four-wheel-drive sports utility vehicle (SUV) or on foot. During the following

years, I made many more trips, most of which were for only one or two days, but a few lasted for nearly a week.

In 2002 I obtained a GPS receiver and began learning how to make use of this technology. This greatly improved my ability to get to the places that I had located on the maps. I could now be certain that I was where I wanted to be when I attempted to make on-site visits to certain sections of the trail.

A little later, I learned about the Terraserver website, and found that I could print copies of small sections of USGS 7.5-minute maps. By taping these sections together and using a set of dividers, I could make measurements that were much more accurate than the measurements I could get on the 30 × 60 minute maps. I also began studying aerial photos that are available on the Terraserver website. In 2005, I started using the Internet mapping program called Google Earth. This program is quite versatile, and when combined with reliable GPS data, makes it possible to obtain highly precise measurements between identified locations.

Included with Simpson's report to Congress was a map entitled "Map of Wagon Routes in Utah Territory Explored & Opened by Capt. J. H. Simpson Topl Engrs, U. S. A. Assisted by Lieuts. J. L. K. Smith and H. S. Putnam Topl. Engrs. U. S. A. and Mr. Henry Engelmann, in 1858–59." From the very beginning of my research, I was aware that this map existed, but it took me two years to obtain a copy of it, and this copy was about a quarter of the original size. It was helpful to have this copy, but it was so small that it was of limited value. After another two years I was fortunate enough to find and purchase a second copy of the reprint of the report, which included a large copy of the map. The text that appears on this map indicates that the actual drawing was done by a J. P. Mechlin, probably a draftsman or cartographer employed by the Topographical Corps, but there is no doubt that the map was drawn under Simpson's direct supervision. The original of this map is in the National Archives, in the Division of Cartographic Records. Obtaining a larger copy of Simpson's map helped a great deal, but I soon discovered that even with the large map, the scale limits its usefulness in determining

William Lee, an eighteen-year-old civilian member of the Simpson expedition.

exact details of the route. After all, it covers all of the area between the Green River in Wyoming and the city of Sacramento. For my purposes, the most helpful aspect of the map is that it shows the shape and general alignment of the various segments of the trail.

For several years, my only direct source of information about the Simpson route was his official report of the expedition. It was not until much later that I learned of the existence of a journal that had been written by eighteen-year-old William Lee, one of the expedition's civilian members. Simpson described Lee as one of his assistants, whose duties were that of a "chronometer-keeper" and "meteorological assistant."[5] In the orders that Simpson issued to the members of the expedition a few days prior to their departure was the following: "Messrs. Edward Jagiello and William Lee will assist the above named officers [Smith and Putnam] in the required observations in the mode which may be found most expedient."[6] The entries in his journal indicate

that Lee spent a lot of his time collecting specimens of plants and small animals, and assisting with the scientific observations. Lee probably owed his assignment to the fact that he was from a prominent family that had some influence with either Simpson or some other army officer.[7] Lee's journal begins on April 11, 1858, when he left Washington, DC. Two days later, he reported to Simpson in Cincinnati, and traveled with him to Fort Leavenworth. Lee was with the Army's Fourth Column when it left Fort Leavenworth on May 31 to march to Utah. He arrived at Camp Floyd on December 19.[8]

The country between Camp Floyd and Genoa is a striking example of what geologists and geographers call "basin and range." Throughout this extremely arid region, numerous mountain ranges run in a north-south direction, appearing at almost regularly spaced intervals. Between the mountains are flat-bottomed valleys covered with thick growths of sagebrush and greasewood. In many of the valleys, there are expanses of alkali flats, which support no vegetation whatsoever.

Simpson's objective was to find the shortest route across this country, but during virtually every step of the way, the expedition was faced with finding two things that invariably conflicted with traveling a straight line. First, they had to find water, and second, they had to find a way to get through, or around, the next mountain range. With a few notable exceptions, every bend in their trail was the result of their search for these two things.

Although the general route of Simpson's western journey has been fairly well known, information about the details of the route and the exact locations of the camps has been very limited. Brief accounts of the expedition have been included in a number of books about the exploration of the West, but the few maps that accompany these accounts provide only a general concept of the route. Possibly the most accurate of these maps appears in W. Turrentine Jackson's *Wagon Roads West: A Study of Federal Road Surveys and Construction in the Trans-Mississippi West, 1846–1869*, which was first published in 1952. But due to the problems of scale, even Jackson's map would not be of much help to anyone wanting to follow the exact route of the expedition.

I believe that my research has uncovered a few misconceptions that have developed about Simpson's route. One common idea about the route shows up in the reprint of Simpson's report that was published in 1983. In the foreword, Steven Zink makes the comment that "present-day US Highway 50 runs along much of the trail Simpson blazed in 1859."[9] The operative word here is "much," and the question is just how much is much? The Simpson expedition's outbound trail covered approximately 560 miles as it traversed the western part of Utah and most of Nevada. I was able to determine that the expedition traveled either directly on the route of US 50, or within a couple miles of it, for about 145 miles. Does this qualify as "much of the trail"?

Another example is found in *Traveling America's Loneliest Road*, an excellent book about the country along the route of US 50 in Nevada that was published in 2000. In referring to Simpson's expedition, this book indicates that

the westbound route first intersected US 50 near Lone Mountain in Eureka County, and from there the expedition "traveled a route that eventually became the present day US 50, west to Genoa in Carson Valley."[10] My research indicates that this statement is only partially correct. It is true that Simpson first struck the route of US 50 near Lone Mountain, but at this point, the expedition crossed that highway, rather than joining it. From here to Genoa, Simpson's westbound route intersected US 50 four more times, but out of the approximately 220 miles between Lone Mountain and Carson City, Simpson traveled on it, or within a couple miles of it, for no more than sixty miles.

Referring to Simpson's return route, the above publication says, "on the return trip east, the expedition stayed to the south, closely following what is now the US 50 route all the way to the present Utah border." This statement, also, is only partially correct. It begins with the usual misconception that the return route was always to the south of the outbound route. In actual fact, out of the approximately 570 miles that Simpson traveled during the return journey, about 115 of those miles were identical to the outbound trail, while about 85 miles of this trail were to the north of the outbound route. Which means that 200 miles of the trail, or about thirty-five percent of the return route, was not south of the outbound route. And does Simpson's return route actually follow US 50 all that closely? Of course, that depends on what you think "closely" means, but if we consider "close" to be anywhere within five miles of the highway, we find that of the 380 miles that US 50 covers between Carson City and the Utah border, Simpson was "close" to it for about 250 miles.

None of this is meant to suggest that Simpson should not be given credit for opening up the US 50 corridor. He did do that, and in doing so, his expedition had a significant impact on the history of the West.

The Simpson expedition also had a significant impact on the place names of the region. Due to the limited exploration of the area, many of the geographical features they encountered had not yet been given non-Indian names. Simpson evidently felt that a part of his responsibility was to make sure that every significant geographical feature had a name. However, he did not necessarily feel that he had to give everything a new name. At one point, he stated that his intention was to preserve the Indian names whenever it seemed to be practical.[11] He did give new names to approximately seventy locations and geographical features, in most instances using the names of military acquaintances and government officials. In a few instances, he used descriptive terms. Many of the names that Simpson bestowed are still in use today, some have been replaced with different names, and a few have been moved to different places. Although it was not his idea, his own name has been used a number of times. At least two springs, a creek, a mountain pass, and a parklike area bear his name today. In the quoted material that appears in this book, whenever the modern name differs from the name that Simpson used, the modern name is inserted within brackets.

Following good military procedure, Simpson identified the expedition's campsites with numbers, using numbers 1 through 38 during the westbound trip. He then started over, using numbers 1 through 35 for the eastbound journey. Thus, the total of the numbers used comes to seventy-three. However, there were only seventy different campsites. The Genoa campsite was designated as both westbound number 38 and eastbound number 1. In Carson City, the expedition probably occupied the same campsite during both the westbound and eastbound trips. And the report makes it very clear that westbound camp number 21 and eastbound camp number 14 occupied same site. In the material that follows, the letters "W" and "E" are included with the camp numbers to indicate westbound and eastbound.

During my research and travels along the route, I found it possible to drive a vehicle to fifty-two of the campsites. Reaching seventeen of the sites requires a high-clearance vehicle of some type. Of the campsites that are inaccessible to vehicles, seven can be reached by walking less than a quarter of a mile, four are about a half mile from a road, and seven require a hike of about a mile.

As I began looking for the campsites, I tried to develop an idea of what sort of an area they would have tried to find. In the report, Simpson included a brief description of one of the campsites.

Our little camp, made up of four wall-tents, three Sibleys, and three common tents, with our twelve covered wagons and two spring or instrument wagons, with all the appurtenances of living men and animals, constitute quite a picturesque scene.[12]

This all seems to indicate that when it came time to choose a site for an overnight camp, they would have looked for a fairly level area with enough space to erect their tents and park their wagons and ambulances. A Sibley tent has a round base of about ten to twelve feet in diameter and resembles the tipi most commonly used by the Native Americans of the central plains. The army at that time used various square or rectangular wall tents and common tents, and the dimensions of those used by the expedition are uncertain. Simpson also mentioned a barometer tent, in which they would set up a tripod and hang the barometers from it. One morning a couple of the mules got a little feisty and ran into this tent, knocking the tripod over. The barometers sustained some damage but, fortunately, they could be repaired.[13] Although Simpson makes no mention of it, it is probably safe to assume that they had some sort of cook tent, or at least a shelter under which the cook could do his work. Taking all this into consideration, the expedition's campsites would have required a fairly large, and preferably level, area.

Two

The Journey Begins:
Camp Floyd to Faust Creek

JAMES HERVEY SIMPSON was a career army officer, and no novice when it came to traveling into unmapped territory to hunt for places where wagon roads could be established. Born in New Jersey in 1813, he was admitted to the US Military Academy at the age of fifteen. After graduating from West Point in 1832, his duty stations took him to Maine, Virginia, South Carolina, and Florida, where he was involved in action during the Seminole uprisings.[1] When the Army established its Corps of Topographical Engineers in 1838, he was among the first officers assigned to this new unit. Having been upgraded from the Topographical Bureau, the Topographical Corps was assigned a multitude of responsibilities, primarily having to do with geodetic mapping, improvement in lake and river harbors, construction of aqueducts, and explorations and surveys related to wagon roads.[2]

During the following decade, Simpson was involved in various engineering projects, most of which related to wagon roads in a number of eastern and southern states. Simpson first traveled to the American West in 1849, when he received orders to join an expedition under the command of Col. John James Abert. The first part of this journey began at Fort Smith, Arkansas, and ended at Santa Fe, New Mexico. Lieutenant Simpson's assignment during this expedition was to locate a route that could be used by military wagons immediately, and could eventually be used by a railroad that would cross the southern portion of the United States. At the conclusion of this journey, Simpson compiled his first report to Congress, *Report and Map of the Route from Fort Smith, Arkansas, to Santa Fe, New Mexico*. In this report, Simpson predicted that it would be at least twenty years before a railroad would be built across the western territories.[3] Thirty years later, when the transcontinental railroad was finally under construction, Simpson, then a lieutenant colonel in the Corps of Engineers, was given the responsibility for determining the suitability of certain sections of the proposed route, and later acted as an inspector to determine the quality of the construction on various railroad projects.[4]

Following the completion of the Fort Smith-Santa Fe survey, Simpson received orders to conduct an exploration of the Old Spanish Trail route between Abiqui, New Mexico, and Los Angeles. Although this pack trail had been in use for about twenty years, not much was known about it by anyone other than the relatively small number of traders who were using it. According to western historian William H. Goetzmann, it was regarded as "somewhere between mystery and legend for even the most informed geographers" of the time.[5] Simpson was looking forward to this assignment with enthusiasm, and there is little doubt that our knowledge of this historic trail would have been significantly improved if he had been allowed to complete it. Unfortunately, this was not to be. As he was getting ready to leave Santa Fe, his orders were changed, and he was instructed to accompany Col. John M. Washington on a punitive raid against a group of recalcitrant Navajos. During this mission, Simpson led a detachment into Chaco Canyon and discovered a number of Anasazi ruins, including Pueblo Pintado, Canyon de Chelly, and Canyon Bonito.[6]

Camp Floyd in 1859, looking to the east from the parade ground. This photograph was taken by one of the two photographers that accompanied the Simpson expedition.

After the completion of this expedition, Simpson submitted another report to Congress. This document had the lengthy title of *Journal of a Military Reconnaissance from Santa Fe, New Mexico to the Navajo Country Made with the Troops under Command of Brevet Lieutenant Colonel John M. Washington, Chief of the Ninth Military Department and Governor of New Mexico.*[7] In 1869, Simpson drew on his experiences during this expedition when he wrote an article for the Smithsonian Institution in which he speculated that Coronado's Seven Cities of Cibola were located in the Zuni area.[8]

After the raids against the Navajos, Simpson was expecting to resume his exploration of the Old Spanish Trail, but his orders instructed him to remain in Santa Fe in the position of Chief Topographical Engineer for the Ninth Military Department.[9]

In the spring of 1851, the army transferred Simpson to the Territory of Minnesota, where he spent the next two years surveying and overseeing the improvement of a number of wagon roads in that heavily wooded country.[10] In early 1853, he was promoted to the rank of captain,[11] and in May of that year he was transferred to Florida again, where he spent about a year and a half supervising survey work with the US Coast Survey.[12] Sometime during the winter of 1857–58, he received orders to join the military forces that

were being assembled to march on the Territory of Utah.

In mid-1857, President James Buchanan became alarmed about events that were reported to be occurring in the Mormon-dominated Territory of Utah. Whether or not his concerns were valid continues to be a subject for debate. Buchanan's reaction to these reports was to issue orders that would send several army regiments westward to put down this so-called Mormon Rebellion. This action became known as the Utah War. Under the command of Brevet Brig. Gen. Albert Sidney Johnston, the army reached Salt Lake City on June 26, 1858, and found the city to be deserted except for newly appointed Territorial Governor Alfred Cumming, the governor's staff, and a few of the leaders of the Mormon church. After marching through the city, Johnston and his troops set up a temporary camp on the west bank of the Jordan River.[13] General Johnston then met with Governor Cumming, and it was decided that it would be best for all concerned if the army would set up a more permanent headquarters some distance away from the city. Johnston then led his command to Cedar Valley, which is about forty miles southwest of Salt Lake City, where they established Camp Floyd.

For all practical purposes, this was the end of the Utah War. However, the army did remain in

Cedar Valley for another four years as a sort of occupying force. Although a number of individual soldiers became involved in some minor scuffles with some of the territory's inhabitants, there were no officially sanctioned hostile encounters between the military forces and the civilian population during the time that the army occupied Camp Floyd.

When Simpson was attached to the Utah Expedition, he was assigned to the position of chief engineer and sent to Fort Leavenworth, where he began working on the maps that the army would need during the upcoming campaign in the west. Sometime during the spring of 1858, Simpson moved his operations to Fort Kearny in Nebraska, in preparation for traveling to Utah.[14]

On the day that General Johnston and his troops marched through Salt Lake City, Simpson was still at Fort Kearny and had missed the entire Mormon War. However, as soon as Johnston had settled in at Camp Floyd, he sent word for Simpson to proceed immediately to Utah. There was work for him to do. Simpson, and a small group of officers and civilian assistants that had been assigned as his staff, left Fort Kearny on July 3, 1858. When the group was about halfway to Utah, Simpson decided to take two of his officers and move ahead of the rest of the party, arriving at Camp Floyd on August 19. The remainder of the group reached the post on September 15.[15]

Simpson wasted no time in getting started on his new duties, and his first assignment was to locate, survey, and make improvements to a new wagon road between Fort Bridger and Camp Floyd. Within two weeks, Simpson had made a rudimentary survey for a new wagon road that would bypass most of the Mormon Trail between Fort Bridger and Salt Lake City. This new route descended Chalk Creek Canyon, instead of following the Mormon Trail down Echo Canyon. When it reached the Weber River, it turned upstream to the area of the Rockport Reservoir, turned west to Parley's Park, then south to the Provo River and followed it down Provo Canyon. At the mouth of the canyon, the new road turned to the west, skirted the northern shore of Utah Lake, and turned southwest to Camp Floyd. Even before the improvements were completed, the army and its contracted freighting company,

Russell, Majors, and Waddell, began using it to get to Camp Floyd.[16]

As soon as Simpson and General Johnston were satisfied that the new road had been put into usable condition, they turned their attention to the country west of Camp Floyd. On October 19, Simpson set out on a preliminary reconnaissance into Utah's West Desert. This was the first step in an ambitious plan to find a central route to California. Leading a party that consisted of about thirty-five men and six wagons, Simpson traveled in a generally southwesterly direction for about eighty miles, before the approach of winter forced him to return. During this trip he traveled almost due west across Rush Valley and camped on Meadow Creek, about four miles north of today's Faust railroad station.[17] The next day he turned to the northwest and traveled through Johnsons Pass, which is located between the Stansbury and Onaqui mountains.

Upon reaching the western base of the pass, the reconnaissance party turned to the southwest and traveled another forty or so miles into the desert. Just as they reached the Dugway Mountains, a snowstorm began to close in on them, and Simpson decided to return to Camp Floyd. During the return trip, they found what proved to be a much better route, which traversed a pass that lies between the Onaqui and Sheeprock mountains. Simpson named this pass after General Johnston, but today it is known as Lookout Pass. The similarity in the names of Johnsons Pass and General Johnston's Pass can lead to some confusion, but they are clearly two different passes, separated by about twenty miles.

Simpson was optimistic about what he had seen during this reconnaissance, and he promptly submitted a formal proposal for a more extensive expedition. The War Department accepted the proposal, and the following spring, with a larger party and provisions for a much longer journey, he was ready to go again.

On the morning of the second day of May in 1859, the men and wagons of the expedition formed up in the post's assembly area, which was probably located just west of Camp Floyd's headquarters buildings. Although Simpson's report does not say anything about it, it seems likely that some sort of military ceremony would have taken place before the expedition began its west-ward journey.

When the expedition left Camp Floyd, it was composed of sixty-four persons. The officers were Captain Simpson; Lt. Alexander Murry, who was in command of the military escort; Lt. Haldiman S. Putnam, an assistant to Simpson in charge of geographical observations; Lt. J. L. Kirby Smith, an assistant to Simpson and the Ordinance Officer for the expedition; and Joseph C. Baily, the Medical Officer. There were twenty enlisted sol-diers, ten of which were mounted members of the Second Dragoons, and ten soldiers from the Tenth Infantry. Although the latter were classified as infantryman, they were not expected to walk, and they were provided with mules for their mounts.

The civilian contingent consisted of a geolo-gist, a taxidermist, two meteorologists and chro-nometer-keepers, a sketch-artist, two photogra-phers, a wheelwright, a blacksmith, two packers, four herders, fourteen teamsters, a chief guide, and three assistant guides, two of which were Ute Indians. The names of the civilians that are known, along with their assignments, are as follows:

Henry Engelmann—geologist, meteorologist, botanical specimen collector

Edward Jagiello—meteorological assistant, chronometer keeper

Wilson Lambert—exact assignment uncer-tain, sometimes scout

William Lee—meteorological assistant, chro-nometer keeper

Charles S. McCarthy—taxidermist, specimen collector

C. C. Mills—photographer

Payte, first name unknown—teamster, some-times scout

John Reese—chief guide

Henry Sailing—wagonmaster

Stevenson, first name unknown—scout and guide

Ute Pete—guide, interpreter

H. V. A. Von Beckh—artist

William Lee was under the impression that one of the Indian scouts would be acting as a hunter

for the expedition, while the other was to be an interpreter for the Indians they expected to encounter.[18]

John Reese was a resident of the small settle-ment of Genoa, which was located on the far western border of what was the Territory of Utah at that time, and which was the goal of the expe-dition. Reese had a fairly extensive knowledge of some, but not all, of the country through which they would be traveling. He had traveled with the first group that Colonel Steptoe had sent to look for a central route in 1854. Simpson's regard for Reese seems to have varied somewhat during the expedition. When the expedition was travel-ing through the valley just to the west of present-day Austin, Nevada, Simpson was feeling good enough about Reese to name the river for him. On the other hand, it is quite clear that on sev-eral occasions Simpson became quite irritated with some of the things that Reese did, and failed to do. Although Reese's son is never mentioned by name in the report, an article published in the *Deseret News* shortly after the expedition had returned to Camp Floyd suggests that he was one of the unnamed members of the expedition.[19]

The party's wheeled vehicles included 12 six-mule quartermaster wagons, 1 six-mule spring wagon, and 1 four-mule ambulance, which carried the expedition's scientific instruments. Simpson mentioned that the wagons were of "such superior character" that they seldom needed any repair.[20] This probably means that the expedition's wheel-wright did not have much to keep him occupied. On the other hand, the blacksmith seems to have been a very busy man. Simpson mentioned that whenever they went into camp, the forge would be fired up and the blacksmith would go to work repairing and replacing the shoes on the horses and mules.

The expedition's livestock included horses for the officers and dragoons, mules to pull the wagons and for the infantry soldiers to ride, and six "commissary beeves" which would be slaugh-tered and eaten during the trip.

Throughout the expedition, Simpson kept a very detailed record of the distances between the campsites and numerous geographical features along the route. He was able to make an accurate determination of these distances because, among

A six-mule quartermaster wagon. Nick Eggenhofer's drawing of a Civil War–era wagon appeared in his book *Wagons, Mules and Men*. Eggenhofer quoted from the army's contract for the wagons' construction; *"The body to be straight, 3 feet 6 inches wide, 2 feet deep, 10 feet along the bottom, 10 feet 6 inches at the top, sloping equally at each end…. The outside of the body and feed trough to have two good coats of white lead, colored to a blue tint; the inside of them to have two coats of Venetian red paint; the running gear and wheels to have two good coats of Venetian red, darkened to a chocolate color; the hub and felloes to be well pitched instead of painted."*

The Simpson expedition included two ambulance-style wagons to carry the scientific instruments. One was pulled by six mules, the other by four. This Nick Eggenhofer drawing of a Civil War–era ambulance shows only two mules, so it was probably somewhat smaller that the expedition's ambulances. On July 9, when the expedition was about halfway back to Camp Floyd, a wheel on the smaller ambulance was broken and the whole thing was dismantled and packed in one of the regular wagons. From Wagons, Mules and Men.

the instruments taken along on the expedition, were two odometers. These instruments and the procedures for using them were mentioned in the written orders that authorized the expedition.

Lieutenant Putman will further keep up an itinerary of the route, according to the prescribed form with which he will be furnished, the distance to be measured by two odometers to provide against error.[21]

Simpson did not give any additional details about these odometers, but they may have been similar, if not identical, to the instrument that had been used by another western expedition six years before. Capt. John W. Gunnison of the Topographical Engineers was equipped with a pendulum-style odometer during his ill-fated railroad survey of 1853. Gunnison's party had explored a route across Colorado and the eastern part of Utah. Moving ahead of the main group, Gunnison and several others set up camp on the Sevier River about fifteen miles southwest of the city of Delta. During the early hours of October 26, they were attacked by a group of Pahvant Indians. Gunnison and seven other members of the party were killed during the short battle.[22] After the fight was over, the Indians seized several items of equipment, including the odometer that the survey party had been using, and carried them away. Several years later, the odometer was found about seventy-five miles to the north in Skull Valley. It is now on display in the Museum of Peoples and Cultures at Brigham Young University in Provo, Utah.[23]

These pendulum-style odometers would be placed into a leather case and strapped to the spokes of a wagon wheel. Each time the wheel made a revolution; the pendulum would swing and trip a counter. By looking at the counter, the operator could see how many times the wheel had revolved. The distance traveled could then be calculated by multiplying that number by the circumference of the wagon wheel.

For almost every day's journey, Simpson recorded the distance traveled in three different places. First, in the narrative portion of his report he frequently mentioned the incremental distances between certain geographical features

and other arbitrary points, such as the campsites. As an example, he reported the very first increment by saying "Our course lay slightly south of west, up a scarcely perceptible ascent, out from Cedar Valley to Camp Floyd Pass, 3 miles distant from Camp Floyd."[24] These incremental distances can usually be added together to arrive at the total distance traveled during a given day. Second, somewhere near the end of his description of each day's journey, Simpson would usually mention the total number of miles they had traveled during that day. Third, the appendix to the report includes a Table of Distances, Altitudes, and Grades. This table lists all of the campsites, along with a number of geographical features, and gives the distances between them. Although these numbers should be the same, more often than not they are different. The differences, however, are usually insignificant, generally about two- or three-tenths of a mile. Occasionally the discrepancy is greater, and most of these instances will be mentioned later.

The expedition also carried a number of scientific instruments that were to be used to determine latitude, longitude, and altitude. Some of Simpson's assistants, including Lieutenants Smith and Putnam, had started their training on the use of these instruments while they were still at Fort Leavenworth. During the expedition, it was the normal practice for these officers, with help from others, including Simpson, to take daily observations. At one point in his narrative, Simpson gave a detailed account of a part of this process.

This afternoon the astronomical transit was set up for observations of the transit of the moon and moon-culminating stars....Also observed as usual for time (or longitude) and latitude. Also took four sets of lunar observations for longitude with sextants and artificial horizons, two sets being on each side of the moon. Lieutenant Smith observed for double altitudes of the stars; Lieutenant Putnam, for double altitude of the moon; and I, for lunar distances, Mr. Lee noting audibly the time....I would ask, "Are you all ready?" If so, each would reply, "Ready!" I would then say, "Count!" While Mr. Lee was counting, Lieutenant Smith would be keeping up the superposition of the reflected and

The area in the foreground was Camp Floyd's parade ground and assembly area. The view is to the east, toward Camp Floyd State Park. State Route 73 crosses the photo just this side of the trees.

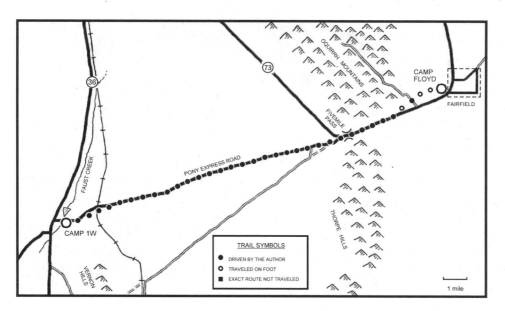

MAY 2, 1859

TRAIL SYMBOLS

● DRIVEN BY THE AUTHOR
○ TRAVELED ON FOOT
■ EXACT ROUTE NOT TRAVELED

1 mile

direct image of the star in the artificial horizon; Lieutenant Putnam, the tangential contact of the reflected and direct image of the bright limb of the moon, also in an artificial horizon; and I, the tangency of the star and bright limb of the moon directly. At the proper instant, I would call out the time, and if the other observers would respond, "All right!" to my query, the angles of time were recorded. We got through at midnight. Also, determined the magnetic variation at this camp, by observations on Polaris.[25]

The expedition also carried along at least one camera, which Simpson referred to as "a photographic apparatus." Two photographers accompanied the expedition as a part of the topographical party. On one occasion, Simpson mentioned that he had "a likeness taken" of an Indian woman.[26] However, Simpson was not convinced that photographs had any real value for the expedition. What he wanted was good images of geographical features, and when he found that the photographs did not provide this, he remarked, "the enterprise has been attended with failure....In my judgment, the camera is not adapted to explorations in the field."[27] I have been unable to determine whether or not any photographs were included with Simpson's report to Congress, but there are several photographs of Camp Floyd in the National Archives that were taken by "the photographer of the J. H. Simpson Expedition."[28] Simpson did feel that it was important to obtain some sort of images of the country they were exploring, and for that reason, an artist was a member of the expedition. This was H. V. A. Von Beckh, and he was assigned "the duty of sketching the country in a manner to illustrate its common as well as peculiar characteristics."[29] Following the completion of the expedition, John J. Young of Washington, DC made watercolor copies of a number of Von Beckh's sketches. At least some of these images accompanied Simpson's official report to Congress. These watercolors are now located in the Cartographic Division of the National Archives in Washington, DC.

Following whatever ceremony that may have been conducted, the men and animals of the expedition left the parade ground and headed west toward today's Five Mile Pass, which is located at the southern tip of the Oquirrh Mountains. Simpson begins his description of the journey as follows:

CAMP FLOYD, MAY 2, 1859.—*The topographical party under my command left this post at a quarter of 8 A.M., to explore the country intervening this locality and Carson River; at the east foot of the Sierra Nevada, for a new and direct route to California. Our course lay slightly south of west, up a scarcely perceptible ascent, out from Cedar Valley to Camp Floyd Pass [Five-Mile Pass], 3 miles distant from Camp Floyd; through this broad champaign pass 3 miles, and thence, nearly southwest 12.2 miles, to Meadow Creek [Faust Creek], in Rush Valley, where we encamped. Journey, 18.2 miles.*[30]

Today's State Route 73 comes south from the town of Cedar Fort and makes a bend to the west at the point where it passes through what was once the army post of Camp Floyd. An examination of some early maps of the area seems to indicate that the headquarters area was located inside the curve of the highway, and just slightly south of Big Spring, which was the source of the small stream that divided Camp Floyd from the community of Fairfield. The assembly area was probably just west of the headquarters buildings.

A careful examination of Simpson's map shows that for the first three miles the expedition's trail was somewhat to the north of today's highway. As the expedition approached the southern foothills of the Oquirrh Mountains, the wagon train turned a little to the south until it merged with the highway and turned to the west, heading directly toward Five Mile Pass.

JULY 2006

Since there is no surviving road or trail along the first three-mile section of the expedition's route, it can only be followed on foot. Leaving my vehicle in the parking lot at Camp Floyd State Park, I began walking westward to the area that was the camp's parade ground and assembly area.

After taking a few photographs, I continued to the west along the expedition's route. Relying on the latitude and longitude coordinates that I had previously programmed into my GPS receiver,

The entrance to Camp Floyd State Park. The structure behind the sign was the army post's commissary and is now the park's headquarters.

I followed what I believe to be the expedition's approximate route to the spot where it joins State Route 73. Although this undrivable section was the very first part of the expedition's route, I had intentionally saved it for one of the last sections to cover on foot. Part of the reason for this was the fact that until that time I had not been at all certain about the location of the parade ground. It was not until early in 2006 that I obtained a copy of a map that shows the locations of the camp's buildings in relation to the alignment of SR 73. After crossing the summit of Five Mile Pass, the expedition entered Rush Valley and began heading slightly south of west. They were following what is now officially designated by the counties of Tooele and Juab as Pony Express Road. This road begins at Five Mile Pass and extends all the way across Utah's West Desert to the Nevada state line. Although it does not always follow the exact route that was used by the riders of the Pony Express, it is never far away. After making its way to the west side of Rush Valley, the expedition went into camp for the night on the east bank of what was then known as Meadow Creek. Henry J. "Doc" Faust established a ranch in this area in 1860, and

the stream subsequently became known as Faust Creek. It appears to me that the campsite would have been either right on, or possibly just to the south, of Pony Express Road.

As he summed up his description of the first day's journey Simpson made some additional comments about the route they had just traveled.

Finding that the California mail party, after threading Camp Floyd Pass, had missed my route of last fall, and had unnecessarily made too great a detour to the northward, I struck directly across to Meadow Creek with the wagons, and thus marked out a short cut which would shorten the road a mile or two.[31]

This statement requires some further explanation. When he said "my route of last fall," Simpson was talking about the trail that he had made during the return portion of the reconnaissance trip he made during the previous October. While traveling eastward toward Camp Floyd, the party camped on Meadow Creek, near what would become the Faust Ranch. From there they followed a straight line in a slightly north-of-east direction to Five Mile Pass. It was this section of the trail that Simpson was talking about when he said "my route of last fall." And it was this section of his route that the mail company employees had missed when they "had unnecessarily made too great a detour to the northward."

The term "California mail party" refers to the company that was owned and operated by George W. Chorpenning, who at that time had a government contract to carry the mail between Salt Lake City and California. This company was the immediate predecessor to the shorter-lived, but much more famous, Pony Express that was operated by the firm of Russell, Majors, and Waddell. Because Chorpenning's mail riders usually used mules rather than horses, it is sometimes called the Jackass Mail. Prior to October of 1858, Chorpenning had been using a route that left Salt Lake City and went around the northern end of the Great Salt Lake and joined the California Trail near City of Rocks. But this was a difficult and dangerous trail during the winter, and Chorpenning was looking for a more southerly route.

Shortly after Simpson returned from his reconnaissance trip, Chorpenning visited Camp Floyd, where he talked with General Johnston and possibly Simpson himself. As a result of this meeting, Chorpenning headed west and took a look at the route that Simpson had followed during his return to Camp Floyd. He liked what he saw, and immediately decided that, at least during the winter months, it would be much better than the route around the northern end of the Great Salt Lake. By the time that Simpson started west again in May, Chorpenning's agents had explored and developed a trail that extended well beyond where Simpson had turned around the previous fall. In that relatively short period of time, they had opened up a new trail that went all the way to the southern point of the Ruby Mountains, and then northwest to the Humboldt River at Gravely Ford. At a number of locations, they had begun to build some rudimentary structures to be used as mail stations.[32] Simpson was well aware of this, and had mentioned Chorpenning's activities in his report on the reconnaissance trip when he submitted it to the Secretary of War in December of 1858.

Immediately on my return, Mr. Chorpening, the contractor for carrying the mail on the Humboldt route from Utah to California, at the suggestion of the general commanding, went, with a small party, over my track for the purpose of examining it in reference to the transfer of his stock to a more southern route, a measure which had been rendered necessary by the obstructions from snow on the Goose Creek mountains. This party returned some time since, and Mr. Taft, who was one of the number, has informed me, after a good deal of exploration, they could find no better route to connect with the Humboldt route and avoid the Goose Creek mountains than that I went over. Since then they have transferred their mail stock to this route, and are now making use of it as a winter route towards California.[33]

A footnote to the report stated that "since the above was written Mr. Chorpenning has been here, and reports that he has got a good hard wagon route all the way to the Humboldt." It is not certain just when this footnote was added, but it would have been after Simpson had finished writing the report, which was December 28, 1858, and before the report was printed, which was in March of 1859. As a result of Chorpenning's activities, for the next few weeks the expedition would not be breaking a new trail, but would be following a route that was already being used by the Jackass Mail.

Three

FAUST CREEK TO PLEASANT VALLEY

Camp 1-W. The expedition's first campsite was at the left, on the east bank of Faust Creek, which was known as Meadow Creek in 1859.

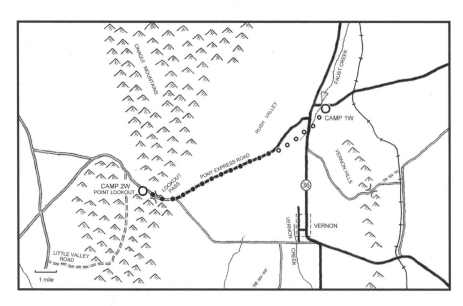

Looking southwest across the southern end of Rush Valley toward Lookout Pass: *"our course lay nearly southwest, seven miles to east foot of General Johnston's Pass."*

MAY 3, CAMP NO. 1, ON MEADOW CREEK.—
Follow up Meadow Creek a mile, and then cross just above old adobe corral....About half a mile above the crossing the mail company has a station, at present consisting of a Sibley tent, and a cedar picket corral for stock is being made. From this station our course lay nearly southwest, seven miles to east, foot of General Johnston's Pass [Lookout Pass], which I discovered last fall, and which I called after the general commanding the Department of Utah.[1]

LEAVING THE CAMPSITE on Faust Creek, the party moved southwest, heading upstream along the east bank of the stream. After traveling about a mile, they forded the small stream near where it now crosses under Utah State Route 36. Heading west from the ford, the expedition began crossing a flat, meadowlike area. After another half mile, they passed the spot where

Simpson and his smaller force had camped the previous October 27, when they were returning from the reconnaissance trip. At this location, the Chorpenning employees had established a mail station. At the present time, the area to the west of the highway is owned by the city of Tooele, and is being leased by the operator of a sod farm. Joe Nardone, who is regarded by many as the foremost authority on the location of the trail and the stations, has determined that the Faust Pony Express station was located at the site now occupied by a large equipment shed. The earlier Chorpenning station was probably located at this same spot, as it seems doubtful that Russell, Majors, and Waddell would have moved the station when they took over Chorpenning's operation in 1860.

"Doc" Faust was working for George Chorpenning as the manager of the Pleasant Valley mail station when Chorpenning made the switch to the central route in late 1858. It was there that

Simpson made Faust's acquaintance when the expedition reached Pleasant Valley on May 9. About five or six months later, the Chorpenning company discontinued the Pleasant Valley section of the route and started going through Callao and Deep Creek, which is now known as Ibapah. When this change took place, Faust and his family moved to Deep Creek, where he operated the new mail station.[2] His time at Deep Creek was short; within a few months he had moved to Rush Valley, where he was placed in charge of the station on Meadow Creek. When the firm of Russell, Majors, and Waddell initiated the Pony Express and took over Chorpenning's operation, they hired Faust, and he continued to manage the station. At about this time, Faust homesteaded 160 acres and began a ranching operation in the grassy area surrounding the station. Since that time until the present, the area around the station has been intensely cultivated, and sometimes used as pasture. When the station was in operation, it was on the creek's western bank, but sometime during the intervening years, the channel has been changed and it now passes to the north and then circles to the west of the station site.

After passing the mail station, the expedition continued across the open meadow in a southwesterly direction for a mile and a half, where the route then merged with today's Pony Express Road at a prominent bend in the road.

APRIL 2006

After determining that the expedition's route followed the east bank of Faust Creek between Pony Express Road and SR 36, I looked for, but failed to find, a road or trail that could be driven through this area. Deciding that I would have to cover this section of the route on foot, I asked my friend Jim Hall to go along. This was one of the rare occasions that I had company during one of my hikes along the trail. Jim was living in Rush Valley at that time, and was researching the early history of the area. Starting from the site of the expedition's camp, we headed south along the east bank of Faust Creek. Although the stream is at ground level in the vicinity of the campsite, we found that the channel quickly becomes much deeper. In less than a quarter of a mile, the banks become as much as eight to ten feet high, and

this continues until the stream is about a tenth of a mile from SR 36. The height of the banks would have made it impossible take the wagons across the steam at any point before reaching the place where they did make the ford. When Jim and I reached SR 36, we crossed the stream and the highway, and then continued across the meadow until we reached the point where the expedition's route comes back to Pony Express Road.

In about a mile more, by a good grade, you reach the top of the pass, and thence, in three-quarters of a mile, by a steep descent, which, for a portion of the way, teams going east would have to double up, you attain to a spot where is a patch of grass, and where we encamped. There is a small spring near us, on the north side of the pass, which, however, our animals soon drank dry, and which doubtless is dry during the summer. Road today good. Journey, 9.9 miles.[3]

The expedition's second campsite was located in a relatively level area about three-quarters of a mile below and to the west of the summit of Lookout Pass. On the north side of the road there is a large Pony Express monument made from native rock. The meager spring that Simpson mentioned is in the shallow canyon just to the north of the monument.

The California mail-stage passed us on its way to Camp Floyd. Cho-kup, chief of the Ruby Valley band of Sho-sho-nees, was a passenger, on his way to see the Indian agent.[4]

Although Chorpenning's mail company had previously relied on pack mules to carry the mail, Simpson's comment about the "California Mail-Stage" points out that by this time the mail company had improved the road enough so that it could be used by a wagon or coach of some type. This mail-stage was probably the type of coach that was known as a mud wagon.

MAY 4, 1859

MAY 4, CAMP NO. 2, THREE-QUARTERS OF A MILE BELOW GENERAL JOHNSTON'S PASS.—*This morning at daylight we found that a driving snow-*

Camp 2-W. Near the Lookout Pony Express station, three-quarters of a mile west of Lookout Pass. The campsite was probably near the center of the photo.

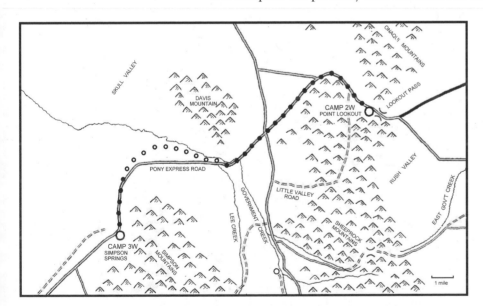

storm had set in from the west and about six inches of snow had fallen. The Sibley tent occupied by some of the assistants had become prostrated, under the combined effects of the snow and wind, and when I saw it its occupants were still under it. Lieutenant Murry reports the spring full again this morning.[5]

WILLIAM LEE was one of the assistants who were sleeping in the tent when it collapsed. His journal entry for the day reads: "On awakening this morning found the tent laying over me, and was hemmed in on all sides by canvas."[6]

Moved camp at 10 minutes after 7 A.M., our course being westwardly down General Johnston's Pass into Skull Valley, and thence southwestwardly, in a somewhat tortuous direction to avoid a low mountain, to a spring which I discovered last fall, and which I called, in my last report, Pleasant Spring, but which now, I find, goes by the name of Simpson's Spring. This spring is on the base and north side of some mountains [Simpson Range], which I call after Captain Stephen Champlin, of the United States Navy. Journey, 16.2 miles.[7]

Traveling west from the camp, the expedition continued to follow Pony Express Road until they crossed Government Creek. Simpson's use of the phrase "a tortuous direction" seems a little overblown, but in order to get around Davis Mountain, the route they followed did have to bend to the left, then back to the right, and then back to the left again. A careful examination of Simpson's map indicates that after crossing Government Creek, rather than following today's road in a straight line to the west, the expedition followed the south bank of the usually dry streambed for some distance before turning to the south again. They rejoined Pony Express Road about three miles north of Simpson Springs.

OCTOBER 2005

Since no roads or trails of any type can be found along the south bank of Government Creek and then back to Pony Express Road, it would have to be covered on foot. I parked on the side of the road and began hiking along the route that I had previously plotted on the map.

Following the south bank of Government Creek for about two miles, I then left the streambed and began curving back toward Pony Express Road, joining it again where it makes a sharp bend toward Simpson Springs. In making this hike, I found that this is one of the rare sections of the route where no indications of the trail can be found. The curve to the north was entirely unnecessary, and subsequent travelers must have straightened the bend within a short period of time. The stage road through this area was just a few yards to the north of today's Pony Express Road, and is still visible in some spots. In his report of the previous fall's reconnaissance, Simpson indicated that the springs that became known as Simpson Springs were "in an arroyo pretty well up the bench of the mountain."[8] This description seems to place the campsite a short distance to the east of the spot that is generally accepted as the site of the Pony Express station. When Simpson and his reconnaissance party had camped here the previous October, he had given it the name of Pleasant Spring. In his 1859 report, he indicated that it was now being called Simpson's Spring. When Sir Richard Burton traveled through this area a little over a year later, his observations were as follows:

At "Point Look Out," near the counterslope of divide, we left on the south Simpson's route [referring to the return route], and learned by a sign-post that the distance to Carson is 533 miles. The pass led to Skull Valley, of ominous sound....Passing out of Skull Valley, we crossed the cahues and pitch-holes of a broad bench which rose above the edge of the desert, and after seventeen miles beyond the Pass reached the station which Mormons call Egan's Springs, anti-Mormons Simpson's Springs, and Gentiles Lost Springs.[9]

Somewhere near the springs, Chorpenning's employees had established a rudimentary mail station and were working on the construction of a small reservoir that was intended to collect the slowly seeping water. John Reese was waiting here for the expedition to arrive, after having gone ahead to scout the country to the southwest. He reported that he had been unable to locate a route across either the Dugway or the

Thomas Mountains that would be any better than the pass that Simpson had reconnoitered the previous fall.

MAY 5, 1859

MAY 5, CAMP NO. 3, SIMPSON'S SPRING. — *My party moved at quarter to six. Course nearly southwest, across desert…to "Short Cut Pass" [Dugway Pass], in a mountain range, which I call Colonel Thomas's range, after Lieut. Col. Lorenzo Thomas, assistant adjutant-general of the Army. Through this pass Chorpenning & Company, the mail-contractors, have made a road, but it is so crooked and steep as to scarcely permit our wagons to get up it.…Encamp 1.3 miles west of summit of pass, where there is little or no grass, and no water. Journey, 23.2 miles.*[10]

BETWEEN SIMPSON SPRINGS and the long and narrow depression in the valley floor known as Old Riverbed, the expedition's route was a short distance to the north of today's Pony Express Road. Although it is getting quite faint, there are places where the old Overland Stage road can still be seen. Simpson said nothing about Old Riverbed in his report of the 1859 expedition, but in his report of the previous year's reconnaissance, he includes a brief description of this area.

At the foot of the mountain which we are skirting on our left, at about 8 miles from our last camp [Simpson Springs], I notice a great deal of bunch grass. At this place the bottom of the valley is broken, and there is quite a low vail, or arroyo, where, if anywhere, water might be possibly got by digging. Indeed, the indications are that there has been water here recently and the green grass in places show that it might probably be got not far below the surface.[11]

In the bottom of Old Riverbed, a short distance north of today's road, a Pony Express monument can be found. This monument is probably located on, or near, the old Overland Stage road. Near the western side of the depression, a very faint trail leaves today's road and climbs up the steep bank to the south. At the top of

the slope, the trail turns to the southwest and remains some distance from today's road, until the trail and the road merge together again at the foot of Dugway Pass.

Along this faint, but still visible, track are several small concrete Pony Express Trail markers and a large stone monument that is believed to be located near the site of the Dugway Pony Express station. In the area between the Dugway Station monument and the base of the mountain, the trail is very faint, but when I hiked this section of the route, I came across several places where it can still be seen.

During his exploration of the previous fall, Simpson and some of his men had ridden their horses to the top of what he called Shortcut Pass, leaving the wagons at the eastern base of the mountain. Simpson called it Shortcut Pass because it was "the shortest route to the Goshoot mountains," but it soon became known as Dugway Pass.[12] When Simpson saw this pass in 1858, he could tell that it would present some problems for wagons.

On account of the steep ascent of the pass, it looks very much as if our expedition had come to an end. We could, by unpacking our wagons and carrying everything up by hand, and doubling the teams, probably be enabled to get over, but this would consume so much of the day that we would not be able to reach the spring before late in the night.[13]

In 1859, Simpson sent Reese ahead of the expedition to look for another pass which, for some reason, he believed to be about five miles to the north. Reese either failed to find it or did not like the looks of it, and the expedition used Shortcut Pass to get over the Dugway Mountains.

We do not know the exact alignment of the route that the expedition followed as it ascended the eastern side of Dugway Pass, but it was probably not the route that is used by today's road. If you look about a hundred feet or so below today's road, you can see an abandoned roadbed. Even this old road may not have followed Simpson's trail, because it is almost certainly the road that was constructed six years after the expedition made its way over the pass. The records of the Utah territorial government show that in 1865

Camp 3-W. Simpson Springs, looking to the west from near the springs. The campsite was in the foreground.

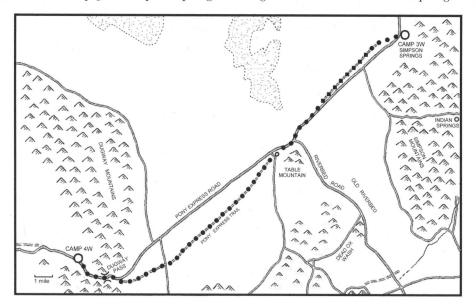

The east approach to Dugway Pass, called Shortcut Pass by Simpson. Today's road is marked by a faint line that slants upward from right to left near the center of the photo. *"The mail-contractors have made a road, but it is so crooked and steep as to scarcely permit our wagons to get up it."*

the Overland Mail Company was granted the right to construct a toll road over Dugway Pass.[14]

After crossing the summit of the Dugway Mountains, the expedition dropped down the western slope and made a waterless camp at the first relatively flat area that they came to.

May 6, 1859

May 6, Camp No. 4, Short Cut Pass.—*1.3 miles west of summit. The grass at this camp being very scant, and it being important to reach water as soon as possible, the expedition, under charge of Lieutenant Murry, left at twelve midnight on its onward march, myself remaining behind with a small party to look at the country by daylight. I with my party moved at twenty-five minutes after*

five.... The road we are following for one mile continues down the pass north of west, and then turns more southwardly, Thomas's range flanking us on our left, or to the east, and the desert on our right.[15]

Simpson made a few errors in his mileage figures for this day's travel. Although the distance figures that Simpson included in his report were usually quite accurate, errors did creep in occasionally. It is doubtful that these mistakes were attributable to the odometers, but probably came from misreading, miscalculations, misunderstandings, or mistakes in copying the numbers. During the course of my research, whenever I ran into distance figures that seemed to be wrong, I always spent a lot of time attempting to figure out where and why the error had

Camp 4-W. This campsite was at the first level area to be found west of Dugway Pass. *"Encamp west of summit of pass, where there is little or no grass, and no water."*

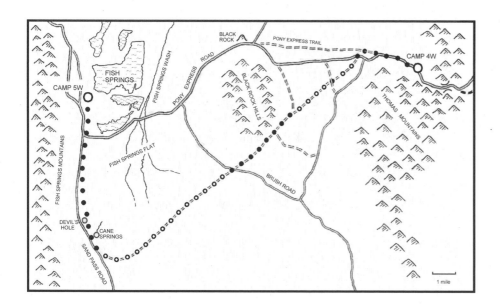

MAY 6, 1859

been made. In many cases I discovered that the confusion was mine, but there were a number of instances when I ultimately had to conclude that Simpson, or possibly one of his assistants, had simply gotten it wrong. The fact that the wagons that were equipped with the odometers were traveling well ahead of Simpson during this day's journey may have contributed to the errors. Whatever the reason, the mileage figures simply do not fit with the terrain that he described. The first error came when he indicated that he followed the road for one mile and then turned "more southwardly." He did begin to turn toward the west at one mile from camp, so he might have been mistaken in the direction rather than the distance. Whichever it was, one thing that is certain is that the steeply rising slopes of the Thomas Mountains would have made it impossible to turn south until they had rounded the northern point of the mountain, and that did not occur until they were three miles from the camp. At this three-mile point, Simpson left the route that would later become the Pony Express Trail, and turned in a southwesterly direction into the little valley that lies between the Thomas Range on the east, and the Black Rock Hills on the west.

> In 6 miles you enter Cedar Valley, made by Thomas's range on your left, and a short range [Black Rock Hills] on your right. Threading this, in 3 miles you emerge from it, and cross a valley 9 miles wide, which, on your right, is a salt-spring marsh and boggy, and therefore forces the road to the south, as indicated on the maps.[16]

Simpson's second error came when he indicated that he entered the valley at six miles. The most logical place to say that you are entering this valley would be at four miles from the campsite. At six miles from the camp, he would have been more than halfway across the little valley, rather than just entering it. He seems to have made another minor error when he said that he emerged from the valley at three miles from where he entered it. The place that would logically fit the description of emerging from the valley would be when he crossed the ridge that divides his "Cedar Valley" and Fish Spring Flat.

The actual distance from where he entered the valley to where he crossed this ridge is four and a half miles.

The final error that he made this day shows up in the Table of Distances, Altitudes, and Grades that appears in the appendix to the report. The entry that follows Camp 4-W reads "Foot of slope," and the distance from the camp is given as 12.6 miles. There is clearly something wrong with this. Either he got the distance wrong, or he mislabeled the point that he was describing. Throughout the journey, Simpson made numerous notations of the mileage at places that he referred to as "foot of slope" and "in the valley." I am quite certain that in this instance the entry should read "in the valley," rather than "foot of slope." When he was 12.6 miles from the camp, he would have been out in the flats, about two and a half miles from the base of the Black Rock Hills. The other possibility is that the distance figure should have been 10.6 rather than 12.6.

Since leaving the summit of the Dugway Mountains, the expedition had been following a trail that had been established by the Chorpenning mail company sometime between the previous October and May. Three months later, Horace Greeley, the editor of the *New York Times*, who was traveling in one of Chorpenning's mail coaches, said that on the way to Fish Springs, he passed by a "salt well" that was probably Devil's Hole.[17] This shows that the stage was following the trail through Simpson's Cedar Valley. However, sometime during the next few months, this route was abandoned in favor of a route that circled around the northern end of the Black Rock Hills.

Slightly over a year after the Simpson expedition, on September 29, 1860, Sir Richard Burton's party decided to take the new route and ran into some serious difficulties. He described his experiences on this section of the trail as follows:

> After roughly supping we set out, with a fine round moon high in the skies, to ascend the "Dugway Pass" by a rough dusty road winding round the shoulder of a hill, through which a fiumara has burst its way.... Arriving on the

summit we sat down, whilst our mules returned to help the baggage wagons....In honour of our good star which had preserved every hoof from accident we "liquored up" on that summit, and then began the descent.

Having reached the plain the road ran for eight miles over a broken surface,...then forked. The left, which is about six miles the longer of the two, must be taken after rains, and leads to the Devil's Hole....We chose the shorter cut, and after eight miles rounded Mountain Point, the end of a dark brown butte falling into the plain. Opposite us and under the western hills, which were distant about two miles, lay the station, but we were compelled to double, for twelve miles, the intervening slough, which no horse can cross without being mired. The road hugged the foot of the hills at the edge of the saleratus basin....We then fell into a saline, resembling freshly-fallen snow....After ascending some sand-hills we haled for the party to form up in case of accident, and Mr. Kennedy proceeded to inspect whilst we prepared for the worst part of the stage—the sloughs....The tule, the bayonet-grass, and the tall rushes enable animals to pass safely over the deep slushy mud, but when the vegetation is well trodden down, horses are in danger of being permanently mired....Beyond the sloughs we ascended a bench, and traveled on an improved road.[18]

JULY 1999

During my first major trip along Simpson's Route, I turned off Pony Express Road just after passing the northern end of the Thomas Range. At this time, I was quite uncertain about the actual location of the trail, but I soon found that wherever it was, I would not be able to follow it in my SUV. Finding a seldom-used two-track road that headed directly south along the western base of the Thomas Mountains, I followed it for about four and a half miles and came to another one that headed west. By following that track, I was able to intersect Simpson's route near the southeast corner of the Black Rock Hills. From that point Simpson's trail follows a two-track that leads in a southwesterly direction to the eastern edge of Fish Springs Flat.

JULY 2001

After some further study of the wording of the report and some maps of the area, I decided to attempt to follow the trail across the little valley on foot. I enlisted the help of Louis Dunyon, my father-in-law, and we drove to the area and got onto the narrow two-track that heads south along the east side of the valley. At about two miles south of Pony Express Road, I got out of the vehicle and started walking across the valley in a southwesterly direction. Lou continued to follow the two-track until he came to the southwest corner of the valley, where he stopped and waited for me. I saw no indication of a trail during this hike, and further research has shown that the route I had followed that day was to the south of Simpson's trail. Since that time, by studying aerial photos, I have located an abandoned road that crosses the valley in an almost straight line between the point that Simpson entered it and the place where he emerged from it.

MAY 2006

Returning to the little valley, I hiked across it again, this time following the old road that I had found on the photos. By using the latitude and longitude tools that are available on the Google Earth program, I was able to determine a number of checkpoints along the route. Then by programming these checkpoints into my GPS receiver, I was able to go to each of them with an accuracy of a few feet. This time I knew exactly where the trail was, and had no trouble in following it across the valley. Although essentially abandoned for somewhere around one hundred and forty-six years, the trail can still be seen almost all of the way. I did come across a few short sections where it has become very faint, but as I continued to walk, it would soon become visible again.

After crossing the valley, the trail dropped down the southern slope of the Black Rock Hills and came to the eastern edge of Fish Springs Flat. From here, the trail headed out into the flats in a southwesterly direction. I wanted to continue to follow the route across the flats, but was unable to find any kind of a road that would let me drive through this area.

JULY 2001

This was the first of many hikes that I would eventually make along the undrivable sections of the expedition's route. In preparation for this hike, I enlisted the help of Jay Banta, the manager of the Fish Springs National Wildlife Refuge, which is a few miles north of the area where I needed to walk. I parked my vehicle on the west side of Fish Spring Flat, near Cane Springs. Jay then gave me a ride to the east side of the flats, near the base of the Black Rock Hills, where I started hiking toward the west.

During my hike across Fish Spring Flat, I found nothing that would even suggest a trail or wagon tracks, and I was satisfied that whatever trail had been here, had long since disappeared. I was wrong about this, and it took me a long time to learn that the trail is still there. When I first learned about the aerial photos on the Terraserver website, this was one of the first places I looked at. However, at that time, the photos of this particular area were of such poor quality that I was unable to see any evidence of a trail. Early in 2006, I decided to take another look and was pleased to find that the poor-quality photos had been replaced with better ones, and a trail could now be seen. It is quite faint, and almost disappears in some areas, but it can be seen, and when I measure along it, the distance between Camp 4-W and Camp 5-W matches the distance that Simpson listed in his report. I am convinced that the trail that can be seen in the new photos is Simpson's route. When I hiked across the flats in 2001, I had probably traveled almost parallel to the trail, but slightly to the north.

This valley crossed, the road takes a sharp turn to the right, and, running northwestwardly, skirts a range of highly-altered calcareous and slaty rocks on your left, and in 1.5 miles passes by Devil's Hole, and in 5.5 miles more reaches Fish Springs, where Lieutenant Murry and command are encamped. Whole journey, 25.3 miles.[19]

The natural well that is still known as Devil's Hole is found next to the road that runs along the eastern base of the Fish Springs Range. It is about twelve feet in diameter, and the level of the water varies significantly. I have seen it when the surface of the water was nearly at ground level, and at other times, it has been as much as six feet lower. William Lee described it as "a singular formation, being a perfect well about ten feet to the water and the water being twenty-eight feet deep and tasting like soap and water."[20] This pool's importance to Simpson's route is that it shows how far south the expedition had to go in order to avoid the boggy ground in the northern part of Fish Springs Flat.

I had narrowed the probable location of the Fish Springs campsite down to about a half-mile area, but was still uncertain about the exact spot until I found William Lee's journal. The biggest problem I had been having was that Simpson's report gives three different figures for the distance they traveled that day. His incremental distances add up to exactly twenty-five miles, his end-of-day figure in the text was 25.3 miles, and the figure in the table of distances is 25.5 miles. When I read Lee's description of the day's journey, I found a clue that helped me get a lot closer to the true location.

Friday, May 6th. Marched until ten A.M., coming to camp at Warm Springs after marching twenty-five miles.... The water of Warm Springs is slightly tinctured with sulphur and is pleasantly warm for bathing.[21]

This information at least told me that the campsite was near a pool of water that was large enough and deep enough for bathing. My first assumption was that this would narrow it down considerably. However, when I took a look at the map again, I found that there are no less than five springs within the half-mile area in question. Realizing that I needed more information, I contacted Jay Banta to see if any one of these springs would fit Lee's description any better than the others. He said that there are two pools that would fit the description quite well, Thomas Spring and South Spring. After visiting the area again and taking some more measurements, I have concluded that South Spring is the most likely candidate. By measuring along the trail, this spring is 4.9 miles from Devil's Hole; Simpson said it was five miles. Another factor is that South Spring is the first pool that the expedition would have

Camp 5-W. Located about a half mile southeast of the Fish Springs Wildlife Headquarters, this pool is called South Spring. It would have been the first spring that the expedition reached after crossing Fish Spring Flat.

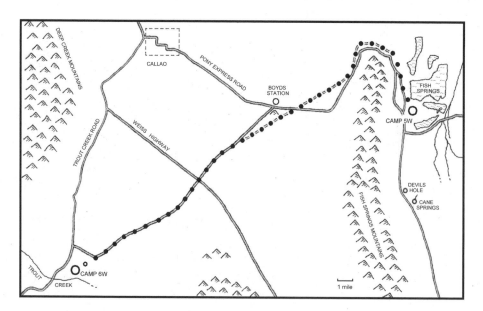

MAY 7, 1859

come to after making their long and waterless trek that day. Why would they have gone any farther? The final factor is that South Spring turns out to be exactly six miles from the northern tip of the Fish Springs Mountain, which is the distance reported by Simpson the next day.

While camped at Fish Springs, Simpson talked to the Chorpenning employee who was in charge of the station. The mail-agent confirmed that it would have been extremely difficult, if not impossible, to bring the wagons directly across the flat rather than making the loop to the south. The agent stated that this area would "scarcely allow animals with packs to cross." The next morning Reese came in and reported that he had just come directly across the flats, and he had "been obliged to unpack his animals to get over the marsh."[22]

By 1913, when this northern route across the flats was adopted as a part of the Lincoln Highway, two bridges had been built across the main drainages of Fish Springs Wash,[23] but the road across the flats still presented serious challenges to automobile travel. Several road guides from the early automobile period noted the presence of a large sign on the east side of the flats, advising motorists that if they got stuck, they should build a large fire and the owner of the Fish Springs Ranch would bring a team of horses to pull them out.

It was at the south side of the Fish Springs Wildlife Refuge that Simpson's route and the route of the Lincoln Highway first came together, but the joining would be brief. Twelve miles farther west, at Boyd's Station, the routes would separate again and would not rejoin for another fifty miles.

During his westward trek, Simpson occasionally mentioned his plans to return by a route that would be some distance to the south. He made one such statement while camped at Fish Springs, when he reported that John Reese had been looking for water in the country to the south of Devil's Hole. That search had been unsuccessful, but an Indian they encountered at Fish Springs claimed to know that there was water in that area of the country. Upon hearing this, Simpson instructed Reese to take the Indian and look again. He then commented that

"if water is found there, I shall change the road accordingly on my return from Carson Valley."[24] Four days later Reese caught up with the expedition in Pleasant Valley and reported that they had found some water, but it was well beyond the area he had explored during his first scouting trip.

May 7, 1859

MAY 7, CAMP No. 5, FISH SPRINGS.—*Took up march at 6 ¼ o'clock. In 3.5 miles pass Warm Spring and a mail-station. Soon after starting it commenced to rain, which softened the road at the outset so much as to cause the wagons, 6 miles from Fish Springs to stall occasionally in a distance of one-quarter of a mile. Detained an hour on this account.*[25]

FROM THE FISH SPRINGS campsite, the expedition headed north along the eastern base of the Fish Springs Range. Their trail would have been along the edge of the flats, rather than up in the foothills where Pony Express Road is located. At six miles from camp, they would have reached the northwest point of the mountain.

At this point, the road doubles the point of the range along which we have been traveling, and continues on the plain of the desert toward the Go-shoot or Tots-arrh Mountains [Deep Creek Range], meaning high mountain range.[26]

Leaving today's road about two miles south of the northwest tip of the mountain, Simpson's route cut across the flats in a southwesterly direction, passing Boyd's Station about a mile to the east. This section of Simpson's route became the route of the Overland Stage, the Pony Express Trail, and the Lincoln Highway. Later, a better road was built, which followed the base of the mountain for another three miles before turning west and heading straight across the flats, and the older road was abandoned. I drove this abandoned section in 1995 while exploring the Lincoln Highway.

The expedition was still following Chorpenning's mail route at this time, but about five or six months later, the mail route changed. The

The northern tip of the Fish Springs Mountains. *"At this point the road doubles the point of the range."*

trail around the south end of the Deep Creek Mountains was dropped in favor of a new route that headed west from Boyd's Station, to go through Callao and Ibapah.[27] When the Pony Express began operating in April 1860, it followed the new route, as did the Overland Stage and the Lincoln Highway. The Simpson expedition continued in a generally southwesterly direction, following Chorpenning's original trail down the length of Snake Valley to the area of Trout Creek.

After making a journey of 29.7 miles, and coming for the first time to grass, the mules beginning to give out, we were obliged about sundown to encamp without water, except that in our kegs. I however found water 2.5 miles ahead, to which we will move to-morrow.[28]

Simpson reported that for most of the day, the expedition had been heading toward the "Go-shoot" or "Tots-arrh" mountains, and he noted that many of the peaks were covered with snow. He then added that about seventy miles from their position; "quartering to the left from our camp may be seen a towering one, which I call Union Peak, on account of its presenting itself in a doubled and connected form."[29] It appears that Simpson considered the Deep Creek Mountains and the Snake Mountains to be one single mountain range, which he referred to as the "Go-shoot or Tots-arrh Mountains." His Union Peak is today's Wheeler Peak, which is a part of the Snake Range, and is actually about fifty-five miles southwest from Trout Creek.

Simpson does not give us much of a description of the area where the camp was located, and the only thing Lee had to say about it was that there was no water.[30] However, by measuring from the Fish Springs campsite, it appears that it was in a roadless area, about a mile northeast of Trout Creek.

August 2002

I drove to the Trout Creek area with the intention of hiking to the sites where I believed Camps 6-W and 7-W had been. Leaving my SUV next to the road about two miles northeast of Trout Creek, I began to follow the route that I thought the wagons may have used. Making my way through growths of unusually tall sagebrush and greasewood that were replaced occasionally by completely barren playas, I came to the site of Camp 6-W. After taking some photographs and GPS readings, I headed for Camp 7-W. A couple of years later, after making some additional measurements on the maps and studying aerial photos of the area, I decided that I had picked the wrong spot for Camp 6-W. The new site was about half a mile to the northwest, and I needed to make another short hike.

July 14, 2005

Returning to the Trout Creek area, I hiked to the spot that I now believed to be a more accurate location for Camp 6-W. This point turns out to be a lot closer to the main road, and is much easier to reach.

During the evening that the expedition spent at Camp 6-W, a Ute Indian, who was known as Black Hawk, came into the camp and visited with them for some time. In spite of the fact that Simpson had earlier stated that he had seen Chief Cho-kup near Lookout Pass and had talked to an Indian at Fish Springs, he made the comment that Black Hawk was the first Indian he had seen since leaving Camp Floyd. Throughout the remainder of the journey, he frequently mentioned the Indians that they encountered, describing at length their appearance, their living conditions, and their habits. At a time when the humane treatment of Indians was not a very popular concept, especially among career army officers, Simpson included the following observation in his official report:

I have made it a point to treat the Indians I meet kindly, making them small presents, which I trust will not be without their use in securing their friendly feelings and conduct. A great many of the difficulties our country has had with the Indians, according to my observations and experience, have grown out of the bad treatment they have received at

the hands of insolent and cowardly men, who, not gifted with the bravery which is perfectly consistent with a kind and generous heart, have, when they thought they could do it with impunity, maltreated them; the consequence resulting that the very next body of whites they have met have not unfrequently been made to suffer the penalties which in this way they are almost always sure to inflict indiscriminately on parties, whether they deserve it or not.[31]

The members of the expedition experienced difficulties with Indians on only a single occasion. While they were in camp one afternoon, one of the cooks became irritated with a couple of Indians who were hovering around the food he was preparing. In an effort to persuade them to leave, the cook pointed to the revolver he was carrying at his side. The Indians immediately took the hint and departed in a huff, shooting an arrow into one of the expedition's animals as they were leaving. When questioned, the cook reluctantly admitted to what he had done, and Simpson promptly issued orders.

I have given orders to the effect that if the like indiscreet act should be committed again the perpetrator would be held to a strict account for it, and should be punished to the extent of his crime. As I have before stated, my policy with the Indians has always been one, so far as it could be, of peace and good-will toward them; and I have never found anything but good resulting from it.[32]

Simpson wanted to maintain good relations with the Indians, but he was not above having a little fun with them. On one occasion, he allowed a few of them to attempt a mule ride. Their efforts met with little success, and Simpson noted that the mules were "so much frightened at their rabbit-skin dress as to cause them to run off with them."[33] Simpson was quite impressed with one Indian, who went by the name of Cho-kup and was the chief of a band of Shoshones. Simpson had first encountered him near Lookout Pass on May 3, when Cho-kup was traveling to Camp Floyd to meet with the Indian agent. Simpson not only named a pass in the Diamond Mountains for this chief, he also wrote a letter of introduction that vouched for his character.[34]

Camp 6-W. In the alkali flats at the foot of the Deep Creek Mountains, about a mile and a half northeast of Trout Creek: *"the mules beginning to give out, we were obliged about sundown to encamp without water."*

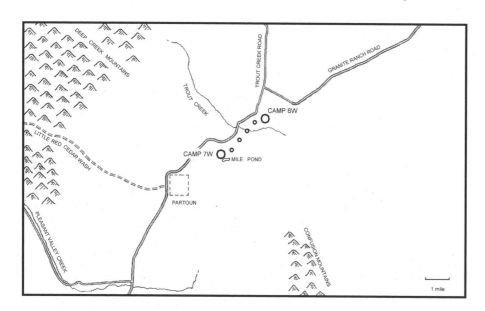

MAY 8, 1859

On the other hand, Simpson showed that he could get a little irritated with some of the Indians' behavior. On one occasion, he admitted that he found some of the natives to be "a little impudent," and he had reacted by giving "some significant evidences of displeasure."[35] Simpson was also a practical man, and his goodwill had certain limits. He mentioned once that he did not allow any Indians, other than those attached to the party, to stay overnight in the expedition's camps. He did make one exception to this policy during the return trip. This involved a crippled Indian named Quah-not, who led them to a much-needed spring. In his appreciation for this Indian's help, Simpson named the spot Good Indian Spring. There will be more about this experience later.

MAY 8, 1859

MAY 8, CAMP NO. 6, GREAT SALT LAKE DESERT.—*Moved at half past five. In one mile, pass on our left an alkaline spring. Water not drinkable. In 1.2 miles more, come to a sulphur spring, where there is an abundance of water and grass, and where we encamped. It being Sunday and the animals and party requiring rest, we have only made this short march of 2.5 miles to get feed and water. The water, though sulphurous, is quite palatable to man and beast.*[36]

THIS CAMPSITE WAS LOCATED about a mile south and slightly west of Trout Creek. When Simpson traveled through this area, the vegetation was low-growing greasewood, mixed with some sagebrush, and some grassy areas near what little water existed. Today the entire area is overgrown with Russian olive trees. During my visit to this area in 2002, I hiked along what I then felt was the expedition's route between the two campsites. Along the way, I looked for the small alkaline spring that Simpson mentioned, but found no sign of it. As I approached the site of Camp 7-W, I made my way through the thick growth of thorny trees and came to a grassy clearing. Maps of the area show this clearing as a small lake called Mile Pond. I found that the clearing was filled with grass, and not a drop of water was to be seen, clearly a result of the

several-year drought that the Great Basin region had been experiencing during the time that I was traveling Simpson's trail. During my explorations, I came to many places where Simpson reported the existence of water, but I found them to be completely dry. Although there was no water in Mile Pond when I was there, the presence of the Russian olive trees is a clear indication that there is a certain amount of subsurface moisture in this area.

MAY 9, 1859

MAY 9, CAMP NO. 7, SULPHUR SPRING.—*Resumed march at 25 minutes of 6, and shaped our course south of west for a wide pass through the Go-shoot Mountains [Deep Creek Range], which we commence ascending in 4.5 miles.*[37]

HEADING SLIGHTLY SOUTH-OF-WEST from the campsite, the expedition would have crossed today's road just north of the small community of Partoun. After traveling four and a half miles from the campsite, they came to the lower end of Little Red Cedar Wash. This usually dry streambed comes out of a shallow canyon about five miles north of the southern tip of the Deep Creek Mountains. A fairly common misconception is that Chorpenning's mail route and the Simpson trail went all the way around the south end of the Deep Creek Mountains. The trail did get fairly close to the southernmost tip of the mountains, but not quite. Simpson's description of the route makes it clear that he was following Chorpenning's route when he used Little Red Cedar Wash as a shortcut to Pleasant Valley.

In 6 miles more you reach the east summit, by a tolerable grade, and thence, in 2.5 miles, descend, by a good grade, to Pleasant Valley, where we find an abundance of grass and plenty of water. A mile more brought us to a spring, the copious source of the stream which runs eastwardly through the valley into a large valley, which I call Crosman Valley [Snake Valley], after Lieut. Col. George H. Crosman, deputy quartermaster-general and chief of the quartermaster's department in the Military Department of Utah. This stream (Pleasant Valley Creek) has a width of 12 feet, is 5 feet in depth, of

Camp 7-W. On the edge of what the maps show as Mile "Pond": "*In 1.2 miles more, come to a sulphur spring, where there is an abundance of water and grass.*" For at least the last ten years, this area has been a grass-covered clearing, surrounded by a dense growth of Russian olive trees.

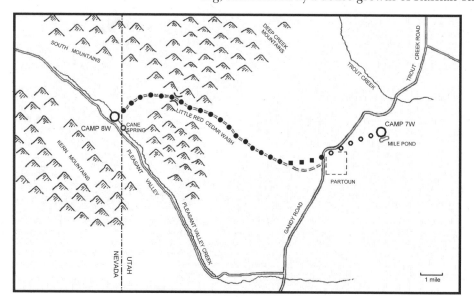

MAY 9, 1859

sandy bottom, and has a rapid current. Near the spring we encamp after a march of 13.4 miles. At this point is a mail-station, a log house. The mail company has done a great deal of work in the pass we have just come through, in removing rocks, filling up gullies, and making side cuts.[38]

During my first extensive trip along Simpson's route in 1999, I drove to Partoun and then started up the narrow two-track trail that goes over the pass. It soon became evident that it was going to take much more time than I wanted to spend that day, so I returned to the main road, and got into Pleasant Valley by driving around the southern point of the Deep Creek Mountains.

SEPTEMBER 2000

Returning to the Snake Valley area, I headed west from Partoun and drove all the way up Little Red Cedar Wash and down the west side of the ridge into Pleasant Valley. The trail was very faint, and for about a mile on each side of the summit, I found it necessary to use four-wheel drive. At the bottom of the western slope, I had to go through three gates and then found myself in the backyard of a ranch house. I stopped there and knocked on the door to get permission to drive through the yard. The rancher, whose name is Bill Henroid, and I were soon engaged in a rather lengthy conversation about the history of Pleasant Valley. He had never heard of James Simpson, but he knew all about the trail over the pass and told me that he had traveled it several times.

The spring near which the expedition camped that night is located next to the creek, about a mile and a half northwest of the Henroid ranch and Utah-Nevada state line. There is a bridge across the creek today, but a locked gate prevents access to the road that crosses the creek and heads eastward into the foothills of the Deep Creek Mountains.

Horace Greeley was quite impressed with Pleasant Valley. He was particularly pleased to find some good water to drink.

We drove rapidly down its [the mountain's] western declivity, and, a little after 5, P.M., reached our next station in "Pleasant Valley," a broad ravine, which descends to the south-west. Here we found water—bright, sweet, pure, sparkling, leaping water—the first water fit to drink that we had reached in a hundred miles; if Simpson's Spring ever dries up, the distance will then be at least a hundred and twenty.[39]

Four

Pleasant Valley to Roberts Creek

Camp 8-W. The campsite was near the ranch building in the foreground, just west of the Utah-Nevada border.

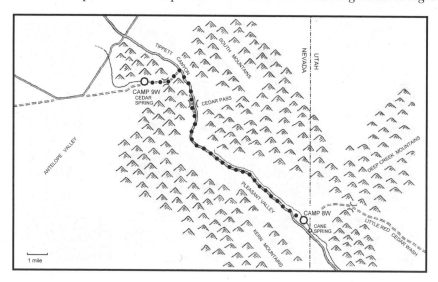

MAY 10, 1859

38

MAY 10, CAMP NO. 8, PLEASANT VALLEY.— *Pleasant Valley, which is very narrow, contains grass all along it, but no water above the spring where we encamped last night except occasionally....From Pleasant Valley to Camp No. 8 [sic, 9], the road, which has a general direction north of west, traverses in 8.5 miles two or three steep but short hills, which, however, did not require the teams to be doubled, to the west summit of the Totsarrh range [Kern Mountains], and thence 4 miles to camp. The mail company have done on this portion of the route some little work, but not enough to make the road what it should be. The road as made does not follow the direct pack-route, but makes quite a detour to the right or north. The mail-man, who has piloted us from the last camp, says a road, however, could be made by the pack-mule route, The difficulty is a very steep declivity into Antelope Valley....Journey to-day, 12.5 miles.*[1]

SIMPSON CLEARLY MADE an error when he said they traveled from Pleasant Valley to "Camp No. 8." They were actually leaving Camp Number 8, which was in Pleasant Valley, and heading for Camp Number 9. The summit that they crossed at 8.5 miles is known as Cedar Pass, and is located on the ridge between South Mountain and Kern Mountain. Today two roads cross this pass. One is a well-traveled and well-maintained dirt road that travels along the eastern side of a knoll that lies in the middle of the pass area. The second road is a very seldom used, but drivable, track that passes the western side of the knoll. Since it is older, it is my assumption that the expedition followed the now-abandoned road. The pack-mule route that the Chorpenning mail carriers were using must have gone through a canyon known as Blue Mass, and then across Moffitt Pass.

The route followed by the expedition during the second half of this day's journey proved to be one of the most difficult sections of the entire route for me to figure out. It was not until after a great deal of study, and several trips to the area, that I finally came to a satisfactory conclusion regarding the alignment of the route and the location of the campsite. The primary cause of my confusion was Simpson's failure to mention an abrupt turn that they made. Simpson's map

shows that after crossing the summit, the trail continued in an almost northerly direction for some distance, and then made a sharp turn to the west. The exact location of this turn cannot be determined from the map, and it is not even mentioned in the report, and it took a long time to find it.

As I began looking at this section of the route, I did not have access to a good copy of Simpson's map, and I was assuming that his trail followed today's well-traveled road all the way down Tippet Canyon into Antelope Valley. A short distance after emerging from the canyon, the road comes to a four-way intersection, and for a long time I thought this was the location of the turn. However, this assumption failed to account for a couple of important items. The first of these was the fact that the table of distances includes a listing for "Ridge east of Antelope Valley," at 2.8 miles beyond the summit. The problem with this is that after crossing the summit, today's main road never goes over anything that can be described as a ridge. The second item was that both the table and the text of the report indicate that the campsite was located four miles from the summit. The problem here is that on the main road, at four miles from the summit, you are still in the canyon, and still a mile and a half short of the four-way intersection. This would mean that the camp would have been somewhere to the south of the turn, but the map shows it as being west of the turn. When I first discovered these problems, I reluctantly concluded that Simpson must have put the campsite at the wrong place on the map. But that still did not account for the location of the turn.

I had been looking at this problem off and on for about four years when it occurred to me that the expedition may not have remained on today's main road all the way to the valley. Perhaps Simpson had found a place where they could get across the ridge that made up the western side of the canyon. Taking another look at the maps, and paying particular attention to the contour lines, I found what appeared to be a pass through the ridge at about a mile above the mouth of the canyon. This turned out to be the right idea, but it was the wrong place.

OCTOBER 2003

My wife Nancy decided to come with me on this trip, and we drove to Tippett Canyon, where we looked for the pass through the western ridge. Not very far from the mouth of the canyon we found a low pass leading to the southwest. Finding no road of any sort through this pass, I took off on foot to see if this route would have been passable for the wagons. After hiking a couple of miles, I found that this area would have presented no serious problems for the wagons, but I was suspicious of the fact that I was unable to find even the slightest indication that any type of wheeled vehicles had ever passed through this area. The mere absence of visible tracks cannot be considered as proof of anything, one way or another, but it did leave me very doubtful. Added to the lack of any indication of a trail was the fact that a route through this little pass would still fail to solve the distance problem. The camp would still be on the wrong side of the turn. Reluctantly, I had to admit that I had not yet solved the puzzle.

After returning home and spending some more time studying my maps of the area, I stumbled across the answer. While taking another look at a USGS 7.5-minute map, I noticed a faint line that had never caught my attention before. This line was some distance to the south of the area I had been concentrating on, and I had simply failed to notice it. It was apparent that the narrow line represented some sort of trail that leaves the main road at about three and a half miles southeast of the four-way intersection. Heading west, this trail appeared to cross the canyon's western ridge and then drop down into Antelope Valley. Suddenly things were beginning to fit, and I could hardly wait to get back to Tippett Canyon to check it out.

MAY 2004

I was accompanied on this trip by Jim Hall, who wanted to get a look at the country between Ibapah and Tippett. Once we had gotten into Tippett Canyon, we had no trouble locating the faint trail I had discovered on the map. We found it to be a seldom-used two-track that crosses the west ridge of the canyon at exactly the distance from the summit that is listed in Simpson's table of distances. When we reached the spot where the campsite would have been, we found a small running stream and a reservoir that is marked on the map as Cedar Spring. This spring would have been the first water that the expedition encountered after leaving Pleasant Valley, and is almost certainly the reason that this particular spot was selected for the camp. Simpson does not mention anything about water in relation to this camp, and I was somewhat surprised to find the spring. It was not until a couple of years later that I read in William Lee's journal that they had "camped at a spring on the side of a hill on the divide between Pleasant and Antelope Vallies."[2]

After finding the small stream at just the right distance from the Pleasant Valley campsite, I was finally satisfied that I had found the route the expedition had used to get from Tippett Canyon to Antelope Valley, and the correct site for Camp 9-W. After finally getting it all figured out, it became apparent that Simpson's map was exactly right, and I had been much too quick to assume that he had made an error.

MAY 11, 1859

MAY 11, CAMP NO. 9, EAST SLOPE OF ANTELOPE VALLEY.—*Moved at 25 minutes of 6. Course, south of west across Antelope and Shell Valleys. Just after leaving camp we have a fine distant view of the mountains hemming in the Antelope Valley at the west and north. After getting across the valley you can see to the east of south, glittering with snow, the high peak of the Go-shoot, or Tots-arrh range (Union Peak), some 60 miles off.*[3]

CEDAR SPRING IS LOCATED at the bottom of a steep-sided canyon that blocks the view to the north and the south. But after less than a quarter of a mile, a westbound traveler comes out of the canyon, and the view in all directions opens up. Wheeler Peak, which Simpson called Union Peak, and which he had previously observed from Snake Valley a few days before, lies about fifty-five miles from where the expedition crossed the southern part of Antelope Valley.

Camp 9-W. Cedar Spring, on the western slope of Kern Mountain. Although Simpson did not mention that there was water here, they probably camped at this location because of the small stream that now empties into the man-made reservoir.

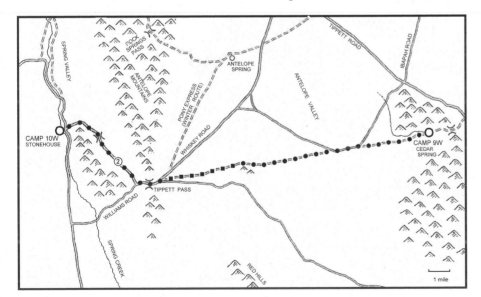

MAY 2004

After spending some time at Cedar Spring, Jim Hall and I continued west, following Simpson's trail about halfway across Antelope Valley. At that point, our progress was halted by an ungated fence, so we turned around and headed home by way of Pleasant Valley and Fish Springs.

JULY 2003

I had been doing some exploring in the southern end of Spring Valley, and had decided to head north into Antelope Valley to see if I could get onto the section of the trail that traverses the western part of the valley. I found that although this piece of the route can be seen from the eastern base of Twelve-Mile Summit, it has become so overgrown with sagebrush that it is impossible to negotiate in a vehicle. However, I was able to find a drivable road that sort of parallels the trail a short distance to the south. I drove eastward on this road and followed it until it turned to the north and joined the route that was used by the expedition and Chorpenning's pack mules and mail coaches. After getting onto the old trail, I followed it until I came to the fence that would later stop Jim Hall and me from crossing the valley after our trip to Cedar Spring.

After crossing Antelope Valley, you ascend a rather low range of mountains [Antelope Range], composed of slaty, stratified rocks, by a tolerable grade, and get into a shallow valley, called Shell Valley on account of its being covered with shale. Crossing this you descend over a formation of dioritic rocks, in 2 miles, by a good grade, into Spring Valley, where there is an extensive bottom of alkaline grass and of spring water, and where we encamp early in the afternoon. Journey, 19 miles.[4]

As mentioned previously, Simpson's route and the route followed by the Pony Express, the Overland Stage, and Lincoln Highway, had separated at Boyd's Station in Snake Valley. These two routes come together again just before reaching Twelve-Mile Summit at the southern tip of the Antelope Mountains. According to Joe Nardone, the Pony Express riders sometimes took a shortcut and crossed these mountains through Rock

Springs Pass, but most of the time they used the Twelve-Mile Summit route.

After crossing Twelve-Mile Summit, the expedition turned northwest and went through Tippett Pass, which is not to be confused with Tippett Canyon, which is fifteen miles away, on the eastern side of Antelope Valley. After crossing the shallow valley that lies to the west of Tippett Pass, the expedition emerged into Spring Valley, at a spot that is known today as Stonehouse. Later, the Pony Express would establish its Spring Valley station at this location.

MAY 12, 1859

MAY 12, CAMP NO. 10, SPRING VALLEY.—Our course lay west of north for about 3 miles, when we turned up a ravine south of west, along a rapid mountain-stream (Spring Creek), which we followed for 3.5 miles, when we left it, and continuing up a branch ravine, in 2 miles, by a good wagon-road grade, attained the summit of the Un-go-we-ah range [Schell Creek Range], whence could be seen lying immediately to the west of us Steptoe Valley.[5]

WHEN THEY LEFT camp on the morning of May 12, the expedition traveled upstream along the east bank of Spring Valley Creek. Simpson felt that the main stream, which he called Spring Creek, flowed out of Stage Canyon. Modern maps, however, indicate that Spring Valley Creek continues to the north, and the stream coming out of Stage Canyon is a tributary. When they reached the mouth of Stage Canyon, the expedition forded Spring Valley Creek and entered the canyon. After traveling three and a half miles up the canyon, Simpson said they left the stream and turned up a "branch ravine." Evidently, he felt that the main stream and the main canyon continued in a southwesterly direction from this point. Today, his branch ravine is considered to be the continuation of Stage Canyon.

Somewhere near the mouth of Stage Canyon, the expedition came across several mules that were running loose. Simpson had his herders round these animals up and put them in with the expedition's herd. Partway up the canyon, they encountered two men from the Chorpenning

Camp 10-W. This campsite was in Spring Valley at a spot now known as Stonehouse. *"Descend by a good grade, into Spring Valley, where there is an extensive bottom of alkaline grass and of spring water."*

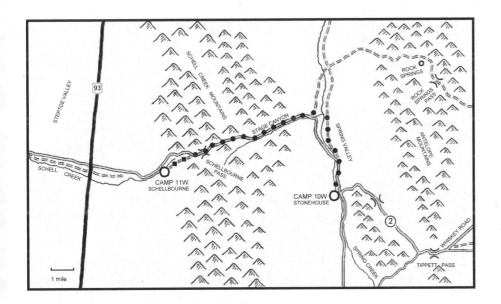

MAY 12, 1859

mail station that was located on the western side of the mountain. One of these was Lot Huntington, who was in charge of Chorpenning's operations in the area between Pleasant Valley and the Humboldt River. Huntington was attempting to track down some mules that had been run off by Indians, and was pleased to find that they were with the expedition. Simpson consistently misspelled this name as Lott Huntingdon, but there can be little doubt that he was the same man who was later killed by Orrin Porter Rockwell at the Faust Pony Express station. In January of 1861, Huntington and five other residents of Salt Lake City were charged with assaulting John W. Dawson, the Governor of the Territory of Utah. Learning that there was a warrant for his arrest, Huntington decided to leave the area. Apparently lacking a horse of his own, he stole one and headed west, taking refuge in the mail station at Faust. Unfortunately for Huntington, the owner of the horse was a good friend of Rockwell, who tracked him to the station and shot him when he attempted to make another getaway.[6]

Descending the west slope of the mountain, which is somewhat steep, about 2 miles more, along a pure, mountain-gushing stream, which I call after Lieutenant Marmaduke, of the Seventh Infantry, brought us to the mail-station on the east side of Steptoe Valley, in the vicinity of which we encamped after a journey of 11.1 miles among good grass, water, and fuel.[7]

The expedition made camp near the site of what would later become Fort Schellbourne, and which is now Schellbourne Ranch. A number of old stone structures that were probably built by the army are still standing near the ranch buildings. The exact location of the mail station is uncertain, but measuring two miles from Schellbourne Pass would put the expedition's campsite about a quarter of a mile below the present ranch buildings. The employees of the mail company told Simpson that they had not yet had a chance to do much to improve the road beyond this point, but they had been getting ready to build a bridge across the stream that flowed through Steptoe Valley. They had already cut and hauled most of the

needed logs. An agreement was reached that if Simpson and his men would build the bridge, the Chorpenning people would deliver the rest of the logs that would be needed. Consequently, the soldiers of the escort worked on the bridge during the day of May 13, and the party stayed at the Schellbourne camp for two nights.

MAY 14, 1859

MAY 14, CAMP NO. 11, EAST SLOPE OF STEPTOE VALLEY.—*Moved at 5.30 o'clock. Course westwardly, directly across Steptoe Valley to Egan Cañon. This valley, trending about north and south, is bound by the Un-go-we-ah Mountains [Schell Creek Range] on the east, and the Montim Mountains [Egan Range] on the west, and is open at either end as far as the eye can reach.... This is a poor, arid valley, perfectly useless for cultivation where we cross it; but farther south, where I crossed it on my return, as my report will show, there is a great deal of good, available pastural and cultivable soil.[8]*

WHEN HE SAID "where I crossed it on my return," Simpson was talking about the expedition's return trip from Genoa. This and a few other statements make it clear that his report was not an unaltered journal. At some point before his report was finalized, Simpson went back to his journal and made some additions to his original entries.

When they left camp that morning, the expedition continued to follow Chorpenning's mail route and the future routes of the Overland Stage and the Pony Express. The Lincoln Highway, however, now turned to the south. Simpson's route and the Lincoln Highway would next come together in Kobeh Valley, about a hundred miles to the west. But they would only cross each other there, and it would be another eighty miles before they merged together again at Eastgate.

Along the axis of the valley a stream [Duck Creek] runs northwardly, which, at the present time, is twenty-five to fifty feet wide; bottom miry; depth, in places, three feet; current moderate. It is said to dry up in the summer.... On account of the marshy approach to the bridge we constructed yesterday over this creek, we were detained three-quarters of an hour.

Camp 11-W. The camp was in this meadow just below today's Schellbourne Ranch. *"Descending the west slope of the mountain brought us to the mail-station on the east side of Steptoe Valley, in the vicinity of which we encamped among good grass, water, and fuel."*

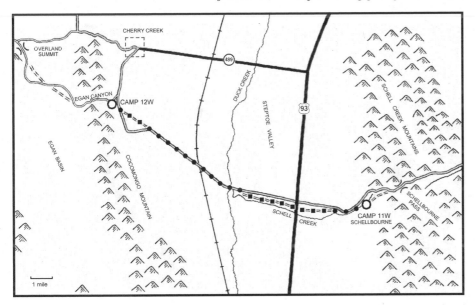

MAY 14, 1859

Duck Creek in Steptoe Valley. This concrete bridge is probably located where Simpson's men spent a day building a log bridge.

Several of the wagons were taken over by hand. At noon, 6.8 miles from bridge, we reached the mouth of Egan Cañon, down which a fine, rapid stream runs, and on which we encamp. Grass on the side of the mountain. Journey 13.3 miles.[9]

After the party had set up camp near the mouth of Egan Canyon, Simpson and Lieutenant Murry made a scouting trip through the canyon. Someone at the mail station had warned Simpson that a lot of work would be needed before they could get the wagons through the canyon. He was pleased to find that very little work would actually be required. Later in the afternoon, the officers set up their instruments and prepared to make some lunar observations after it got dark.

MAY 15, 1859

MAY 15, CAMP NO. 12, MOUTH OF EGAN CAÑON.—*Moved at quarter to 6. The pioneer party went ahead, in order to prepare the road. Our course is westward up Egan Cañon, by an easy ascent, to Round Valley [Egan Basin], about 2.5 miles, thence six miles across Round Valley, and by a ravine which required some work, to the summit of the Montim range [Cherry Creek Range], and thence 9.5 miles across Butte Valley, to the vicinity of a small well on the west side of the valley.... The Humboldt range [Ruby Range] has appeared ahead of us to-day, looming up above the range limiting Butte Valley on the west, and is covered with snow. It is the most imposing range I have seen since leaving the Wahsatch Mountains, and is to be seen stretching far to the northward. Our day's travel has been 18.1 miles.[10]*

IMMEDIATELY AFTER LEAVING camp, the expedition entered a narrow, steep-walled canyon that first took them almost due west, and then turned to the southwest for a short distance before coming out into the Egan Basin. Once out of the canyon, they turned to the northwest and crossed this small valley, then climbed to the summit of the Cherry Creek Range. The trail that Simpson described as going up a ravine is

Camp 12-W. On the west side of Steptoe Valley: "we reached the mouth of Egan Cañon, down which a fine, rapid stream runs, and on which we encamp."

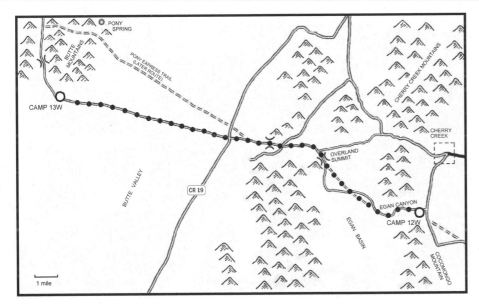

now abandoned, and a better-traveled two-track road turns west near the Egan Basin Well, then after a short distance turns north to climb the mountain. Simpson's table of distances lists two summits in the Egan Mountains. The first one was at 5.2 miles from the camp, and is shown on some maps as Overland Summit. The second was at 8.3 miles and is on the main ridge of the Cherry Creek Range.

JULY 1999

During my first long trip along Simpson's route, I drove through Egan Canyon, then got onto the abandoned trail and followed it to where it rejoins the better-traveled dirt road a short distance below Overland Summit. It was slow going, but presented no real difficulties for my four-wheel-drive SUV. A few years later, during one of the trips that Nancy made with me, we traveled through this area again, but this time we remained on the better road to Overland Summit.

Because the slope in both directions is so gentle, it is a little difficult to know when you have reached Overland Summit. The actual summit lies about halfway between where two branches of the same two-track road reach the Pony Express Trail. This other road comes from the town of Cherry Creek and splits into two branches about a tenth of a mile to the east. About two miles from Overland Summit, the trail comes to a surprisingly wide and well-traveled graveled road. It was at this point during my first two trips to this area that I lost the trail. Not knowing exactly where I was, I got onto the wide road and followed it to an open-pit mining operation, where it came to a dead-end. During my second trip, I thought I was going to avoid this trap, but I got confused and did the same thing again. Both times, I had to work myself down into the valley on the west by using an almost non-existent two-track that took me past Mustang Hill before I could get back onto the Pony Express Trail. But the third time was the charm. This time I had studied the maps a little better, and had my GPS to keep me going in the right direction. Instead of turning onto the mine road, I crossed it and got onto a faint two-track that turned out to be the Pony Express Trail. This road took me over the main ridge

of the Cherry Creek Mountains, then down the western slope into Butte Valley.

From the Cherry Creek summit, the expedition dropped into Butte Valley and crossed it in a slightly north-of-west direction. They made camp for the night in the southern foothills of the Butte Mountains. Simpson's map shows that this campsite was in close proximity to one of Chorpenning's mail stations.

We are encamped at the foot of a dark brown, isolated, porphyritic rock, near the summit of which is a small dug well, 10 feet deep and 2 feet wide. The water in this well can only get here on the principle of the siphon bringing it from some distant source.... (Subsequent to this date, in the summer, this point had to be abandoned by the mail company as a station on account of the well drying up. I have learned, however, that they have since found water in the vicinity, probably about 2 miles to the southeast, where a Sho-sho-nee told us there was water.)[11]

Simpson does not say when or how he heard about the new source of water, but this information was at least partially correct. The mail station that Chorpenning established at the southern tip of the Butte Mountains, and near which the expedition camped, was later abandoned and another station established. However, this new station was about three miles to the northeast, near Pony Springs, not to the southeast, which would have been down in the bottom of the valley. The move to the new site required a significant change in the mail route. The new trail split away from the older route at the east side of the valley, near the base of the Cherry Creek Range. Traveling in more of a northwesterly direction than Simpson's trail, the new route climbed into the Butte Mountains and crossed the ridge just a short distance below Pony Springs. Dropping down the west side of the mountain, it rejoined the older route about three miles north of Simpson's camp. The date of this change is elusive, but it probably took place before the mail route was taken over by Russell, Majors, and Waddell.

Richard Burton arrived at what he called "Butte Station" on October 5, 1860. It was probably the Pony Springs site. His description of his evening at the station is nothing if not colorful.

Camp 13-W. On the west side of Butte Valley: *"We are encamped at the foot of a dark brown, isolated, porphyritic rock."*

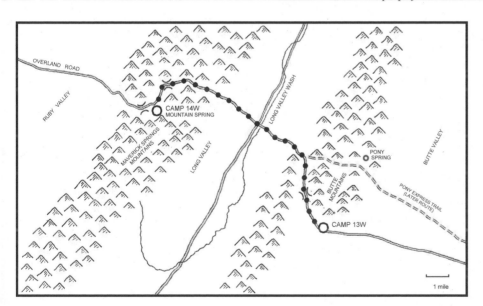

The good station-master, Mr. Thomas, a Cambrian Mormon…bade us kindly welcome, built a roaring fire, added meat to our supper of coffee and dough-boy, and cleared by a summary process amongst the snorers places for us on the floor of "Robber's Roost," or "Thieves' Delight," as the place is face-tiously known throughout the countryside.…It is about as civilised as the Galway shanty, or the nor-mal dwelling-place in Central Equatorial Africa. A cabin fronting east and west, long walls thirty feet, with portholes for windows.… The length was divided by two perpendiculars, the southernmost of which, assisted by a half-way canvass partition, cut the hut into unequal parts. Behind it were two bunks for four men.… The floor, which also fre-quently represented bedsteads, was rough, uneven earth, neither tamped nor swept, and the fine end of a spring oozing through the western wall kept part of it in a state of eternal mud. A redeeming point was the fireplace, which occupied half of the northern short wall.[12]

Nothing but a small mound of rocks can be found at the site of the first mail station, near which the expedition camped.

MAY 16, 1859

MAY 16, CAMP NO. 13, WEST SLOPE OF BUTTE VALLEY.—*Moved at 20 minutes of 6. Course con-tinues a little north of west. In 2 miles reach sum-mit of divide between Butte and Long Valleys, by a very gradual ascent, and 2.5 miles more, by and easy descent, reach Long Valley.*[13]

AS THEY LEFT the Butte Valley camp, the expe-dition started out in a westwardly direction, but soon made a turn to the north and began climb-ing a gentle slope. After crossing the ridge of the Butte Mountains, they turned toward the north-west and dropped into Long Valley.

Crossing this dry valley, which is 2.7 miles wide, 3.1 miles more up a tolerable grade brings you to the summit of a low range [Maverick Springs Range] running north and south, dividing Long from Ruby Valley, about one mile below which, on the west slope, we encamp, at a spring [Mountain Spring] just discovered by Lott Huntingdon, of the

mail party, and which therefore I have called after him. It is a good camping-place, and grass and fuel are convenient. Journey to-day, 12 miles.[14]

During the last few miles of this day's journey, the expedition traveled up today's Murry Canyon to the summit of the Maverick Springs Range, then dropped down the western side of the ridge to make camp at Mountain Spring. In this area today there is a man-made pond that is fed by the spring. The USGS 7.5-minute map for this area indicates that the Mountain Spring Pony Express station was located near this spring. However, Joe Nardone's research indicates that the station was about two and a half miles back along the trail, near the lower end of Murry Canyon, where he has found an abandoned well and the ruins of a couple of stone structures.

Included in this day's report is the first of a number of comments about a wagon train that had traveled through the area that Simpson was planning to explore during his return trip. The story was that this had occurred sometime during the previous year. It is quite clear that Simpson had been completely unaware of this wagon train until he heard about it from Lot Huntington, while the expedition was camped at Schellbourne. Simpson now learned that John Reese, his own guide, had come across the trail of the mysterious travelers while scouting for the expedition's return route.

He represents that he has found a route generally parallel to the one we are on, and some 30 miles to the south, which is practicable for wagons, and furnishes water and grass at intervals of 15 to 20 miles. Indeed, a good portion of the way is an old wagon-road.[15]

In his account of the return trip, Simpson adds more information about this wagon road. We will get back to this matter later.

MAY 17, 1859

MAY 17, CAMP NO. 14, HUNTINGDON'S SPRING, EAST SLOPE OF RUBY VALLEY.—*Move at quarter to 6, and, shortly after attaining sum-mit of Too-muntz range [Maverick Springs Range]*

Camp 14-W. This campsite was near what later became known as Mountain Spring: "we encamp at a spring just discovered by Lott Huntingdon, of the mail party."

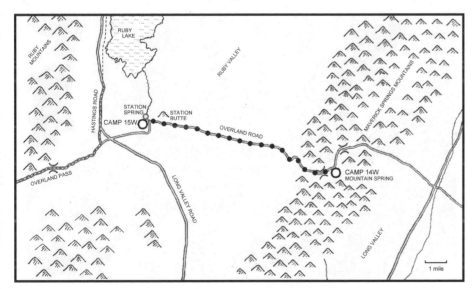

Found just off the road near the Butte Valley camp, this pile of rocks is possibly the remains of the structure that was used by the Chorpenning mail company prior to the advent of the Pony Express.

pass down a cañon, which I call Murry's Cañon, after Lieut. Alexander Murry, the commanding officer of the escort.[16]

THE NAME MURRY CANYON seems to have migrated. Simpson said that he gave this name to the canyon they traveled through as they descended the western slope of the Maverick Springs Range. Today's maps show it on the eastern side of these mountains. I have been unable to find a name for the canyon on the western side.

In 3.9 miles we reach the mouth of the cañon, and immediately cross Ruby Valley, requiring 5.3 miles more of travel to mail-station in the valley, where we encamp at 9.30 A.M. Journey, 9.2 miles. Road good....At our camp is a spring which sends out a small stream of pure water, flowing along the valley northwardly.[17]

This day's travel brought the expedition to Station Spring, near which the Chorpenning company had established a station. A year later, the station was taken over by Russell, Majors, and Waddell, to be used as a station for the

Pony Express. Simpson says nothing about the station itself in his report, but it is clearly designated on his map. Horace Greeley did mention the station building, describing it as being constructed of "red or Indian Pine."[18] This structure may have survived to this day, although not at its original location. Several years ago, a small building that was believed to be the mail station was dismantled and moved to the city of Elko, where it was put back together and now stands in front of the Northeastern Nevada Museum.[19] During the summer of 2005, I was wandering around in the tall greasewood brush on the south side of Station Spring when I came across what appeared to be some sort of concrete marker. I could see four rusted bolts protruding from the concrete, and it appeared to me that they had once been used as fasteners for some sort of a metal plaque. It seems quite likely that I had stumbled across the site of the mail station.

MAY 18, 1859

MAY 18, CAMP No. 15, RUBY VALLEY.— *Moved at 5½ o'clock. Struck immediately for*

Hastings's Pass [Overland Pass], lying south-west from mail-station, the foot of which we reach in 2.5 miles, and the summit by a remarkably easy ascent in 3.3 miles more. This pass leads through the Humboldt range [Ruby Mountains] from Ruby Valley into the valley of the South Fork of the Humboldt which some call Huntingdon's Creek [Huntington Creek]. For the first time we in this pass get into Beckwith's, here coincident with Hastings's road, both of which at the present time are very indistinct.[20]

SIMPSON'S MAP SEEMS to indicate that from the campsite, the expedition continued almost due west for some distance before turning to the southwest. Today you must follow a narrow two-track that heads directly south along a fence line for about a half mile before turning to the west. After traveling two and a half miles, the expedition came to the Hastings Road and started up the slope that leads to Overland Pass, a summit that is located at the southernmost tip of the Ruby Mountains. Hastings Road was the route that was opened and promoted by Lansford Hastings in 1846. In August of that year, Hastings led a vanguard of three parties of emigrants down the eastern base of the Rubies, breaking an entirely new trail that he had never traveled. A few weeks later, the Donner-Reed party made their way along this new wagon road. In 1849 and 1850, the Hastings Road was traveled by a number of California-bound gold rushers, but had seen little use since then. In 1854, Capt. E. G. Beckwith, of the Army's Topographical Corps, traveled a portion of this road while looking for a suitable route for a railroad. Beckwith had followed the Hastings Road from Salt Lake City to Hope Wells in Skull Valley. From Hope Wells, which is now known as Iosepa, the Hastings Road turned northwest to cross the Cedar Mountains through Hastings Pass. Beckwith left the Hastings Road at Iosepa, and continued in a southwesterly direction to cross the Cedar Mountains through a narrow pass that leads, in a southwesterly direction, from Cochrane Spring. From there to the Ruby Mountains, Beckwith's route remained some distance south of the Hastings Road. The two routes rejoined at the western edge of Ruby Valley, then split apart again west of Overland Pass.

At the highest point of the pass, I found a marker made from two sections of railroad rail that have been welded together to form a T. It is one of a number of so-called T-rail posts that have been placed along various emigrant trails in the Western states. The small plaque on this post is inscribed with a quotation from an emigrant journal: "The pass is an excellent one, no rocks, nor very steep, and the road is very firm.—Madison Moorman, 1850."

Descending from the summit, by the finest kind of grade, in about 4 miles we leave Beckwith's and Hastings's roads, which go, the former northwestwardly to join the old road along the Humboldt, 10 miles above Lassen's Meadows, the latter northwardly to join the same road at the mouth of the South Fork of the Humboldt; while we strike southwestwardly, over an unknown country, toward the most northern bend of Walker's River.... We also now leave Chorpenning's or Mail Company's extension of my route from Hastings's Pass, it also turning northward, and joining the old road near Gravelly Ford, which they follow by way of the sink of the Humboldt and Ragtown, on Carson River, to Genoa....From this point, therefore, to where we expect to strike the old road on Carson River, we will have to be guided entirely by the country as it unfolds itself.[21]

About four and a half miles west of the summit, the road comes to a fork. The right-hand branch turns north, climbing up a short hill. The left branch continues straight ahead for a short distance, then turns southwest. There was no fork at this point when the expedition arrived; the road simply made a bend to the north, which was the direction that had been taken by all previous travelers. To the best of Simpson's knowledge, no one had ever turned to the south from here before. If anyone had ever gone in this direction, they had left no trail.

There is another T-rail post at this fork. The inscription on this one reads: "The road wound first to the northwest and finally wholly to the north, now going steadily down into the valley.—Heinrich Leinhard, 1846." Leinhard was with a group of emigrants that were traveling just a few days behind Lansford Hastings. Leinhard was

Camp 15-W. Station Spring in Ruby Valley. "At our camp is a spring which sends out a small stream of pure water flowing along the valley northward."

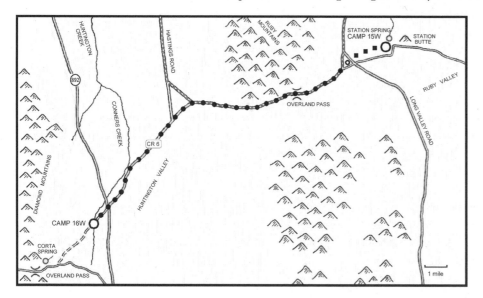

The cabin that was used for the Ruby Pony Express station. Several years ago it was moved from Ruby Valley to the city of Elko, Nevada.

apparently talking about the Hastings Road as it traveled north along the western base of the Ruby Mountains.

Simpson mentioned that the Hastings Road, Beckwith's trail, and Chorpenning's mail route all turned to the north and joined the California Trail on the banks of the Humboldt River, but each of them reached it at a different place. The Hastings Road continued in a northward direction and came to the river near the mouth of the South Fork of the Humboldt, about ten miles southwest of Elko. A short distance north of today's fork in the road, the Beckwith trail and Chorpenning's mail route split away from the Hastings Road, and turned west to go though Railroad Pass. A few miles farther west, these two routes split apart. Beckwith continued west and reached the Humboldt about twenty-five miles southwest of Winnemucca. The Chorpenning route turned to the northwest, crossing Pine Valley, then climbing over the low Cortez Mountains, and reached the Humboldt River at Gravely Ford, a well-known crossing on the California emigrant road, near present-day Beowawe and about seventeen miles southwest of Carlin.[22] This was a part of the route that Chorpenning had opened in late 1858. And Chorpenning was paying close attention to what Simpson was doing in 1859. Shortly after Simpson returned from the expedition,

Chorpenning began making plans to adopt the new route that Simpson had found between the Ruby Mountains and Carson Lake. By early 1860, Chorpenning had dropped the Humboldt River route entirely, and had switched to Simpson's route. During the first three months of 1860, Chorpenning established several relay stations along Simpson's route, and was planning on several more when his contract with the Post Office was canceled and given to Russell, Majors, and Waddell.[23] Turning to the southwest from the southern end of the Ruby Mountains, the Simpson expedition of 1859 first began to break new trail through unknown territory.

After reaching the west foot of Hastings's Pass, in the valley of the South Fork of the Humboldt, we struck for a pass in the next western range, which we could see lying to the southwest of us, about 9 miles off, and which looked favorable for admission into the next valley.[24]

In his comments relating to this day's travel, Simpson mentioned that he had with him a map that he called "the Topographical Bureau map." He noted that the map showed the route followed by John Charles Frémont in 1845, "but as he has never submitted a detailed report of this reconnaissance, and his track is no longer visible, and it goes too far south for our purposes, his exploration is of no service to us in our progress."[25] This comment suggests that Simpson felt that Frémont's 1845 exploration had little, if any, bearing on the objectives of his expedition. On the other hand, Simpson did show Frémont's route on his map, and it indicates that Frémont had traveled through the very pass that Simpson's party would cross the following day.

After crossing the Overland Pass at the southern end of the Ruby Mountains, the expedition turned to the southwest and headed toward another Overland Pass, this one located in the Diamond Mountains, about thirty miles north of the town of Eureka.

In 4 miles we struck the South Fork of the Humboldt [Conners Creek], a rapid stream, stony bottom, 6 feet wide, ½ foot deep, course northwardly. We follow up this creek for about a mile, and then leaving it, in about 2 miles, come to a small mountain-stream flowing over a stony bottom, where we encamp at 1 o'clock.…Journey 17.6 miles.[26]

The stream that Simpson called the South Fork of the Humboldt appears to be a combination of today's Conners Creek and Huntington Creek. Conners Creek empties into Huntington Creek, which empties into the South Fork of the Humboldt about thirty miles to the north near Twin Bridges. Earlier in his description of this day's journey, Simpson had mentioned that they were headed for "the valley of the South Fork of the Humboldt, which some call Huntingdon's Creek," but he never did mention the name of the "small mountain-stream" on which they camped. Evidently, it was Conners Creek, and Simpson seems not to have realized that it was the same stream that he called Huntingdon's Creek.

The expedition would have first come to Conners Creek about three miles upstream from where it empties into Huntington Creek. Simpson's comment about following this creek for a mile, then leaving it and later coming to a small stream, seems to mean that he believed they left one stream and, after traveling two miles, came to a different stream. However, I have been unable to find a second stream in this area, and have reached the conclusion that there was only a single stream involved, and it

was Conners Creek. It appears to me that when they came to Conners Creek, they followed it for about a mile, veered away from it and traveled two miles, then came back to it and made camp. William Lee said that they "camped on Huntingdon Creek, a branch of the Humboldt."[27] The campsite would probably have been near the spot where the Pony Express Trail crosses this now usually dry streambed.

MAY 19, 1859

MAY 19, CAMP NO. 16, VALLEY OF SOUTH FORK OF THE HUMBOLDT.—*Raised camp at 25 minutes of 6, and directed our course west of south to pass of the mountain-range directly west of us. In 2 miles cross a small rapid mountain-rill.…In two more miles we commence ascending the pass, which on the east side is quite steep, all the teams doubling but the leading one, and ropes being used to keep the wagons from upsetting.…Descending from pass by an easy grade down the west slope of the range, albeit in places slightly sidling, in 3 miles and at quarter to 1 P.M., encamped in splendid and abundant grass, near the small stream which comes down the pass. Day's travel 7.1 miles.*[28]

DURING THIS DAY'S JOURNEY, the expedition made its way across the Overland Pass in the Diamond Mountains, possibly the steepest climb of the entire journey, then descended Telegraph Canyon and set up camp about a mile above the canyon's mouth. Somewhere along the way, the mule that William Lee was riding got away from him, and he "had some trouble to catch her."[29]

Simpson gave the name of "Cho-kup" to the pass and the canyon on the west slope of the mountain. This was the name of a Shoshone chief who visited the camp that afternoon. This was Simpson's second encounter with Chief Cho-kup. The first was a couple of weeks before, in Rush Valley, when Cho-kup was on his way to Camp Floyd. Apparently, Cho-kup had concluded his business with the Indian agent and caught up with the expedition. During his eastbound journey, Cho-kup had been a passenger in one of Chorpenning's mail wagons, and it is probably reasonable to assume that he returned the

Camp 16-W. Conners Creek in Huntington Valley, at the east foot of the Diamond Mountains: "Come to a small mountain-stream flowing over a stony bottom where we encamp." The low spot in the mountains is Overland Pass which they would cross the next day.

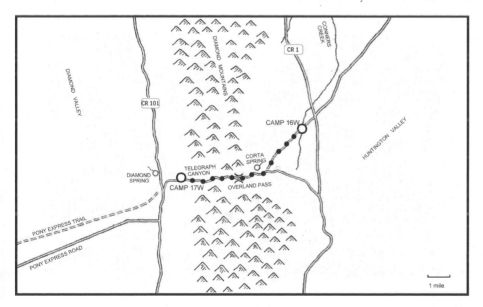

Camp 17-W. In Telegraph Canyon on the west slope of the Diamond Mountains. *"Descending from pass by an easy grade we encamped in splendid and abundant grass, near the small stream which comes down the pass."*

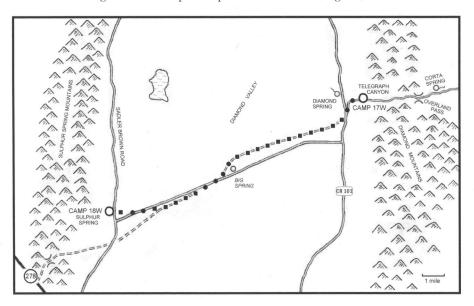

MAY 20, 1859

same way. That, however, does not explain how he got to Telegraph Canyon, which was not on Chorpenning's mail route at that time. Whatever his means of transportation, he had obviously been traveling faster than the expedition.

JULY 1999

During the second day of my first extensive trip on Simpson's route, I spent an entire afternoon in a failed attempt to find a trail that I could use to get over this pass. I started up the mountain on several different trails, but each of them disappeared before I was able to reach the pass. I later learned that I had actually been on the correct trail for a time, but when it ran into a boggy area, I had decided it was a dead end and turned around. Late in the evening, I gave up and made my way around the northern end of the Diamond Mountains, going through Railroad Pass. Coming south again on the west side of the mountain, I camped for the night near the mouth of Telegraph Canyon.

AUGUST 2001

Equipped with a more detailed map than I had with me in 1999, I approached the Conners Creek area from the south, and had no trouble finding the two-track road that goes over the Diamond Mountains. It took about four hours to cross the mountain and drive down Telegraph Canyon to Diamond Springs. But I still had not covered the two and a half mile section of the trail between the campsite on Conners Creek and the road that reaches the pass from the south.

AUGUST 2005

Nancy and I drove to the Connors Creek campsite, where we got onto the Pony Express Trail and headed southwest toward the pass. When we reached the boggy place where I had turned around in 1999, I shifted into four-low and kept on going. Finding solid ground and the old trail on the far side, we soon reached the better-traveled road that comes from the south. Shortly after that, we made it over the top of the mountain and dropped down Telegraph Canyon to Diamond Valley.

MAY 20, 1859

MAY 20, CAMP NO. 17, WEST SLOPE OF CHO-KUP'S PASS.—*Moved at 5.30 o'clock. In 1 mile reach foot of pass in Pah-hun-nupe, or Water Valley [Diamond Valley].... Six and eight-tenths miles farther brings us to a large spring, in marsh, where we water. Plenty of grass about it, though not of best quality. This valley is in some portions argillaceous and in some arenaceous. The latter glitter with small crystals of quartz, of very pure character, which we amuse ourselves in picking up, and facetiously call California diamonds.... In 5.6 miles more reach a large spring on west side of valley, at foot of mountain range, where we encamp in pure salt grass, which the animals eat with avidity.... Road to-day good, though it might cut up early in the spring.... Day's travel, 13.3 miles.*[30]

IMMEDIATELY AFTER LEAVING the mouth of Telegraph Canyon, the expedition's trail turned sharply to the left, skirting the bottom of the hills, then went through the Thompson Ranch. From this ranch, the expedition followed the Pony Express Trail almost all the way across Diamond Valley. Simpson's comment about the "California diamonds" originally led me to believe that this may have been the origin of the name of the valley, but western historian John Townley indicates that it was named for Jack Diamond, an early prospector who spent some time in the area.[31] Showing some geographic confusion, young William Lee's journal indicates that he believed they were now in Smith Valley.[32]

At about a mile and three-quarters south of the Thompson Ranch, a cross-valley road heads in a slightly south-of-west direction. The expedition's route crosses this road about midway across the valley. About 2.3 miles from the crossing, the expedition left the track that the USGS 7.5-minute map shows as the Pony Express Trail, veered a little to the west, and after another two miles reached Sulphur Spring. Aerial photos show a faint trail in this area, and it is quite certain that the mail riders also went to Sulphur Spring, which Joe Nardone has identified as a Pony Express station.

Camp 18-W. Sulphur Spring on the west side of Diamond Valley. A stainless steel Pony Express station marker can be seen in the center of the photo. *"Reach a large spring on west side of valley, at foot of mountain range, where we encamp in pure salt grass."*

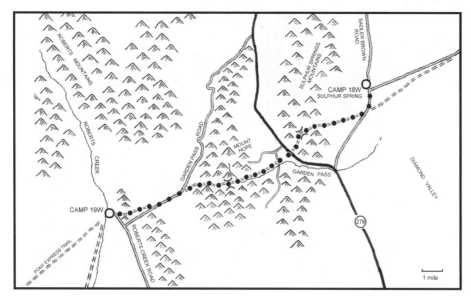

MAY 21, 1859

The expedition's camp for the night was near Sulphur Spring. The site of the Pony Express station is just west of the main road. The spring itself must have dried up many years ago, but a caved-in cistern can still be found at the station site.

═══════════════════════

MAY 21, 1859

MAY 21, CAMP NO. 18, WEST SIDE OF PAH-HUN-NUPE VALLEY.—*Raised camp at 5.25 A.M. Keep up the Pah-hun-nupe Valley, or south, two miles; then turn to the right up toward the pass of west range bounding the valley; two miles more commence ascending pass.*[33]

FROM SULPHUR SPRING, the expedition headed south for a couple of miles, rejoined the track that the maps show as the Pony Express Trail, then began to turn to the southwest to follow the Pony Express Trail over a low pass near the south end of the Sulphur Springs Range. Today's main road does not follow the old trail over the ridge, but continues south until it reaches the mouth of Garden Pass Canyon. The trail across the ridge is essentially abandoned, and I had bypassed it during my first couple of trips through this area. In 2003, while returning from a trip to another area, I drove north from US 50 and made my way along this section of the trail. In most places it is a fairly good two-track, but a couple of washouts required the use of four-wheel drive.

After crossing the Sulphur Springs ridge, the expedition dropped down to Garden Pass Creek at a point near the southeastern base of Mount Hope. Here they crossed the stream and headed into another range of hills, traveling in a slightly south-of-west direction.

In five miles more, by a very gradual ascent, reach second highest summit of pass, whence can be seen, to the south and southwest, a low ridge trending apparently northwest and southeast.... The pass we have come through, a most excellent one for a wagon-road, the only steep portion being for about 100 yards at the summit.... Immediately to our north is a conical peak [Mount Hope], which, as we found afterward, in our journey westward,

continued for days a most notable landmark, and which I call Cooper's Peak, after Adjutant-General Cooper of the Army.[34]

Simpson's "second highest summit" was directly south of the mountain that he called Cooper's Peak, and is now known as Mount Hope. Some modern maps show a peak in the northwestern part of the Roberts Creek Range that bears the name Cooper Peak, but it is clearly not the peak that was given that name by Simpson. This is possibly another case of a migrating name.

JULY 1999

During my first visit to this area, I was relying on a USGS 30 × 60 minute map, which does not indicate the existence of a road on the south side of Mount Hope. I did have an idea that the Pony Express Trail went this way, but I could not find where it started west from the Garden Pass area. After spending some time in this failed attempt, I left the area and drove south to US 50, then headed west to the Roberts Creek road, which I followed back to the north until I reached Roberts Creek Ranch.

AUGUST 2001

When I was exploring the Roberts Creek area in 1999, I had noticed what I thought might be the western end of the road that came from Garden Pass, so I decided to make an attempt to find the trail from the west. Leaving the Roberts Creek road, I headed east on a well-traveled dirt road for about three miles, when I came to a bend where a narrow two-track veered off to the right. As I drove along this seldom-used road, I noticed several of the red and white fence posts that are sometimes used to mark the Pony Express Trail in this part of the country. Satisfied that I was now on the Pony Express Trail, and on Simpson's route, I continued to the east and had no difficulty in following the old road along the south side of Mount Hope all the way to Garden Pass.

In 6 miles from summit, by an easy grade, at a quarter to 1 o'clock, reach the She-o-wi-te, or Willow Creek [Roberts Creek], where we encamp. The short, steep hill which we passed down just before reaching camp, may be turned at the south

Mount Hope, from the southwest. *"Immediately to our north is a conical peak, which, as we found afterward, in our journey westward, continued for days a most notable landmark, and which I call Cooper's Peak."*

by making a short detour. She-o-wi-te Creek, a fine one, 4 feet wide, 1 foot deep, and quite rapid. It sinks about 1 mile below camp....Journey, 14.9 miles.[35]

As Simpson was describing the route they had traveled that day, he stated that the road was good, "except short hill referred to, which can be avoided." While visiting this area, I noticed that there is a small knoll on the north side of the road just before it comes to the Roberts Creek Road. In taking a closer look, I found a very faint two-track trail going through the low pass on the north side of the knoll. I have concluded that this knoll is the "short hill" that Simpson mentioned. The expedition went through the low pass, but today's well-traveled road does just what Simpson said could be done, and avoids the short hill by going past it on its south side. During one of my visits to this area, I spent some time visiting with Jim Esqueviara, the manager of the Roberts

Creek Ranch, who mentioned that he has been told by Pony Express Trail researchers that the mail riders used the trail that went past the north side of the knoll. In 2004, Nancy and I found this trail and followed it to the ranch.

Due to limitations of scale, Simpson's map fails to show that his trail made a turn as it approached the campsite. Nevertheless, it is quite certain that just after coming out of the little draw, the expedition would have turned toward the northwest until they reached Roberts Creek. I believe that the expedition's campsite would have been very near the present-day ranch buildings. Esqueviara is quite certain that the Pony Express station was just north of the ranch house.

Simpson indicated that the natives of the area called the stream She-o-wi-te, which he understood to mean Willow Creek, and that is what he decided to call the stream. That name did not last very long. Sometime during the following year, a Chorpenning employee by the name of

Bolivar Roberts set up a relay station at the spot where the expedition had camped. When the Pony Express took over the mail route, Roberts went to work for Russell, Majors, and Waddell. When Burton came through this area in October of 1860, he mentioned that it was known as "Roberts's Springs Valley," having been named for Bolivar Roberts.[36] It is interesting to note that the stream on which the expedition camped two days later soon became known as Willow Creek. Is this another case of a migrating name or just a coincidence?

Simpson decided to remain at this camp for an extra day "to recruit our animals and observe the Sabbath." Reese came into the camp and reported that he had located water and a passable route to the southwest. During the late afternoon, Simpson and two other members of the expedition hiked to the top of a peak that was located a short distance northeast of the campsite. He reported that from the peak they could see the Humboldt [Ruby] Mountains and the We-a-bah Mountains behind them, and "to the west several ranges, the most distant ones covered with snow."[37]

In the text of the report, Simpson mentions nothing about Frémont traveling through this area, but his map seems to show that Frémont's trail crossed Roberts Creek at a point that was near the Simpson expedition's campsite.

Five

Roberts Creek to Middlegate

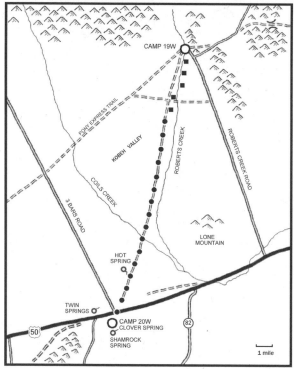

Camp 19-W. The campsite was near the buildings of the Roberts Creek Ranch. "This evening I ascended, with Messrs. Jagiello and McCarthy, the high peak to the northeast of our camp."

MAY 23, 1859

M AY 23, C AMP N O. 19, S HE -O -WI -TE , OR W ILLOW C REEK .—*The guide reports two passes, one north of west, and the other west of south. Neither is in the most direct line of approach to our ultimate point, but the latter is much the nearer of the two and therefore we take it, bearing off, however, still more southwardly in order to certainly reach water within a reasonable distance. (We found, however, the next day that we could have taken a more direct course (southwest,) as laid down on the map, and have saved about 10 miles. Wagons should take this latter course, which they will find practicable.)*[1]

T HE EXPEDITION'S DIRECTION of travel this day illustrates how the need for water influenced Simpson's decisions about the route. Apparently unaware that there was a good source of water to their southwest, they headed almost due south toward a place where the guide knew they would find a running stream. This was one of a few instances in which Simpson later decided that they had gone the wrong way. A glance at the map will show that if they had traveled southwest from the camp on Robert's Creek, they could have gone directly to the Dry Creek area, which is where they ended up three days later.

The Chorpenning company, and then the Pony Express and the Overland Stage, took this southwest route when their routes were established through this area, and so did Burton's party, traveling in their ambulance-style coach. In early 1860, Chorpenning established a stage station at Dry Creek, on the western edge of the valley. A year later, Russell, Majors, and Waddell installed an Overland Stage station at Grubb's Flat, about halfway between Roberts Creek and Dry Creek.[2]

A UGUST 2001

During my first visit to the Roberts Creek area in 1999, I had been very uncertain about where Simpson had gone after leaving the campsite. As a result, when I left the ranch, I followed the well-marked Pony Express Trail, but I did not follow it all the way to Dry Creek. After about eleven miles, I came to Three-Bars Road, where I turned south to US 50. A couple of years later in August 2001, I was ready to make another

attempt to find the expedition's trail between Camps 19-W and 20-W. By this time, I had figured out that the expedition had headed nearly straight south from the campsite, and on my USGS 30 × 60 minute map, I had located a narrow road that seemed to go in the right direction. The map also showed that I could get to this road by leaving the Roberts Creek Road at a point about two miles south of the ranch, and heading west. It looked like this ranch road would lead to the two-track that followed Simpson's route south to US 50. This time I was successful, and I was able to follow the expedition's route across Kobeh Valley.

O CTOBER 2003

By cutting into the trail from the east in 2001, I had missed the two-mile section of the trail immediately south of Roberts Creek Ranch, so I returned to the spot where I had intersected the trail during that trip. The maps that I had been relying on did not show any trail or road leading from that point to the ranch buildings, so I was prepared to make a hike out of it. Nancy was with me on this trip, and was planning to wait for me in the SUV while I walked to the ranch and back. I climbed over the fence that follows the north side of the access road, and started making my way through the sagebrush toward the ranch. In less than a hundred yards, I came to an old road that seemed to be going where I wanted to go. I immediately turned around and followed the road until I came back to the fence, just a few yards from where we had parked. There is a heavy growth of unusually tall sagebrush in this area, and I had failed to notice the road where it came to the fence. Finding an unlocked gate at this point, I was able to open it and follow the old road all the way to the ranch house. Although we were not on the expedition's trail, I was quite sure that it was just a few yards to the east, on the far side of the streambed. When Nancy and I reached the deserted ranch buildings, a pickup truck pulled up and stopped. This was when we met Jim Esqueviara, the manager of the ranch. He was friendly enough, but wanted to know what we were doing. I told him about my project and we spent some time in a very enjoyable and enlightening conversation. A descendent of a Basque sheep ranching family, Esqueviara has spent his entire life in this area. He is quite familiar with the Pony Express Trail through this valley, and always assists the Pony Express Association with their annual re-rides as they come through the ranch. He showed us where he believes the Pony Express station had been located, which is just a few yards north of the ranch house. He also showed us his collection of old horse and ox shoes that he has found near the old station site.

> *About 4 miles farther cross a wash or creek [Coils Creek] running southeast, the bed of which is 12 feet wide, and which at times must void a great deal of water, though at present it only exists in pools. Bunch-grass along it, but too alkaline for use. Two miles farther, pass, on our right, about a mile off, a mound, in which are some warm springs, one of them so warm as scarcely to admit the hand. The mound is the product of the springs, and is a calcareous tufa. Three and a half miles more brought us to a small spring [Clover Spring], which I call after Private Shelton, of the dragoons, who found it.... No grass of any account about the spring, and not a sufficient quantity of water for the animals. They are consequently driven about 1.5 miles to the mountain slopes [Twin Spring Hills]. Day's travel, 17.5 miles.*[3]

During the first couple of miles of this day's journey, the expedition was heading just slightly west of south, paralleling Roberts Creek, which would have been a few yards to the west. About two miles south of the ranch house, they came to a place where the streambed was no longer in a deep wash, and at this point they probably crossed to the west side. There would have been no water to contend with at this point, because Simpson had earlier mentioned that the creek sank about a mile below the campsite. At eight miles from camp, they came to a small, willow-lined stream, and traveled parallel to it for a while. This must have been Roberts Creek again. From the campsite, Roberts Creek runs almost due south for nearly eight miles, then turns toward the west for a short distance, then bends to the south again and runs parallel to the trail for a while before emptying into Coils Creek.

After traveling about twelve miles, they reached Coils Creek, which Simpson described as both a wash and a creek, with only a few pools of standing water, which is a good description of what I saw when I came to it. At that point, the expedition was about three miles to the west of a very large knoll that is known as Lone Mountain today, but is labeled as Mt. Lowry on Simpson's map. Continuing south, they passed about a half mile to the east of what is shown on today's maps as Hot Springs. After another two and a half miles, they crossed the future route of the Lincoln Highway and today's US 50.

In his description of the return trip, Simpson mentioned that they crossed this day's trail at a point about two miles east of a pair of springs he named Twin Springs. Modern maps show a Twin Springs just north of US 50, about nine miles west of Lone Mountain. If we can assume that these are the springs that Simpson was talking about, it gives us a good indication of the point where the routes crossed each other, and also the points where the outbound and return routes crossed US 50.

Simpson indicated that it was 17.5 miles from the camp on Robert's Creek to the small spring where they set up camp for the night. He called it Shelton Spring, but I am quite certain that it is the spring that is labeled as Clover Spring on modern maps. Although the USGS 7.5-minute quadrangle shows a road leading from US 50 to Clover Spring, that road has been fenced off and abandoned, and I have been unable to drive to this campsite.

AUGUST 2000

I parked on the side of US 50 and hiked south until I found what I thought was Simpson's Shelton's Spring. I could tell that there had once been some water here, but it was now totally dry and had the appearance of having been so for a long time. From this dry spring, I headed west until I came to a fairly well-traveled road that skirts the eastern base of Twin Springs Hills. I followed this road back to US 50 and my SUV.

Back home, after some additional study of my maps of this area, and after taking some more measurements of the distances involved, it

Camp 20-W. Clover Spring, in the southern part of Kobeh Valley. *"Three and a half miles more brought us to a small spring, which I call after Private Shelton, of the dragoons, who found it."*

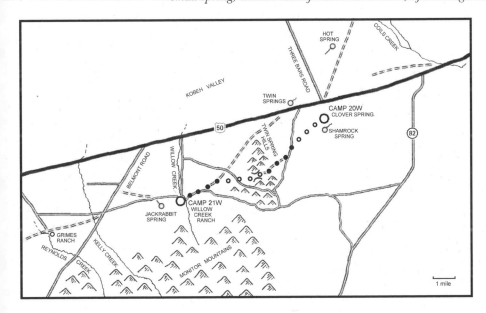

MAY 24, 1859

became apparent that I had been at the wrong spring. This hike had been made before I started using GPS and, simply put, I had been lost. The route that I had followed had taken me too far to the east and then too far to the south. I was able to determine that the dry spring I had found was actually Shamrock Spring, which is about a half mile south of Clover Spring, which was where I had wanted to go.

October 2003

I returned to the Kobeh Valley area to make another attempt to find Clover Spring. I was now equipped with a GPS receiver, and with its help I was able to go directly to the correct site, where I found a couple small pools of water, each of them about ten to twelve feet in diameter and a couple feet deep.

The slopes to which the animals were driven during the evening that the expedition was camped at Clover Spring must have been on the northeast side of Twin Spring Hills, which are about two miles to the southwest.

May 24, 1859

May 24, Camp No. 20, Shelton's Spring.—*In consequence of our having made a longer march yesterday than the guide thought we should, our to-day's travel will be only about 7 miles. Our course lay south of west, through a pass at the foot of Antelope Mountain [Monitor Mountain], and continues over the foot-hills on the north side of the same, to a rushing stream [Willow Creek], 3 feet wide and 1 deep, where, at 9.15 A.M., we encamp, in good grass and abundant cedar timber. This stream, which the Diggers call Wonst-in-dam-me (Antelope) Creek, coming from a high mountain, is doubtless constant, and, indeed, the Indians so represent it.... Colonel Cooper's Peak, on account of its cone-like shape and isolated position, has been all day a very conspicuous object. Journey 7 miles.*[4]

WHEN THEY STARTED OUT on the morning of May 24, the expedition headed in a southwesterly direction, and after about two and a half miles, they began climbing toward a low pass in the Twin Spring Hills. After another mile, they crossed the summit of the pass and turned more toward the west. About two miles from the summit, they reached a spot that they would return to during the eastbound journey. From this point at the western base of the Twin Spring Hills, the return trail would leave the outbound trail and veer to the north. It was the return route that would later be used by the early Lincoln Highway. During the return journey, Simpson indicated that this junction of the trails was 1.6 miles east of the campsite on Willow Creek.[5] It is doubtful that the outbound trail between the summit of the Twin Springs Hills and this point was ever used by wheeled vehicles again.

May 2003

Leaving US 50 near Twin Springs, I drove south on a fairly well-traveled dirt road that skirts the eastern base of the Twin Springs Hills. About two miles south of the highway, at the point where I believe that Simpson's route would have crossed this road, I found a seldom-used two-track heading in a southwesterly direction toward the pass. I am certain that this two-track follows the route that the expedition used to cross the Twin Springs Hills. Turning onto this trail, I was able to drive to within about a quarter mile of the summit of the ridge. From there I hiked across the summit and down the western slope. When I reached the spot where the westbound trail intersects with the expedition's return route, I turned around and headed back across the pass.

At three and a half miles from the summit, the expedition reached Willow Creek, where they probably crossed to the west bank of the stream and set up camp in a small meadow. During the days of the Lincoln Highway, this spot was known as "The Willows." It is now the Willow Creek Ranch.

There is a minor, but intriguing, mystery connected with this place. In my meager collection of old road maps, I have a couple of Nevada maps that were published in the 1940s, which show this spot as "Willows Station." The unanswered question is, why was it called a station? In this area of the country, the term "station" is historically associated with the Pony Express, a stagecoach line, or the telegraph line, but I have found no historical evidence that would indicate that any of these ever came to the Willow Creek Ranch.

MAY 25, 1859

MAY 25, CAMP NO. 21, WONS-IN-DAM-ME OR ANTELOPE CREEK.—*Course westwardly, over a shoot or branch of Kobah Valley. In 4.3 miles cross Saw-wid Creek [Kelly Creek], a rapid stream, 3 feet wide and 1 deep, which comes from the Antelope Mountains [Monitor Mountain], on our left, and sinks 500 yards below our crossing.... Colonel Cooper's Peak still conspicuous.... At 12 m. reach foot of range, on west side of valley, after a journey of 13.7 miles, and encamp on a small creek, which I call Clarke's Creek, after John Clarke, one of the men.... this stream, or one to the north of it, can and ought to be struck directly by wagons from Camp No. 19, and thus some 10 miles saved.*[6]

WHEN THEY LEFT the Willow Creek campsite, the expedition followed what is now a fairly well-traveled dirt road for 1.3 miles, where they reached the normally dry wash that comes from Jackrabbit Spring. Simpson did not say anything about this particular spot in his account of the westbound journey, but during the return trip, when they followed a different route to reach this point, he indicated that it was at this spot that they rejoined their outbound trail.[7]

Simpson's map shows that from the junction of the two trails, the westbound route followed a straight line in a slightly north-of-west direction. Once I had determined the locations of this junction and the next campsite, all I had to do was draw a straight line across the valley. None of the modern maps that I have been able to study show any indication of a road or trail along this alignment. This did not surprise me, because I doubted that anyone had ever followed the expedition's westbound route across this valley. However, I later discovered something that caused me to change my mind about this. I was examining some aerial photos of this area when I noticed some faint indications of a trail that seemed to follow the line that I had plotted across the valley. This long-abandoned trail shows up quite well in the area between Jackrabbit Spring and Belmont Road. West of Belmont Road, it shows up occasionally. In the area north of US 50, it is not visible at all.

JULY 2005

Nancy and I drove to the Willow Creek Ranch, and then turned west on Simpson's trail until we came to the spot below Jackrabbit Spring where the outbound route leaves the main road. Using my GPS receiver, I was soon able to find some of the traces of the old two-track that I had been able to see on the aerial photos. I then spent several hours following the old trail on foot. Due to the appearance of this old trail, I am convinced that not only was it Simpson's route, but it had also been used by many other wagons before being abandoned.

Simpson reported that after crossing this valley, they camped on a small stream, which he named Clarke's Creek. When I first began to study this section of the route, I assumed that this stream was Dry Creek, which flows eastward out of the Simpson Park Mountains. The maps do show other streambeds or drainages in this area, but Dry Creek is the only one that is significant enough to have a name printed on the maps. Then, one day, as I was re-reading Simpson's description of the campsite, I noticed a statement about the existence of a second stream in this area. As he was describing the area where they were camped, Simpson said: "As I have before remarked, this stream, *or one to the north of it*, can and ought to be struck directly by wagons from Camp No. 19" (emphasis added).[8] It is quite certain that when Simpson said "this stream," he was talking about the stream on which they were camped. The phrase "or one to the north of it" has to mean that there was a stream somewhere to the north of the camp. This sent me back to the maps to look for any indication of a stream somewhere to the north of Dry Creek. I found nothing. I then noticed that about a half mile to the south of Dry Creek, there is an unnamed streambed that runs roughly parallel to Dry Creek for some distance, then empties into it about a mile east of the road that leads to the Dry Creek area. I began to wonder if this smaller stream could have been Simpson's Clarke's Creek. I then made a measurement from the Willow Creek campsite,

Camps 21-W and 14-E. Located at today's Willow Creek Ranch: *"[traveled] over the foot-hills to a rushing stream, where we encamp, in good grass and abundant cedar timber."*

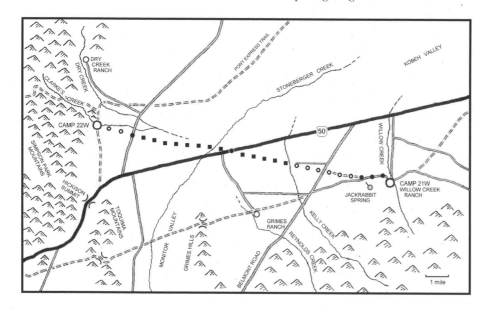

and I found that the trail would have reached this other stream right at the eastern base of the Simpson Park Mountains. This would agree with Simpson's statement that the camp was at "the foot of range, on west side of valley." When I measured from this point to Hickison Summit, I found that the distance was very close to the four miles indicated by Simpson. I was able to use Hickison Summit as a reliable reference point because in this area, it is the only practical way to cross the ridge of the Toquima Mountains, which the expedition did the next day.

JUNE 2004

At this time, I was still uncertain about the site of Camp 22-W, still thinking that it was somewhere on Dry Creek. Nancy and I left US 50 near the eastern base of Hickison Summit, and followed a two-track road that leads north to the Dry Creek area. It later became evident to me that the expedition had followed this route on their way to Hickison Summit, but being unaware of it at the time, we drove right past the actual campsite without knowing it. When we reached Dry Creek, we got onto the Pony Express Trail, which we followed to the east, stopping occasionally to look for possible campsites along the streambed.

JUNE 2005

A year after our 2004 trip, and after I had figured out that the unnamed stream was Clarke's Creek, Nancy and I returned to the Dry Creek area. I parked on the side of the well-traveled road that leads from US 50 to Dry Creek, and hiked to the west along the south bank of what I believe is Clarke's Creek. After reaching the site of the camp, which is right on the two-track that we had driven the previous year, I took some photos and GPS readings, and then returned to the car. The streambed was dry that day, but I could see that there had been a good-sized stream flowing through it fairly recently, probably within the previous week or two.

While camped on Clarke's Creek, the expedition was thirty miles southwest of their camp on Roberts Creek. Since leaving that camp, they had traveled for three days and had covered thirty-eight miles. Simpson commented that future travelers should come directly from

Roberts Creek to Clarke's Creek. A few months later, when Chorpenning's employees laid out their mail route, they took Simpson's advice and did just that, establishing a mail-station on Dry Creek, about two miles northeast of the expedition's campsite. A short time later, when Russell, Majors, and Waddell took over Chorpenning's contract, they sent the Pony Express riders along the same route. Heading west from Dry Creek, the mail riders took a route that went almost directly west through the Simpson Park Mountains, going past the southern base of Eagle Butte. This route proved to be too steep and rugged for the Overland mail coaches, and they headed south to follow Simpson's trail across Hickison Summit.

In October 11, 1860, Richard Burton's party, in their makeshift coaches, left their camp on Roberts Creek and followed the Pony Express route to Dry Creek.

At 6 A.M. we entered the ambulance, and followed a good road across the remains of the long broad Sheawit Valley. After twelve miles we came upon a water surrounded by willows [probably Rutabaga or Coils Creek], with dwarf artemisia beyond; it grows better on the benches, where the subsoil is damper, than in the bottoms....Resuming our way, after three miles we reached some wells [probably Grubbs Well] whose alkaline waters chap the skin. Twenty miles further led to the west end of the Sheawit Valley, where we found the station on a grassy bench at the foot of low rolling hills. It was a mere shell, with a substantial stone corral behind, and the inmates were speculating upon the possibility of roofing themselves in before the winter. Water is found in tolerable quantities below the station, but the place deserved its name, "Dry Creek." [9]

The question of where the stage road went after leaving Dry Creek is answered by Burton as he describes his travels during the following day.

Shortly after 8 A.M. we were afield, hastening to finish the long divide that separates Roberts' Creek Valley from its western neighbour, which, as yet unchristened, is known to the b'hoys as Smokey Valley. The road wound in the shape of the letter U round the impassable part of the ridge. [10]

Camp 22-W. About a mile south of Dry Creek Ranch in the north end of Monitor Valley, the narrow road goes through the usually dry streambed that is marked by the juniper trees: *"reach foot of range, and encamp on a small creek, which I call Clarke's Creek."*

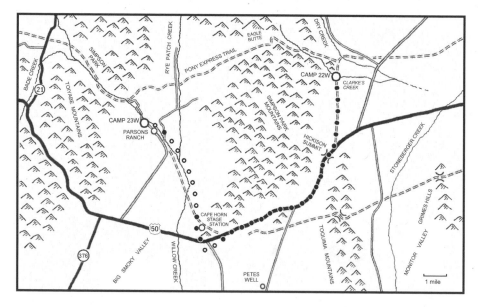

MAY 26, 1859

A route that heads south from Dry Creek, over Hickison Summit, around Cape Horn, and then northwest across Big Smoky Valley does indeed make the shape of the letter U. John Townley's Pony Express Guidebook includes a map that clearly shows the stage road following this route, and a larger map includes the following note: "Cape Horn 'dogleg' laid out in June, 1861 for Overland Stage."[11] It would not have taken much to lay it out; Simpson's track would have still been clearly visible just two years after the expedition traveled this route.

The Eagle Butte route was a good one for Chorpenning's mules and the pony riders that came later, but emigrant George Harter's experience in 1864 shows that taking wagons west from Dry Creek was not a good idea. Harter's journal does not explain why they decided to go past Eagle Butte, but he does give a vivid description of the problems they encountered.

Next day drove nineteen miles over a level desert and camped at Dry creek. Poor feed. Here we took Fools cutoff, which is all the term implies. Traveled four miles up a steep and rough mountain....Reached the summit at noon, turned the stock loose on good grass. After dinner hitched the wheel animals to the wagon and started down. After going a little ways we cut down a good sized pine tree and chained it behind on the wagon, and drove down about a mile to a spring and camped.[12]

It is unlikely that very many wagons ever used this route.

MAY 26, 1859

MAY 26, CAMP NO. 22.—*Skirt the foot of the Pah-re-ah Mountains [Simpson Park Mountains]; course, southwardly; the pass immediately back or west of camp, which would shorten the route considerably, not being practicable for wagons, though pack-animals can use it.*[13]

WHEN SIMPSON MENTIONED the pass west of the camp, he was talking about the Eagle Butte route, and, as George Harter later learned, it was definitely not a practical route for wagons.

In 2 miles commence turning gradually westward, and in 2 miles farther, up an easy wagon-grade, reach summit of pass [Hickison Summit]....From this pass the Pe-er-re-ah (meaning Big or High) Mountain [Toiyabe Mountains] appears directly before us, some 12 miles off, trending north and south. The road down the west side of the Pah-re-ah range is carried on the ridge of the spur, which furnishes a passable grade, though that down the cañon is not bad, and is entirely practicable for wagons without work though a little sidling.[14]

When the Lincoln Highway was established through this area in 1913, it followed a pre-existing road that crossed the Toquima Mountains about three miles south of Hickison Summit. In the mid-1920s, it was decided to move the highway to the north, and use Hickison Summit to cross this ridge. Immediately to the west of the summit, a rather shallow canyon extends to the southwest. A paved road runs along each side of the canyon. The one on the west is the now-abandoned Lincoln Highway. Today's US 50 runs along the eastern slope of the canyon. Simpson said that the expedition could probably have followed the bottom of the canyon, but he decided to stay higher up on the ridge. The problem is, he did not say which ridge they followed. Was it on the eastern side or the western side of the canyon? Mileage measurements will not answer this question, because the distances along both possible routes are identical. Simply because the older automobile road is on the western side of the canyon, my first inclination was to consider that route first. During one of my trips to the area, I hiked the entire length of the western ridge. Not only did I fail to find any indication of any road or trail, I also ran into a couple of places that would have presented some serious difficulties for the wagons. Because of the roughness of the terrain along the western ridge, I have concluded that Simpson was probably talking about the eastern ridge. For the first mile or so, the trail must have been a short distance above US 50; after that, it probably followed the same alignment as the highway until it neared the bottom of the canyon.

After reaching, in 7 miles from summit of pass, the valley called Won-a-ho-nupe [Big Smoky

Valley], we turned northwest diagonally across it to the pass, through the Pe-er-re-ah Mountains [Toiyabe Mountains]. In 10 miles from summit of pass, through the Pah-re-ah range [Simpson Park Range], we came to a rapid creek (Won-a-ho-nupe) [another Willow Creek], 8 or 10 feet wide, 1½ deep, and running southwardly between steep sand-banks, 15 feet high. In 4 miles more cross this stream at mouth of cañon, and encamp one-fourth of a mile above on the stream, in good grass and where cedar abounds. Journey 18.2 miles.[15]

The southernmost tip of the Simpson Park Mountains is known as Cape Horn. US 50 goes through a road cut that is something like a hundred yards north of the tip. Approaching this point from the east, one can look to the north and see a dirt road crossing the ridge about a quarter of a mile from US 50. This was probably the stage road, but I do not believe that the expedition followed this route. It appears to me that this was a shortcut that was developed after the stage line began to operate. The Cape Horn Stage Station was located near the spot where this dirt road reaches the western base of the ridge. A pile of volcanic rocks marks this spot today. As the expedition approached Cape Horn, they were traveling in the flats a short distance south of US 50, and they passed by the southernmost tip of the ridge before turning to the north.

Traveling almost due north for another mile and three-quarters, they came to a stream that was flowing southward in a deep wash. Simpson said the Indian name for this stream was Won-a-ho-nupe, which means willows, and he gave it the name of Willow Creek. Although the upper part of this stream flows through Simpson Park Canyon, it has retained the name that Simpson gave it. The stage road and Simpson's eastbound trail crossed this stream about two and a quarter miles north of Cape Horn, but during the westbound trip, the expedition remained on its east bank until they reached the mouth of Simpson Park Canyon. Crossing the stream at that point, they continued up the stream for another quarter mile and set up camp in a level area just north of Wes Parson's ranch.

An entry in William Lee's journal suggests the possibility that the expedition may have strayed

some distance from the path that Simpson reported.

Thursday, May 26th. Marched 19¼ miles, but going about a mile and a quarter out of the way unnecessarily, it was considered eighteen miles. Saw several antelope to-day. We camped on a fine stream with plenty of wood and grass. Killed a rattlesnake in the tent.[16]

A possible explanation for the extra distance that Lee reported would be that when the expedition reached Cape Horn, they may have continued toward the west for some distance before making the turn to the north. This would have taken them out into the flats of Big Smoky Valley, before they realized that the best route would be through Simpson Park Canyon. Since the path they had inadvertently followed would not be a part of the trail that Simpson was planning for future travelers, he would have eliminated it from the official report. This would also explain the mile and a quarter difference between the mileage that Simpson reported in the text, which was 18.25 miles, and the mileage that appears in the table of distances, which is 17 miles. Lee usually reported the distance traveled each day, but his figures frequently varied a little from the figures that Simpson recorded.

MAY 2003

Today, no road or trail follows the expedition's outbound route between Cape Horn and the mouth of Simpson Park Canyon. However, there is a dirt road that leads from US 50 to the site of the Cape Horn Stage Station, so I parked there and hiked in a northerly direction toward the canyon. After just a little less than two miles, I arrived at the spot where Simpson came to the stream that was flowing "between steep sand banks 15 feet high." From there I followed the eastern bank of the streambed for another two miles before returning to my SUV.

MAY 27, 1859

MAY 27, CAMP NO. 23, WON-A-HO-NUPE CANYON.—*Leave at 6.10 A.M. Course westwardly up the cañon.... The road is winding through the*

Camp 23-W. Near the mouth of Simpson Park Canyon. Willow Creek crosses the photo just behind the small juniper tree. *"Cross this stream at mouth of cañon, and encamp one-fourth of a mile above on the stream, in good grass and where cedar abounds."*

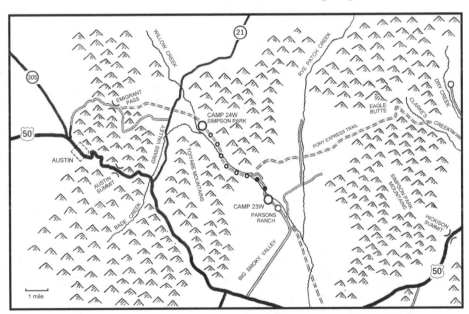

MAY 27, 1859

cañon, but of easy grade, the only bad places being the frequent crossings of the creek, which occasionally are somewhat boggy....At 11 o'clock, after a journey of 4.9 miles, we come to a small lake and the cañon expands into a sort of park about 4 by 3 miles in area.[17]

LOCATED NEAR THE mouth of Simpson Park Canyon is a spot that is shown on some maps as the Givens Ranch, but is now owned by Charles "Wes" Parsons. I have visited with Wes on several occasions, and have found him to be friendly and personable, with an extensive knowledge of the history of this area. I initially met him during my first major trip along the route in 1999. I had crossed Big Smoky Valley on US 50 and turned north on a dirt road that leads to the lower end of Simpson Park Canyon. Nearing the mouth of the canyon, I came to a cluster of ranch buildings, and, as I drove into the yard, I was greeted by a half-dozen furiously barking dogs. Wes came out of one of the sheds and quieted the dogs a little. I introduced myself, and explained what I was doing. When I told him that I was hoping to follow Simpson's trail through the canyon, he told me that the road was not drivable. He went on to explain that in the past, there had been a good road through the canyon, and it had been maintained periodically by the county. But that had all changed during the wet years of the early 1980s, when the road had been washed out in several places and has never been repaired. Parsons claims that the reason for this is that the Forest Service now controls the land, and their policies do not allow any heavy equipment to be brought into the canyon. At the end of our conversation, Wes gave me some directions on how I could circle around the mountain and get fairly close to the upper end of the canyon. I thanked him and went on my way, but I would be back, several times.

AUGUST 2001

My plan during this trip was to drive as far into the canyon as possible, and then hike the rest of the way to Simpson Park. After stopping to visit with Wes for a while, I drove into the canyon until I reached the place where the road now ends. From there, I hiked through the rest of the

canyon and across Simpson's Park. This trip took me past the locations of Camps 13-E, 23-W, 12-E, and 24-W. The problem was that at that time, I was still quite uncertain about the exact locations of these campsites, and I only had a general idea of where to look. When I reached Simpson Park, I found a small lake of perhaps four or five acres. During two subsequent visits to this area, I found no water at all, not even a trickle in the streambed. On my third return to Simpson Park, I found that there was a small amount of water in the lake. By this time I was confident that I had determined the exact locations of the campsites, and, now equipped with a GPS receiver, I made my way to each of them to take photos and obtain on-site GPS readings. During each of these return visits, I reached the park by driving to Grass Valley, and then walking along the Pony Express Trail from the northwest.

MAY 28, 1859

MAY 28, CAMP NO. 24, SIMPSON'S PARK, PE-ER-RE-AH RANGE.— *Renewed journey at 10 minutes to 6 A.M. Leave Valley of Won-a-ho-nupe Creek and strike west for Simpson's Pass [Emigrant Pass], which we reach by a very easy ascent in 4.7 miles....The pass at summit is as much as a mile wide, and both backward and forward the views are beautiful. The mountains near our camp of May 25 are very conspicuously back of us; and ahead of us, limiting Reese Valley, which we are approaching, is a low range trending generally north and south, and beyond them a very high range covered with snow, called by the Indians the Se-day-e or Lookout Mountains [Desatoya Mountains].*[18]

THE PASS THAT SIMPSON seems to have named for himself is now known as Emigrant Pass, and it crosses the Toiyabe Mountains a few miles to the north of the town of Austin. Although there are a couple of gates that must be opened and closed, there is a good dirt road across this pass and I have driven it in both directions with no trouble at all.

Descending from the summit of Simpson's Pass, west side, by not a very steep but sandy grade, and along a short sidling place, near foot of

Camp 24-W. Simpson Park. The author found a small lake here in 1999, but it was gone a year later. *"We come to a small lake and the cañon expands into a sort of park about 4 by 3 miles in area."*

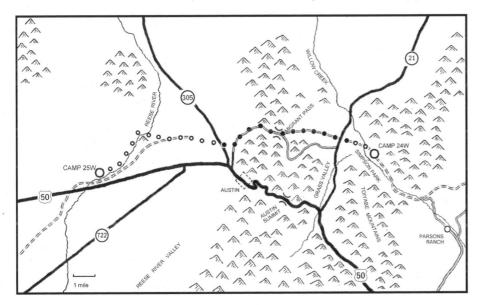

Reese River near the expedition's westbound ford. *"Reese River is 10 feet wide, 1½ deep; current moderate; and is the largest stream we have seen this side of the Jordan."*

ravine.... in 2.8 miles reach Reese Valley, which, in 3.7 miles more, we traverse to Reese River; this we cross by ford, and in 2.6 miles more up the river, or southwardly, reach our camping ground....Day's travel, 13.8 miles. Road generally good.[19]

The "short, sidling place" must have been in the lower end of Midas Canyon. Today the road that comes from Emigrant Pass turns south at the upper end of this canyon, while Simpson's trail continued to the west. This leaves a one-mile section of the trail that cannot be driven.

JUNE 2004

Parking on the side of State Route 305, near a Pony Express Trail crossing marker, I hiked up Midas Canyon until I reached the dirt road that leads to Emigrant Pass. In the lower part of the canyon, I found faint traces of an old trail, but they gradually faded, and had disappeared entirely before I reached the upper road.

The key to figuring out the route across the Reese River Valley was determining where the expedition forded the river.

The text of Simpson's report does not give much of a description of the spot where the crossing took place, so the only practical way to find it was to measure from the summit at Emigrant Pass, which can be identified with some accuracy. Simpson said it was 2.8 miles from the pass to the valley, and since there is only one feasible route going down the west slope of the mountain, the spot where they reached the valley can be accurately identified. The distance from that point to the ford was 3.7 miles, and Simpson's map shows that this section of the trail followed a straight line. Thus, the next step was simply to swing an arc of 3.7 miles and see where it intersected the river.

About three miles north of US 50, on the east bank of the Reese River, a low, rounded knoll can be found. Just after flowing past this knoll, the river makes a sharp bend to the east, goes a few hundred yards, and then turns to the north again. When I struck my arc from the "in the valley" location, I found that it hit the river about halfway between the two bends. This would mean that the crossing was on the section of the river that flows to the east. As I was plotting my straight line across the eastern half of the valley, I found that it was very close to the route that the USGS 7.5-minute quadrangle identified as the Pony Express Trail.

Leaving the lower end of Midas Canyon, the expedition started across the Reese River Valley. At about two and a quarter miles, they passed the spot where a section of their return route would rejoin the outbound route after having split away from it for a short distance. From this spot, the Pony Express riders and the Overland Stage would veer to the southwest, following Simpson's return trail. But during the westward journey, the expedition passed this spot and continued almost due west, directly toward the river, which was still about a mile and a half away. It is quite doubtful that anyone else ever followed this section of the outbound trail, and there are no visible indications of a trail through this area today.

MAY 2003

During previous trips to the Reese River Valley, I had made several unsuccessful efforts to find a way to drive into the area between Nevada State Route 305 and the river. Although the maps do show several different roads in this area, I was unable to find a way to get onto any of them. On this day, I drove north from US 50 on SR 305, parked on the side of the highway near the Pony Express crossing, and began hiking toward the river. After reaching the river near the expedition's westbound ford, I turned to the southeast, and, in about a half mile, I came back to the Pony Express Trail, which at this point is following Simpson's eastbound route. Turning back to the east, I followed the Pony Express Trail back to my SUV. During this hike, I had followed Simpson's westbound trail from the mouth of Midas Canyon to the Reese River, and his eastbound trail from the river back to the mouth of the canyon.

After crossing the river near the low knoll, the expedition began following the west bank toward the south. After traveling another two and a half miles, they stopped and set up camp for the night. This campsite is just a little over a mile northeast of the bridge that US 50 uses to cross the river. Simpson noted that the Indian name for the river was Pang-que-o-whop-pe,

which he understood to mean Fish Creek. This was one Native American name that he did not attempt to preserve. He gave it the name of Reese River, after the expedition's guide, who claimed to have crossed it many miles to the north several years earlier when he was traveling with the Huntington party, which was scouting for Colonel Steptoe.

JULY 2002

I had been unable to find a way to drive to the site of Camp 25-W, so I parked near the US 50 bridge, and made my way to it on foot. From the campsite, I continued in a northeasterly direction, following Simpson's outbound trail along the west bank of the river. At that time, I was still uncertain about the location of the river crossing, and I was looking for a likely spot. When I reached the low knoll, I used an old diversion dam to cross to the east side of the river, and then turned back to the south. I soon came to Simpson's eastbound route, which I followed back to US 50. On the way back, I passed the place where the Pony Express, the Overland Stage, and the early Lincoln Highway had crossed the river. There is no bridge at this point now, but I did see some large rocks on both banks that probably served as abutments for a bridge.

MAY 29, 1859

MAY 29, CAMP NO. 25, REESE RIVER. — *Moved at 5 minutes to 6 A.M. Course southwestwardly, to a depression or pass [Smith Creek Summit] of the low range bounding Reese Valley on its west side, which we reach by an easy grade in 13.5 miles.*[20]

WHEN THE EXPEDITION left camp on the morning of May 29, they continued upstream along the west bank, staying fairly close to the river. After just a little less than a mile, they passed the spot where the Pony Express Trail, the Overland Stage, and the early Lincoln Highway would cross the river. From this crossing, the Pony Express Trail and the stage road left the river and continued west for about a mile before turning south. The Lincoln Highway continued straight west. Simpson's map seems to show that the expedition

Camp 25-W. On the west bank of Reese River, which is a few yards to the right of the photo. This spot is about a mile northeast of where the river is crossed by US Highway 50.

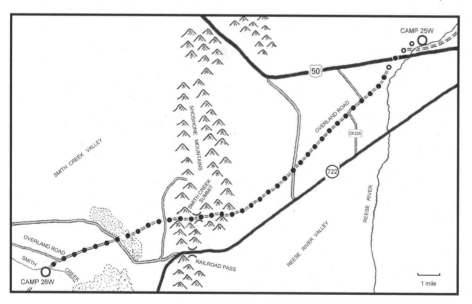

MAY 29, 1859

remained fairly close to the river for the next two miles, and then merged with the Pony Express Trail once again.

AUGUST 2001

The Pony Express Trail is well marked where it crosses US 50, but the right-of-way fence prevents vehicles from leaving the highway at this point. However, about four miles to the west, I was able to find a dirt road marked with a sign that reads "Reese River Farm District." Heading south on this road for a couple of miles, I came to where it intersects the Pony Express Trail. Turning back to the north on the trail, I followed it until I could see US 50 again. I knew that I was fairly close to where the expedition camped on the Reese River during the return trip. Although I was still quite uncertain about the exact location of the campsite, I parked here and hiked eastward to the river. After taking some photographs, I returned to my SUV, turned around, and followed the trail back to the south. Driving past the farm district, I continued to follow the trail to the south until I reached the point where it starts to climb up the eastern slope of the Shoshone Mountains. At that time, I was thinking that the expedition had probably gotten over these mountains through Railroad Pass, which was still a few miles to the south, so I turned off the trail and made my way to State Route 722, which I followed over Railroad Pass. Later, additional study of the report and the maps of the area convinced me that the expedition had continued along the trail that I had been following, and had crossed the mountain through Smith Creek Summit rather than Railroad Pass.

From summit of pass see another valley to the west of us, ranging generally north and south, and bounded by the Se-day-e or Lookout range [Desatoya Mountains], on its west side. In 2 miles from summit reach west foot of pass in valley by a tolerable descent, and without difficulty. This valley is exceedingly forbidding in appearance. To the south the bottom is an extended clay flat, perfectly divested of vegetation, terminating toward the south in a small lake. In the distance it all looked so much like a sheet of water that I sent a dragoon ahead to examine it; but, with my spy-glass, seeing him

gallop over it, I concluded it was passable; so gave the word forward. I struck magnetically S. 60° W., to the green spot across the valley Sanchez pointed out as our camp-ground, and on going to it passed over a portion of the clay flat referred to.[21]

From the western base of Smith Creek Summit, the expedition turned to the southwest, crossed an area of sagebrush and greasewood, and then a large playa where there is no vegetation at all. After crossing this old lake bottom, they crossed another sagebrush flat and came to Smith Creek, a short distance upstream from where it emptied into what Simpson described as a lake, but today is another large and dry playa.

JULY 2002

Returning to the Reese River Valley, I got back on the trail at the point where I had left it the previous year, and drove across Smith Creek Summit without encountering any problems. Upon reaching the valley, I came to an occasionally-used road, which travels along the western base of the Shoshone Mountains. To the west, I could see the faint trace of the old stage road heading in a southwesterly direction through a heavy growth of sagebrush. I made a short-lived attempt to follow the old road in my SUV, but after a quarter of a mile, I found that further progress was blocked by a deep washout. As I was turning around on the narrow trail, a piece of sagebrush penetrated the sidewall of one of my tires. After changing to one of the two spare tires that I habitually carried with me during my desert trips, I returned to the road at the base of the mountain and headed south until I reached the main road that crosses Smith Creek Valley. Turning to the west, I went about a mile, and then turned to the north onto the first of the old lakebeds. Driving across this dusty and barren playa, I circled back to the northeast until I intersected the old stage road at the point where it comes out of the sagebrush. Parking there, I hiked back along the abandoned road until I came to the place where I had gotten the flat tire.

In 5.8 miles from foot of pass, at 3½ P.M., after a journey of 21.2 miles, came to a creek, where we encamp in tolerable grass. The creek is 5 feet

Approaching Smith Creek Summit in the Shoshone Mountains. Today's State Route 722 crosses these mountains through Railroad Pass, about two miles to the south.

wide, 2 deep, and, running with considerable rapidity, spreads out in many rills, and sinks in the lake referred to. Abundant grass can be found at the mouth of the cañon of this stream. Both the stream and cañon I call after my assistant, Lieut. J. L. Kirby Smith. This valley [Smith Creek Valley]...I call after Capt. I. C. Woodruff, Corps Topographical Engineers.[22]

The old stage road crosses the main valley road at a point that is three and a half miles from where that road leaves State Route 722 in Railroad Pass. Continuing southwest, the old road is essentially abandoned, but can be easily driven in a high-clearance vehicle. After another two and a half miles, the stage road comes to an old ranch site that is labeled "Old Hay Ranch" on my maps of this area. Here the stage road and the Pony Express Trail turn to the west, heading for Smith Creek

Canyon. During the outbound trip, the expedition continued another mile to the southwest, where they came to Smith Creek and went into camp. I have been to this site on four occasions, and have never seen any water in the creek bed. It appears that all of the water is being diverted for use at the Smith Creek Ranch, which is located in the mouth of the canyon.

The expedition remained at the camp on Smith Creek for two days, because the guide had gone missing. Reese had left the camp in Simpson Park on the morning of May 28, at about the time the expedition was breaking camp, telling Simpson that he would meet the expedition the following evening. This meant that he should have come into the camp on Smith Creek sometime during the evening of the twenty-ninth. On the morning of the thirtieth, Simpson noted that Reese had not yet arrived.

His next comment shows that he was not exactly pleased. "And as he is alone, contrary to my orders, which require him always to come in with the last man of his party, I am not gratified."²³

Simpson decided to wait where they were for Reese's return, and the expedition remained in camp that day. While they were waiting, Simpson sent out a small party to reconnoiter Smith Creek Canyon, which could be seen to the west of the camp. Although these scouts reported that the canyon was not practical for wagons, the expedition did travel through it during its return journey. At the end of the day, Reese was still missing. They remained in camp again the next day, and Simpson sent out a search party. The party failed to find the guide, but they did find a promising site for the next camp.

The following morning, although Reese was still unaccounted for, Simpson decided to move the expedition forward after sending out another search party. Shortly after the expedition had departed from the campsite, Simpson was surprised to see someone coming through the sagebrush toward the wagons.

I noticed apparently an old, decrepit-looking man approaching the train from the west side, and supporting himself by a couple of crutches or sticks. At first I took him for a Digger Indian. On more close scrutiny, however, I found it to be Mr. Reese, our guide, who, as soon as we reached him, sank down exhausted into a sage-bush. His clothes were nearly torn off him, and altogether he presented a most pitiable aspect. As soon as he could collect his mind he informed us that the day before yesterday, when on the other or west side of the Se-day-e Mountains, about 17 miles off, his mule gave out and that he has ever since been on foot, trudging over the mountains to find us. He had no clothing except what he had on his back, and as he had lost his matches he could make no fire, though the night was quite cold.²⁴

After getting something to eat and drink, Reese climbed into one of the wagons and immediately went to sleep. Simpson sent one of the soldiers to find the search party, and the expedition moved on.

JUNE 1, 1859

JUNE 1, CAMP NO. 26, SMITH'S CREEK, WOODRUFF VALLEY. — *Our course today has been magnetically S. 25° W., between the base of the Se-day-e range [Desatoya Mountains] on our right and the clay flat and small lake of Woodruff Valley on our left. In 1.6 miles from camp cross a fine rapid stream, 5 feet wide, 2 deep, bottom somewhat soft, which I called after Mr. Engelmann, the geologist of my party. It expends itself in the lake. Two and a half miles farther cross another small stream running in the same direction, and after a day's march of 10.2 miles come to a swift creek [Campbell Creek] running east from the mountains, which I call after Lieutenant Putman, Topographical Engineers, one of my assistants.²⁵*

AS SIMPSON'S PARTY LEFT the camp on Smith Creek, they were heading in a slightly west-of-south direction. I have been unable to find any information that would indicate that any early travelers ever used the route that the expedition followed on June 1 and 2. In this area, Simpson's map includes a feature that I have been unable to explain. Although it has no significant bearing on the location of the route or the campsite, it does give rise to questions that remain unanswered. The map shows two separate trails in the area that the expedition traveled during the last half of this day's march. The distance involved seems to be about seven miles. The trail splits near the second small stream that Simpson mentioned, and the two branches come back together a short distance beyond the spot where they crossed Campbell Creek. The map seems to show that the site of Camp 27-W was closer to the eastern branch of the trail. The only similar situation occurs between Camps 29 and 30 of the return route, and in that case, Simpson explains quite clearly that he wanted to indicate that there was an alternate route that would be preferable to the route they actually followed. But he says nothing at all about the two trails in Smith Creek Valley, nor does he give any indication of which of the branches they actually followed. In visiting this area, I have found that Campbell Creek flows through a deep wash that parallels today's road.

Camp 26-W. The dry streambed of Smith Creek slants across this infrequently used stockyard. The campsite was probably on the far side of the creek. *"Come to a creek, where we encamp in tolerable grass. The creek, running with considerable rapidity, sinks in the lake."*

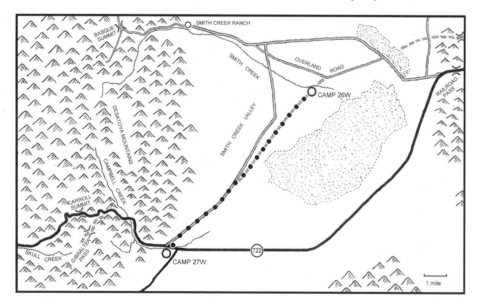

JUNE 1, 1859

This photo was taken from Simpson's Gibralter Pass, looking north to Carroll Summit. The faint line slanting slightly upward from the right is Highway 722, which was constructed in the mid-1920s as a Lincoln Highway project.

It is possible that the wash was between the two trails, but that does not explain why there were two trails. Today the established road is on the west side of the wash, and I have been unable to find any indication of a trail on the east side.

AUGUST 2001

My goal for this trip was to cover the expedition's outbound trail across Smith Creek Valley. After getting into the valley by way of Railroad Pass, I headed west on the main road until I intersected the expedition's trail. Turning to the southwest on what is now an abandoned two-track, I was able to make my way to the site of Camp 26-W. After crossing Smith Creek's dry streambed, I continued to the southwest until the old two-track intersected the well-traveled road that runs along the west side of the valley. From there it is a little less than four miles to where that road comes to SR 722, near the mouth of Campbell Creek Canyon.

After setting up camp on Campbell Creek, Simpson made a twenty-four-mile trip to take a look at a pass that he hoped to use the next day. While Simpson was exploring to the southwest,

Lt. Putnam was reconnoitering the canyon of Campbell Creek, which leads in a northwesterly direction from the campsite. Putnam reported that this canyon would be too narrow for the wagons, unless a significant amount of excavation was done. His report and Simpson's description of the route they followed the next day make it quite clear that the expedition did not follow the route of today's State Route 722 across Carroll Summit. As far as I can determine, there was no road across this summit until 1924, when, at the urging of the Lincoln Highway Association, a road was constructed through Campbell Creek Canyon and Road Canyon.

JUNE 2, 1859

JUNE 2, CAMP NO. 27, PUTNAM'S CREEK.—*Moved at 5 minutes of 6. A.M. Course southwestwardly to the base of the Se-day-e Mountain and then generally westwardly through what I call the Gibraltar (or south) Pass, examined by me yesterday. The teams reached summit of pass, 5 miles from last camp, at 10 o'clock, without doubling. The only exceeding steep place is about three-fourths*

Camp 27-W. Campbell Creek is on the far side of the road. The campsite was probably on the south bank, near the hay derrick. *"Come to a swift creek running east from the mountains, which I call after Lieutenant Putnam, one of my assistants."*

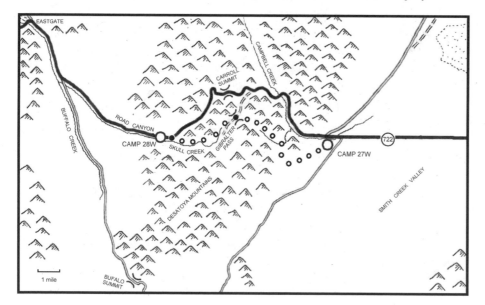

JUNE 2, 1859

of a mile up, where the ravine is left and a minor ridge surmounted to get over into the south branch of Putnam's Creek. The ascent of this minor ridge is steep, and the descent on the west side still more so. To accomplish the latter without accident we had to lock and rough-shoe the wheels.... Two and one-half miles thence up Putnam's Creek by a good grade brought us to summit of pass,...and 3.7 miles more down Gibraltar Creek [Skull Creek] (a small stream) to a point in the cañon [Road Canyon], where, at half past 4, we encamped....Journey 8.7 miles.[26]

THE ROUTE THAT the expedition traveled this day was one of the most challenging for me to find and travel. By the time I had gotten around to attempting it, I had learned that the route usually followed some sort of existing road or trail. This section would prove to be an exception. The only existing road through this area is State Route 722, which goes up Campbell Creek Canyon, crosses Carroll Summit, and descends through Road Canyon, but Simpson makes it clear that this was not the route they followed. After discarding the Carroll Summit possibility, I took a look at the Buffalo Canyon road, but soon determined that the distance involved was much greater than what Simpson reported. So I came back to the north, and started looking on the maps at what appeared to be a low place on the ridge at the upper end of Skull Creek Canyon. I finally concluded that this unnamed pass, located about a mile south of Carroll Summit, was Simpson's Gibraltar Pass. In order to arrive at this conclusion, it had been necessary to analyze very carefully, item by item, Simpson's description of the route they followed that day.

He started out by saying that from the camp, they headed in a "southwestwardly" direction until they reached the base of the mountain. While describing his scouting trip of the previous day, he mentioned that the foot of the pass was two miles from the camp. While studying the maps of the area, I found a small canyon, the mouth of which is two miles from Campbell Creek. This apparently unnamed canyon leads in a westerly direction into the Desatoya Mountains.

Simpson went on to say that after reaching the base of the mountain, they turned "generally westwardly" and, at a distance of five miles from

camp, came to the summit of Gibraltar Pass. He then added that on the way to the summit, "the only exceeding steep place is about three-fourths of a mile up." He did not bother to explain what, or where, this steep place was up from. After pondering this for some time, I concluded that he probably meant that the steep place was three-quarters of a mile from the mouth of the small canyon. The next part of Simpson's sentence states that in getting to the steep place, "the ravine is left and a minor ridge surmounted to get over into the south branch of Putnam's Creek." I have interpreted this as meaning that they got out of the small canyon by climbing over a ridge, then dropping down into another canyon, in which flowed a branch of Putnam's Creek. As I was studying the map, I noticed that a small tributary stream flows into Campbell Creek at a point about three-quarters of a mile above the mouth of Campbell Creek Canyon. This drainage flows out of the interior of the mountains in an easterly direction, then turns to the north about a half mile before reaching Campbell Creek. This stream can certainly be described as a south branch of Campbell Creek, or Putnam's Creek as Simpson called it. If you go up the small nameless canyon for three-quarters of a mile, then climb over its north ridge, you will then drop down into the south branch of Campbell Creek, which is exactly what Simpson said they did.

After getting into the canyon of the south branch of Putnam's Creek, Simpson wrote: "Two and one-half miles thence up Putnam's Creek [meaning its south branch] by a good grade brought us to summit of pass." When I measure the distance between the point where they came to the south branch of Campbell Creek, and the summit of the pass at the top of Skull Canyon, I get almost exactly two and a half miles.

From the summit, Simpson said they followed a stream, which he called Gibraltar Creek, for 3.7 miles and camped in the canyon. The only stream that flows westward from this summit is Skull Creek. Measuring from the summit along this stream for 3.7 miles brings you to a point just west of where Skull Canyon opens into Road Canyon. I believe the expedition's camp was at a small, but fairly level, area in Road Canyon that is now occupied by a roadside rest stop.

That night William Lee made the following entry in his journal:

Thursday, June 2nd. Marched eight and three-quarters miles over about the roughest road I think white man ever traveled, through a canyon which was very precipitous and steep. We got into camp about four o'clock after a hard day's work for the mules and men.[27]

JULY 2002

I came to this area prepared to hike the eastern half of the route that I now believed the expedition had followed through the Desatoya Mountains. I parked near a corral that was just off the dirt road that heads south from State Route 722 near the mouth of Campbell Creek Canyon. From there I hiked westward toward the mouth of the nameless canyon, and began following a trail that appeared to have been made by livestock or wild animals. After entering the canyon, I traveled about three-quarters of a mile, and then the trail began turning north and climbing up a ridge. When I reached the summit of the ridge, I could see that the trail dropped down a very steep incline into a larger canyon that came from the west. At the point where I reached it, this second canyon was just entering a bend that took it to the north, in the direction of Campbell Creek Canyon. It was apparent that I was looking into the south branch of Campbell Creek. I am quite certain that as I stood on this first ridge, the steep drop just below me was the place that Simpson was talking about when he said they had to "lock and rough-shoe the wheels." At this point, I was only about halfway to the summit of the mountain, and as evening was approaching, I decided to turn around and head back to my SUV.

When I arrived back at the corral, a rancher was there, unloading some hay for his horses. I asked if he knew the name of the little canyon. He said he had never heard of one. Feeling that I ought to explain why I was parked at his corral, I told him a little bit about my project, and explained that I was convinced that Simpson had taken his wagons over the mountain through this canyon. His response was straightforward: "Well, if he did, he was the silliest son-of-a-bitch I ever heard of." He went on to suggest that a much

more practical route would have been through Buffalo Canyon. I thanked him for his information and headed for Austin to spend the night.

Early the next morning I returned to the area, drove up Campbell Creek Canyon for about three and a half miles, and got onto a seldom-used two-track road that leads to Simpson's Gibraltar Pass and into the upper end of Skull Canyon. Parking near the summit, I started hiking in a southeasterly direction, down the canyon of the south branch of Campbell Creek. I followed the canyon until I was just below the ridge where I had turned around the previous evening. After returning to my SUV, I drove along the two-track road until I came to a dead end in the upper part of Skull Canyon. This was the second time that I had been on this short section of dirt road.

AUGUST 2001

During an earlier trip into the Desatoya Mountains, I had camped overnight in a little side-canyon just below Carroll Summit. When morning came, I drove down Road Canyon, parked near the mouth of Skull Canyon, and hiked up the canyon until I had reached the area near Gibraltar Pass.

After having hiked the entire distance between Camps 27-W and 28-W, it is my conclusion that although it would not have been an easy trail to travel, it would not have presented the wagons with any insurmountable difficulties. It is true that, aside from the short section of two-track road in the upper portion of Skull Canyon, I found no visible indication of a wagon trail, but that is not really surprising, since it is doubtful that anyone else ever traveled this section of Simpson's route.

Simpson noted that Reese found his mule, complete with saddle and all equipment, somewhere in the vicinity of the Road Canyon camp.

JUNE 3, 1859

JUNE 3, CAMP NO. 28, GIBRALTAR CREEK. — *Raised camp at 6.15, and continued down Gibraltar Cañon [Road Canyon]. For about a mile it continued rough from isolated rocks; after this no difficulty. Creek sinks 1.7 miles below camp. Five and a half miles farther strike a small creek*

Camp 28-W. A roadside rest area in Road Canyon. *"3.7 miles more down Gibraltar Creek (a small stream) to a point in the cañon, where, at half past 4, we encamped."*

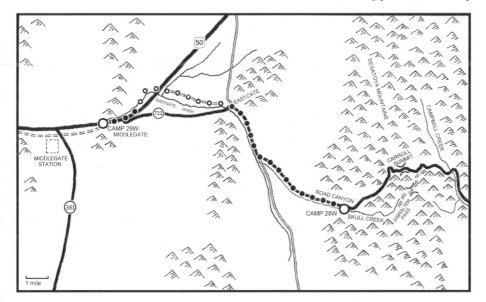

This old signpost stands beside the abandoned road on the north side of Eastgate Wash. Placed here during the days of the Lincoln Highway, it held a sign that was intended to guide early automobile travelers.

and a spring, which might be called an extension or re-appearance of Gibraltar Creek.... Half a mile farther pass through a gap or gate between some stupendous rocks of a dark-gray and brown porphyritic character.... This defile from the cañon to the valley I call The Gate of Gibraltar [Eastgate]. It is about 50 yards wide, and of champaign character. From this gate, following the course of Gibraltar Creek [Eastgate Creek] (very small), in a southwest direction, we cross in 7.2 miles a valley or plain, and arrive at a second gate or gap [Middlegate] in a low range, running north and south, where, at 4 P.M., we encamp near the sink of Gibraltar Creek.[28]

WHEN THEY LEFT Camp 28-W, the expedition continued down Road Canyon, following today's State Route 722 to Eastgate. Eastgate Creek skirts the base of the steep cliffs that make up the Eastgate formation, crosses under SR 722, and begins to flow into a gradually deepening wash. Although Simpson's map does not give a lot of detail, in this area it does show that the expedition's trail was north of what is labeled as "Gibraltar Creek." In his description of the westbound route, Simpson said nothing about which side of the stream they traveled on, or if, and where, they crossed it. However, when the expedition returned to this area during the return trip, he did say something that has a bearing on the westbound route. During the eastbound trip, Simpson indicated that when they left Middlegate, they followed their earlier trail for some distance and then, "After crossing an arroyo, or creek, immediately *leave old road*" (emphasis added).[29] There can be little doubt that this arroyo was Eastgate Wash, and this statement makes it quite clear that during the eastbound trip, they crossed the wash going from south to north. And since they were traveling on their old trail, it follows that they made this crossing at the same place where they crossed it when they were traveling

Eastgate Wash, about a mile and a half northeast of Middlegate, where it was crossed by the expedition.
"Cross an arroyo where the water yesterday, according to Mr. Reese, was running, but now exists in small pools."

west. All of which indicates that during the westbound trip, they had been on the north side of the wash before making this crossing.

SEPTEMBER 2003

During a couple of earlier visits to this area, I had spent some time attempting to find a road that could be used to get into the area on the north side of Eastgate Wash. I finally gave up, and concluded that this would be another section of the trail that would require some hiking. Parking where US 50 crosses Eastgate Wash, I began walking east. When I first started out, I was attempting to stay fairly close to the wash, and the path that I followed took me through a dense growth of greasewood. After about a mile, as I was coming out of the greasewood, I came across an old road. I realized at once that I had been moving parallel to it for some time, but had been unable to see it because of the dense vegetation. It was apparent that the road had seen a lot of use in

the past. In some places, it was worn down to as much as a couple of feet below the surrounding terrain. But it was also very apparent that it had been abandoned for many years. I began following the road, and it led me all the way to Eastgate, where I turned around and headed back to the west. Then I made what was to me a very important discovery.

Nearing the end of my hike, when I was less than a quarter of a mile east of US 50, where I had parked my SUV, I found a rusty metal post.

What does a rusty post have to do with Simpson's trail? It provides reliable evidence that an automobile road once followed Simpson's trail along the north side of Eastgate Wash.

The post that I found is almost identical to other old signposts that I have observed on verifiable sections of the Lincoln Highway in Nevada. All of these posts are made from cast iron pipes with about two inches of thread on the upper end, which means that they were probably used for some other purpose before being put to use as signposts. They all have faint traces of white paint, and holes drilled into them at locations that would allow the attachment of road signs that were placed along the Lincoln Highway in the early 1920s. These posts have been found on the route of the Lincoln Highway at White Pine Summit near the ghost town of Hamilton, in the Grimes Hills on the east side of Monitor Valley, and near the summit where the early Lincoln Highway crossed the Pancake Mountains. I think that it is quite certain that the abandoned road along the north bank of Eastgate Wash was first traveled by Simpson's expedition, then used as a wagon road, and then by the early Lincoln Highway. Later, during the mid-1920s, as the final stage of a major construction project, which shifted the Lincoln Highway from New Pass to Carroll Summit, the road between Eastgate and Middlegate was shifted to the south side of Eastgate Wash, and the road on the north side of the wash was abandoned.

The expedition's campsite for the night was near a gap in a low ridge that is known as Middlegate. This spot is not to be confused with Middlegate Station, which is about two miles farther west, near the junction of US 50 and State Route 361.

Six

Middlegate to Genoa

Camp 29-W. On the east side of the Middlegate gap. *"Arrive at a second gate or gap in a low range, where, at 4 P.M. we encamp near the sink of Gibralter Creek."*

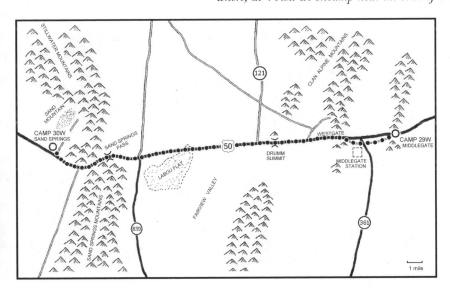

JUNE 4, 1859

— *Moved at 6.... Immediately after passing through Middle Gate, strike southwestwardly over a pulverulent prairie to a third gate, which we reach in 3½ miles, and which I call the West Gate [Westgate].*[1]

By noting that they passed through the Middlegate gap after leaving camp, Simpson makes it clear that the campsite had been on the east side of the ridge. Heading west from the campsite, US 50 follows a straight line that takes it about a quarter of a mile north of the old Middlegate Overland Stage Station, the site of which is now occupied by a restaurant and motel. The expedition's camp had been on the south bank of the creek, and there seems to be no good reason for them to have crossed it before reaching the site of Middlegate Station. The old stage road and the Lincoln Highway also remained on the south bank of Eastgate Creek, following Simpson's route to the station. About three-quarters of a mile west of the station, this old route veered to the north, rejoined the route now used by US 50, and passed through the Westgate gap.

After threading this defile pass over another thirsty-looking marly prairie, surrounded by low, ashy-looking mountains [Chalk Mountain], with passes between. In 5 miles get across this valley and attain summit of a low ridge [Drumm Summit], whence we descend to another shallow valley... which I call Dry Flat Valley [Fairview Valley], on account of the whitish clay flat we cross and which is as smooth and hard as a floor. Indeed, the glare from it was almost blinding.[2]

While studying this section of the route, I ran across an unexplainable error in Simpson's distance figures. In his table of distances, Simpson listed a checkpoint, which he referred to as "In Alkali Valley," and indicated that it was 10.2 miles west of Drumm Summit and 1.2 miles east of Sand Springs Pass. In describing this area, he said the valley floor was whitish in color and as smooth and hard as a floor. This is a good description of Labou Flat in Fairview Valley, but the distance figures do not work. Simpson's figures would put the Alkali Valley point well to the west of the center of the valley, and partway up the eastern

foothills of the Stillwater Mountains. The actual distance from Drumm Summit to the center of Labou Flat is closer to 5.7 miles, and, curiously, Labou Flat is also 5.7 miles from Sand Springs Pass. As a practical matter, this error is unimportant and has no effect on the location of the trail, but what makes it even more curious is that the same error, relating to the very same spot, was repeated during the return trip.

Twenty miles from camp we attain the summit of the range dividing Dry from a valley I call Alkaline Valley [Salt Wells Basin], on account of its general whitish alkaline appearance from saline efflorescence. Descending this ridge 1.7 miles, and turning northwardly and skirting it for 2.7 miles, we come to our camp-ground [Sand Springs], where the guide party, which is in advance of us, has dug a number of small wells.... Journey, 24.5 miles.[3]

This campsite was located near a spot that soon became known as Sand Springs. The springs are about six-tenths of a mile northwest of where the road to Sand Mountain leaves US 50. I have been to this area several times, and have never seen any surface water, but a meager growth of bunch grass marks the spot where the springs are shown on the maps. Although I have been unable to locate the small wells that Simpson mentioned, I did find the remains of a very old concrete water trough. The ruins of the Sand Springs Pony Express station can be found a short distance farther to the north.

Sometime during this day's march, some confusion developed about the difference between where they were and where Simpson wanted to be. Reese and some members of his scouting party were somewhere ahead of the wagons. One of the scouts returned to the wagon train, bringing a note from the guide. The note informed Simpson that the place Reese had selected for the coming night's campsite was about twelve miles from Walker Lake, and they could camp on the shore of that lake the following night.[4] This information was an unpleasant surprise to Simpson because he never had any intention of going anywhere near Walker Lake. In fact, he had been under the impression all along that their route would take them some distance to

Sand Mountain. The Sand Springs campsite was just a short distance from the foot of this large sand dune. It seems strange that Simpson failed to mention the dune in his report.

the north of it. In his usual habit of understatement, he described this news as "unpalatable," and commented:

The consequence is, that as the point I have been aiming at is the north bend of Walker's River, and not the Lake, we are a great deal too far to the south, and must therefore make the necessary corresponding northing.[5]

John Reese was usually a reliable guide, but in this case, he had gotten it wrong. As it turned out, the expedition was exactly where Simpson wanted to be, and the lake that the guide was talking about was Carson Lake, not Walker Lake. Whether Reese actually thought Carson Lake was Walker Lake, or simply erred when writing the note, is never made clear, but when Simpson got the word from Reese that they were southeast of Walker Lake, he was not at all happy. He immediately got out the map that the Topographical Bureau had sent with him, and spent some time studying it very carefully. Based on Reese's erroneous information, he began to suspect that the map was flawed. In this instance, he should have put more faith in the map than in his guide. It would be my guess that Simpson was rather poor company in camp that evening.

During this day's march, when they reached the base of Sand Springs Pass, they turned to the northwest. It ought to be noted, however, that

the shortest route to their eventual destination would have been almost due west. But, at this point, both Simpson and Reese were still under the impression that they needed to get a lot farther north. If they had continued in a more westerly direction, they could have crossed the south end of Salt Wells Basin and gone through a low pass that lies between the northern end of the Cocoon Mountains and the southern end of the Bunejug Mountains. There is a certain amount of irony in the fact that this low spot eventually became known as Simpson Pass.

The expedition passed by both the eastern and western approaches to this pass during the outbound and the return trips, but they never did attempt to take the wagons through it. During the westbound trip, they did not even think about it. During the eastbound trip, Simpson commented that he considered going this way, but Reese talked him out of it by claiming that it was "too full of sand to allow the passage of wagons."[6] Within a year, stagecoaches were traveling through Simpson Pass on a fairly regular basis. Burton describes his trip from Sand Springs to Carson Lake as follows:

About 11 A.M. we set off to cross the ten miles of valley that stretched between us and the summit of the western divide still separating us from Carson Lake. The land was a smooth saleratus plain, with curious masses of porous red and black basalt protruding from a ghastly white.... in one place the horses sank to their hocks and were not extricated without difficulty. After a hot drive... we began to toil up the divide, a sand formation mixed with bits of granite, red seeds, and dwarf shells.... Arrived at the summit, we sighted for the first time Carson Lake, or rather the sink of the Carson River.... Our conscientious informant at Sand Springs Station had warned us that upon the summit of the divide we should find a perpendicular drop, down which the wagons could be lowered only by means of lariats affixed to the axle-trees and lashed round strong "stubbing posts." We were not, however, surprised to find a mild descent of about 30°.[7]

What had happened to all the sand?

Perhaps because he was preoccupied with the problem of where they were, as opposed to where he wanted to be, Simpson failed to mention that they were camped at the foot of one of the largest sand dunes in the country. Young William Lee did notice it, however, and felt that it deserved to be mentioned it in his journal. "Near where we camped there is a large hill about a thousand feet high and perfectly bare—not a shrub or stone on it, all sand."[8]

JUNE 5, 1859

JUNE 5, CAMP NO. 30. ALKALINE VALLEY. — *Up at half past 3 A.M., but in consequence of mules straying off to get grass and water, the train did not move until 5. Course north of west along west foot of Black Mountains [Stillwater Mountains], to the north end of what turned out to be Carson instead of Walker's Lake. The guide, therefore, at fault, and neither the Topographical Bureau map nor my calculations wrong. As the map will indicate, it will be perceived that before I made the turn to the northwest, pursuant to the representation of our whereabouts by our guide, my course was direct for the bend of Walker's River, the locality aimed at from the commencement of the expedition at Camp Floyd. The consequence is that we have lost about 12 miles by our guide's errors, and will have to retrograde, for a distance, our steps.*[9]

FORTUNATELY FOR THE EXPEDITION, Simpson eventually got it figured out that the map was

correct, and Reese was confused about the name of the lake they were approaching. What is missing from the report is an explanation of just how Simpson discovered that it was actually Carson Lake.

While camped at the northern end of Carson Lake during the evening of June 5, Simpson added some additional information about the trail they had followed that day.

The road today has been along the east edge of Alkaline Valley [Salt Wells Basin], and the west foot of the Black Mountains [Stillwater Mountains]. In the valley it has been heavy, and on the benches, on account of the basaltic rocks, rough.... Journey, 16.6 miles.[10]

It appears that as the expedition left the Sand Springs camp on the morning of June 5, they headed due west out into the mudflats of Fourmile Flat. Their reason for doing this is uncertain, but Simpson's map makes it very clear that their initial direction was west. It is possible that it took them a mile or so to learn that traveling across these flats was not as easy as it might look. Simpson mentioned only that the trail was "heavy," which means that the ground was soft. During the return trip, when they crossed Fourmile Flat in the opposite direction, he indicated that "the Alkaline Valley where we crossed it will evidently be impassable from mire in wet weather."[11]

After traveling about a mile into the flats, the expedition turned to the north, and made its way to the tip of a small ridge that protrudes into the flats and forms a separation of sorts between Fourmile Flat and Eightmile Flat. US 50 crosses the tip of this ridge, and the expedition probably crossed it at about the same place. According to John Townley, the Pony Express and the Overland Stage came to this point after traveling in a northwesterly direction from Sand Springs Station.[12] Townley's map shows that the mail riders and the coaches crossed Simpson's trail at this point, then headed due west across the flats to Rock Springs, the only reliable waterhole between Sand Springs and Carson Lake.

After leaving the tip of the ridge, the expedition continued in a northwesterly direction, but now they moved onto a low bench that runs

Camp 30-W. Sand Springs in Salt Wells Basin, which Simpson called Alkaline Valley. *"We come to our camp-ground, where the guide party, which is in advance of us, has dug a number of small wells."* The author has been unable to find any wells, but this concrete cistern must have held water in the past.

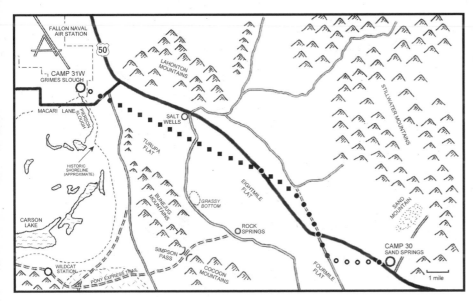

JUNE 5, 1859

along the east side of Eightmile Flat. It was here that they encountered the volcanic rocks that Simpson mentioned. After traveling along the bench for about three and a half miles, they turned a little more to the west, crossed the northern part of Eightmile Flat, then crossed US 50 again about three and a half miles southeast of Salt Wells. From here, they headed toward Turupa Flat and the northern tip of the Bunejug Mountains. After another three miles, they came to the northern shore of Carson Lake and the stream that Simpson called the outlet.

Although this route crosses several roads and trails, it does not appear that any part of it travels along any modern road or trail. During one of my several trips to this area, I spent most of a day slowly working my way along several sections of two-track, traveling through the sand dunes along the eastern edge of Fourmile Flat, and then across the foothills above the eastern edge of Eightmile Flat. I should not have bothered, because I eventually figured out that the distance along these roads does not fit the mileage figures reported by Simpson, nor do they come anywhere close to corresponding with the shape of the trail on Simpson's map. In the end, I had to do my best to superimpose the alignment shown on Simpson's map onto a modern map, and completely ignore the modern roads and trails.

We are encamped at the head of the outlet from Carson Lake into the Sink of Carson, where our only fuel is dry rush. This outlet is about 50 feet wide and 3 or 4 feet deep, and voids the lake rapidly into its sink, which is some 10 or 15 miles to the northeast of us.... The Carson River to the northwest, where it empties into the lake, can be seen quite distinctly, marked by its line of green cottonwoods.[13]

It is clear that the party's camp for the night was on the northeast shore of Carson Lake, but determining the exact location of the campsite proved to be very difficult. The major problem is that the shore of Carson Lake is no longer where it was in 1859. As a matter of fact, for all practical purposes there no longer is a Carson Lake. A massive irrigation project that began in the early 1900s has changed the hydrology of the entire

area, and the reservoir behind the Lahontan Dam now holds most of the water that once flowed into Carson Lake. The small amount of water that now gets to the lake is found several miles south of where the expedition camped that night.

Simpson did provide one helpful clue when he said the camp was on the bank of a stream that he called the outlet of the lake. Since he described the outlet as being 50 feet wide and three or four feet deep, I felt that I should be able to find some evidence of a stream of this size. During my first several visits to the area, I was unsuccessful in finding anything that I could recognize as a streambed, and I was beginning to believe that the construction of irrigation canals and ditches had completely wiped out any signs of the stream. This was before I learned about the Terraserver website and had begun to study some of the aerial photos that are available on the Internet. When I did begin to use this website, a study of the photos of this area revealed the general shape of the lake as it must have existed before the irrigation project. Then I noticed what appeared to be some sort of a channel running in a northerly direction from the old lakeshore. Comparing the aerial photos with topographical maps of the area shows that this channel is a combination of what is now called Pierson Slough, which is found on the south side of Macari Lane, and Grimes Slough, which runs north from Macari Lane. I am quite certain that this is the channel that Simpson called the outlet, and I believe that the campsite was about a half mile north of Macari Lane, and about a mile south of the southern end of the Fallon Naval Air Station's main runway. Interestingly, William Lee used the word "slough" to describe the stream that he saw flowing out of Carson Lake.

Sunday, June 5th. Marched seventeen miles and came to camp on a slough at the northern end of Carson Lake.... The mules seemed to feel that they were near water, for it was hard to restrain them. Having had nothing to eat since last night, I was very glad to get to camp. Met here with a band of Pah-Utes; they seemed very healthy and were fishing in the lake. Noticed some decoy ducks among them.[14]

The eastern shore of Carson Lake. The expedition's artist, H. V. A. Von Beckh, drew a sketch that John J. Young later copied in painting this watercolor.

SEPTEMBER 2005

Parking on the side of Macari Lane, I hiked northward, following the east bank of Grimes Slough until I reached the area where I believe Camp 31-W was located. If I understand the maps of this area correctly, this spot is on property that is a part of the Fallon Naval Air Station, but, unlike most of the station's property, this area remains unfenced. The fenced part of the air base lies directly to the north. During this short hike, I noticed that a narrow dirt road approached this area from the west. A year later, with a slightly different set of GPS coordinates; I attempted to get onto this road with my vehicle, but was barred by a locked gate. Since I could not see any No Trespassing signs on the gate or the fence, I climbed over the gate and hiked the half mile to the location of the campsite.

JUNE 6, 1859

JUNE 6, CAMP NO. 31, NORTH END OF CARSON LAKE. — *We retrograde today in our course, southerly direction, and skirt the east shore of Carson Lake.*[15]

BY RETROGRADE, SIMPSON did not mean that they returned along the entire previous day's trail, only that they were returning back toward the south. Simpson's map does show that they did travel back along the earlier trail, but for only about a mile. At that point they left it and headed straight south, traveling between the western

base of the Bunejug Mountains and the eastern shore of the lake. There is a good dirt road through this area today, but the expedition's trail was somewhat farther to the west and closer to the lake. Three weeks later, during the return trip, Simpson mentioned that the rising waters of the lake had covered the trail they made through this area during the outbound trip.[16]

Somewhere along the eastern shore of the lake, William Lee and at least one of his fellow assistants, possibly Edward Jagiello, stopped to take a break.

We stopped under the shade of some cottonwood trees for about two hours, where we had a refreshing nap and let the animals graze; but contrary to our expectations, we found that the train, instead of camping on the lake, had concluded to push on. So we had a smart ride of about eight miles to catch up, and found them making a noon halt.[17]

This comment seems to imply that Simpson may have said something about making another camp on the shore of the lake, but when the main body of the expedition reached the southern end of the lake, it kept on going. Lee and his companion had to hustle to catch up.

In 9.7 miles leave the lake at its southern end, and, passing over and through some sand-hills, in 5.7 miles come to a small spring of calcareous water [Lee Hot Springs], where there is no grass. Here there has been a number of these springs, and

Camp 31-W. Looking south toward Carson Lake. The campsite was on the east bank of Grimes Slough, a short distance from the Fallon Naval Air Station's primary runway.

JUNE 6, 1859

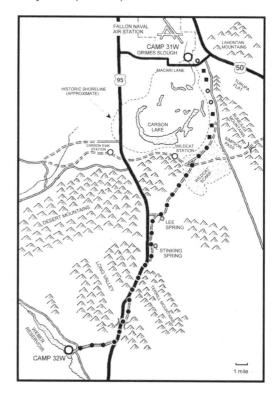

the locality for a very considerable area is nothing but calcareous tufa, formed by the springs, which are all closed but one.[18]

If I am right about the location of the shoreline at that time, they were about a quarter of a mile from the lake's southeastern shore when they reached the point that was 9.7 miles from the previous night's camp. During the return trip, the expedition came back to its outbound trail at this same spot. It is also at about this point that the Pony Express and the Overland Stage rejoined Simpson's return trail after coming through Simpson Pass. On this day, the expedition continued in a southerly direction and crossed the barren flats of Wildcat Scarp. In doing this, they compounded the error they had made when they traveled all the way to the northern end of the lake. It would have saved them a lot of time and effort if they had turned to the west at this point. Their failure to make this turn may have been caused by Reese's faulty recollection of the area, but it is much more likely that it was due to Simpson's determination to get to the big bend of the Walker River. Whatever the reason, if they had turned to the west, they would have missed Walker River entirely, and their route would have been shortened by approximately twenty miles. Three weeks later, when the expedition was on its way back to Camp Floyd, Simpson had figured this out, and they did follow the shorter route back to Carson Lake.

SEPTEMBER 2001

Nancy and I drove southeast from the city of Fallon, and got onto the dirt road that travels along the eastern side of what was once Carson Lake. Near the southeast corner of the lake, we came to an area that is known as Wildcat Scarp. As we drove into the scarp, the road we had been following abruptly vanished. The scarp is an expanse of soft clay soil that seems to melt and run as soon as it gets wet. Burton described it as "a plain too barren for sage."[19] The occasional rain that falls here quickly eliminates the tracks of anything that crosses the scarp. In order to get across this area you simply drive over the dusty flats, doing your best to avoid the random washes and gullies. In wet weather, such an attempt

would surely end in disaster. On the far side of the scarp we found the road again, and started climbing into the foothills that lie to southeast of the White Throne Mountains. About five miles southwest of the scarp, we came to Lee Hot Springs, which is still sending up a column of steam. Heading west from the hot spring, we soon came to US Highway 95.

Three miles more brought us through some heavy sand-drifts to a very small spring of miserable mineral-water, so nauseous as not to permit me to take even a swallow.[20]

A small seep called Stinking Springs is located just slightly over three miles from Lee Hot Springs and about a quarter of a mile east of US 95. A note on the USGS 30 × 60-minute map indicates that the water is undrinkable.

After proceeding a few miles further, in consequence of the day being very warm and the sandhills heavy, halted at 3 o'clock and turned out the animals to graze upon the little grass which exists in bunches around. At 5 start again, and still ascending to crest of dividing ridge between Walker's Lake Valley and Saleratus Valley [Lahontan Valley], in 9.4 miles reach summit. Just before doing so, Lieutenant Murry sent word that some of the mules were giving out, and he was afraid he would be obliged to halt. I sent word back to him to try and hold on till he could reach the summit, and after that there would be no difficulty. He managed, by exchanging some of the mules, to get the wagons all up to the top of the divide, but it was midnight before we reached Walker's River, 6.9 miles distant, and as the night was quite dark, we considered ourselves very fortunate that we got along without accident....Journey to-day a hard one....Distance 31.2 miles.[21]

Simpson said only that they took their break a "few miles" beyond Stinking Springs, which is not enough information to determine the exact location of their rest stop. About five and a quarter miles south of Stinking Springs, an earlier, and now-abandoned, version of US 95 veers away from today's highway. Simply because it was an older road, it is probably safe to assume that

Camp 32-W. Weber Reservoir on the Walker River, about twenty miles north of Walker Lake. The campsite would have been near the center of the photo, under the waters of the reservoir.

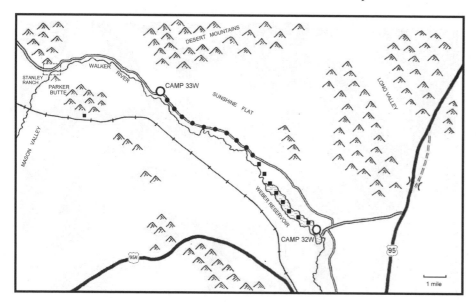

it was the route that the expedition followed. At four and a quarter miles from this split, the old road crosses the summit and begins to drop toward Walker Lake. About four miles south of the summit, the old road rejoins today's US 95. After another three quarters of a mile, the expedition turned and headed directly west toward the Walker River, reaching it near the site of today's Weber Reservoir. After a lot of map work and several trips to the area, it is my conclusion that the campsite is now covered by the waters of the reservoir, about a quarter of a mile to the northwest from the dam.

June 7, 1859

June 7, Camp No. 32 Walker's River.—*In consequence of getting into camp so late last evening, and the teams requiring rest, we lay over at this point till this afternoon. The river we are encamped on (Walker's) is the largest I have seen this side of Green River; is about one hundred yards wide and from six to ten feet deep at its present stage, which seems to be high.…Its banks, which are vertical, are about four feet above the surface of the water.*[22]

As subsequent events will show, there is no doubt that the river was running high at that time, but since it was not over its banks, and since Simpson had never seen it before, one has to wonder about what he saw that led him to conclude that it was higher than normal. William Lee took advantage of the morning layover and went for a swim. "Got up this morning pretty early and took a fine swim in the river."[23]

Raise camp at 3 P.M. Sun scorching hot. Course northwestwardly along the left or north bank of the river, being forced occasionally by the river from the bottom to the sand-bench.…After marching ten miles, at 7 o'clock encamped again on the river.…Pete came in from guide's party, and reports bend of Walker's River six miles ahead, where I expect to camp to-morrow.[24]

This day's journey followed the Walker River upstream in a northwesterly direction. It appears from Simpson's description that they stayed as close to the river as was practical for the wagons. This would probably mean that the Weber Reservoir now covers the first couple of miles of their trail.

September 2001

Nancy and I had reached the Weber Reservoir after following US 95 south from Lee Hot Springs, then turning west on a fairly well-traveled dirt road. Now, as we were preparing to follow the expedition's trail along the Walker River, I was concerned about being able to make it all the way from the Weber Dam to Wabuska, which is on US Highway 95A. My map indicated that the road would be going through an Indian reservation, and I suspected it might be closed to travel, as are other reservations that I have visited in the past. I soon found that my qualms were unwarranted. The road itself is a good dirt road, and unlike many of the dirt roads through similar areas in Nevada, there was not a single gate to be opened and closed. Although it does go through a few sandy washes, the road presents no difficulties for high-clearance vehicles. Camp 33-W, the second camp on the Walker River, was near the western edge of Sunshine Flat, at a point where a side channel of the river makes an ox-bow loop that brings it next to the road. This loop was filled with running water when Nancy and I first saw it in 2001. During subsequent visits in 2003 and 2004, it was completely dry.

June 8, 1859

June 8, Camp No. 33, Walker's River.— *Moved at twenty minutes after 5. Continue 6.3 miles up valley of Walker's River, as far as the North Bend, and, at 8 A.M., encamp in tolerable grass.*[25]

Sometime during this morning's travel, the expedition crossed the trail of the first group of emigrants known to have made the overland journey to California. On October 11, 1841, the Bidwell-Bartleson party crossed the Walker River somewhere between Sunshine Flat and the big bend of the river. There is nothing in Simpson's report about this group, and it seems likely that he was unaware of its existence. And

Camp 33-W. On the north bank of the Walker River, near Sunshine Flat. Water occasionally flows through the oxbow channel at the left of the road. The river's main channel is about one hundred yards farther to the left.

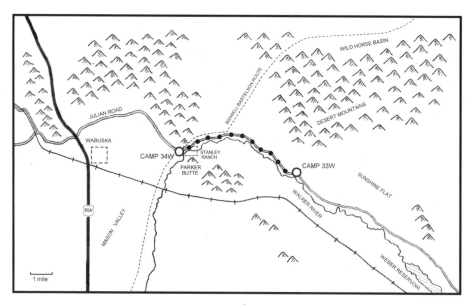

it is not surprising that he failed to notice their trail, because well before reaching this point, the entire party had abandoned their wagons and had continued their journey mounted on horses and mules. In 1859, the 18-year-old trail would probably have been difficult to see.

When the Bidwell-Bartleson party left Missouri in May 1841, it was comprised of about sixty people and fourteen covered wagons. Just west of Soda Springs in Idaho, about half of the group split off and headed for Oregon. The rest of the party, which included both John Bidwell and John Bartleson, turned south and followed the Bear River into Utah. When they reached the northeast shore of the Great Salt Lake, they turned west and made their way past the north end of the lake. Reaching the Park Valley area, they turned south until they passed by the eastern base of Pilot Peak, then turned to the west again. Somewhere west of Pilot Peak, they abandoned their wagons and most of their worldly goods. Packing what they could on the backs of their draft animals, they continued west until they stumbled across the Humboldt River, which they followed to its sink. Heading south from Humboldt Sink, they passed by the western side of Carson Lake, then managed to find their way through the rugged Desert Mountains and came to the Walker River, striking it somewhere near its bend. According to the journals of John Bidwell and James Johns, after reaching the river they followed it upstream for about four miles, then left it to travel in a southwesterly direction.[26] It seems quite likely that they left the river at the point where it began to turn to the east. Upstream from this point, the river is running almost due north.

After crossing the Bidwell-Bartleson Trail, the Simpson expedition came to a sweeping bend in the Walker River, where it changes its direction of flow from nearly north to east and then southeast. Simpson described this area as the "North Bend," and stated that this is where they camped. This statement caused me a lot of problems.

When I first began looking at this part of the route, I relied on Simpson's statement, and placed Camp 34-W at the spot where the river reaches its farthest point to the north. At the time, this bend in the river seemed to be a dependable landmark, and I relied on it to determine the location of the

two previous campsites, and the two campsites that followed. Later, after obtaining a good copy of Simpson's map, I noticed that the symbol for this camp was shown as being some distance upstream from the high point of the bend. This discovery sent me back to my modern maps, and after a lot of re-plotting and re-measuring, and another trip to the area, I finally concluded that the map was accurate, and Simpson's description should not have been taken quite so literally. The campsite had to be at the point where the north-flowing part of the river first begins to enter the bend to the east. Once again, I found that the map was more accurate than I had at first assumed.

After adjusting the location of Camp 34-W to fit better with Simpson's map, I had to relocate the other two Walker River campsites. It was when I did this that I found that the site of Camp 32-W would have been under the waters of today's Weber Reservoir. Previously, I had placed the camp some distance downstream from the dam, but this area had never seemed quite right, because I had found that this was an area that would have been difficult for the wagons to reach because of the river's steep banks.

SEPTEMBER 2004

Placing Camp 34-W at the very beginning of the big bend puts it on the western edge of the Stanley Ranch. The road that follows the northern bank of the Walker River bypasses this ranch by going around a hill to the north. While I was still under the impression that the campsite was farther to the east, Nancy and I had driven by the ranch a couple of times without stopping. However, in September of 2004, having figured out that the campsite was on the ranch property, we stopped and asked for permission to drive to this new location. Permission was readily granted, and David and Molly Stanley seemed genuinely interested in my project. They told me that they were aware that Frémont had traveled through this area, but they had never heard of James Simpson. They said that I was welcome to go anywhere on the ranch that I wanted, and we spent a couple of hours wandering around the campsite area, taking photographs and GPS readings.

Molly Stanley mentioned that on a few occasions since they began living on the ranch, the

Camp 34-W. On the northwest bank of Walker River, near the northern end of Mason Valley. *"Continue up valley of Walker's River, as far as the North Bend, and, at 8 A.M., encamp in tolerable grass."*

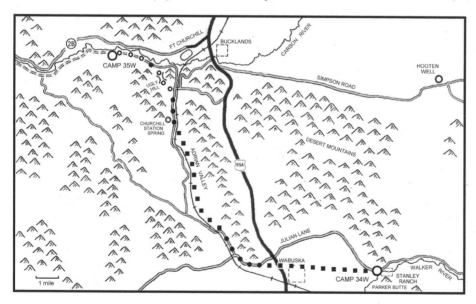

JUNE 9, 1859

river has risen high enough to cover the entire area between the ranch buildings and Parker Butte, which is almost half a mile to the south. This is probably the way Simpson saw it in 1859. He had previously mentioned that the Walker River was running high, and the following day he reported that the Carson River was also running much higher than normal. Since the headwaters of both rivers are within a few miles of each other in the Sierra Nevada, it is probably safe to assume that the Walker River was over its banks in the area near Camp 34-W. This would have forced the expedition to choose a campsite that was up on the bench, rather than down in the grassy area next to the normal channel of the river.

June 9, 1859

June 9, Camp 34, North Bend of Walker's River.—*Our course lies northwestwardly to Carson River....Six miles from camp we pass some hot and cold springs to left of road in valley. Leaving the valley of Walker's River and striking for Carson River, we cross the point of a low mountain—ascent and descent good—and in three and one-half miles more get into an old wagon-road which we follow.*[27]

WHEN THE EXPEDITION left camp, they struck off in a westerly direction across the northern end of Mason Valley, passing just north of today's small community of Wabuska. When I first attempted to plot the route through this area, I was still thinking that Camp 34-W was about two miles farther east than it actually was, which caused me to believe that the expedition turned north at Wabuska to follow today's US Highway 95A to the Carson River. Relying on this mistaken assumption, I made several failed attempts to find the features that Simpson noted during this day's journey. After I finally determined the correct location for Camp 34-W, it became apparent that the expedition had crossed US 95A and had continued to the west for a couple of miles more before making the turn to the north. This would have taken them into the southern end of Adrian Valley, which they could then follow to the Carson River. Once I started looking at this possibility,

it did not take long to locate a couple of the features that Simpson had noted in his report.

The first of these were the "hot and cold springs" that Simpson said they passed at six miles from camp. I had earlier assumed that these were today's Wabuska Springs, but it now became apparent that they were somewhere west of the highway. After a little exploring, I found a cluster of springs at almost exactly six miles from the campsite. The next feature that Simpson mentioned was the point of a low mountain that he listed in the table as the "Divide between Carson River and Walker River," and indicated the distance as being 6.7 miles from the camp. I found that at this distance from the Stanley Ranch, the dirt road that leads from Wabuska to Adrian Valley goes over the southern tip of the westernmost ridge of the Desert Mountains.

An even more significant landmark was a spring that Simpson said they passed at fourteen miles from camp, describing it quite colorfully as being "embowered among wild roses and willows." I had been unable to find even the slightest indication of a spring anywhere along US 95A between Wabuska and the Carson River, but when I studied the Adrian Valley route on a USGS 7.5-minute map, it did not take long to find a spring that is located at almost exactly fourteen miles from the Stanley Ranch. This spring is identified on the map as Churchill Station Spring. Then there was a ridge that Simpson called the "Ugly Hill." The expedition first crossed this ridge during the westbound trip. During the return trip, they came back across it, and within a short distance crossed over a second ridge, which Simpson referred to as "another spur."[28] Before finding the Adrian Valley route, I had been looking for the ugly hill just to the west of US 95A. At one point, I felt that I had identified it, and had gone so far as to spend a couple of hours hiking over it. But I always realized that there was a problem with this location, because there was no other spur to the east of this hill. Upon shifting the expedition's trail to Adrian Valley, it became evident that Simpson's ugly hill was a part of the ridge on the west side of this narrow valley, and the second spur was the ridge on the east side. The hill that I had climbed earlier is a part of the second ridge, but is about a mile south of where

Churchill Station Spring, at the northern end of Adrian Valley. *"In this cañon, on left side, fourteen miles from last camp, embowered among wild roses and willows, is a small spring of good, cool water, about which there is a little grass."*

the expedition crossed this ridge during their eastbound journey.

SEPTEMBER 2004

A couple of months after I had figured out that the expedition had traveled through Adrian Valley, Nancy and I made a trip to the area. Although the road is not paved, it is fairly well traveled, and the only difficulty that we ran into was one deep mud hole alongside the railroad tracks, about three miles west of Wabuska. We got through that by shifting into four-low and giving it the gas.

Although made almost in passing, Simpson's mention of the "old wagon road" is intriguing. One has to wonder where it went and who used it. I have been unable to find anything that would even hint at the answers to these questions. Nevertheless, this point on the route is significant because it marks the spot where the expedition was no longer breaking a new trail. As previously mentioned, they had first begun breaking new trail when they left the southern

end of the Ruby Mountains, some 270 miles back. They now found themselves on an established wagon road once again, and they would continue to travel on established roads for the remainder of the westward journey. Simpson's map shows a short section of this road coming to his route from the southwest. When Nancy and I were in Adrian Valley, we spent some time looking for this road, but failed to find it. However, since making this trip, additional study of maps and aerial photographs leads me to believe that in this area, the expedition's trail was probably closer to the railroad than it was to today's dirt road. If this conclusion is correct, it would mean that we were never in the right place to see the old wagon road. Aerial photos of the area show an old road that comes to the tracks from the southwest at about the correct spot, and it is marked as a trail on the USGS 7.5-minute map of the area. After leaving the railroad, this road goes through some bends and ends up reaching US 95A near Wabuska.

Looking west toward the ridge that Simpson called the ugly hill. *"Pass over the steepest and roughest hill, or spur, we have seen."*

One mile more brings us to a cañon which we thread, and in which we find a considerable patch of grass and rushes. In this cañon, on left side, fourteen miles from last camp, embowered among wild roses and willows, is a small spring of good, cool water, about which there is a little grass; a plenty of the latter one half-mile south.[29]

During our trip through Adrian Valley, Nancy and I stopped for a while at Churchill Station Spring. It is still a good source of water, and is surrounded on all sides by a lush growth of willows. Much to Nancy's disappointment, we were unable to find any wild roses.

Two miles farther, pass over the steepest and roughest hill, or spur, we have seen. We would like to continue down the valley until we strike Carson River, and then turn up its valley to the left, and thus avoid this spur, but the height of the water

prevents. At this hill we were detained two and one-half hours. All the teams had to double to get up, except Payte's, which seems thus far to carry off the meed of power and good management. Three miles more along and up Carson River upon its bank brought us to a good spot on the river, where we encamp in good grass....Journey, 19 miles.[30]

At about a mile and a half north of Churchill Station Spring, the expedition left the road and turned to the west. They were still about a mile and a half from the northern end of the western ridge and the Carson River's normal channel, but the scouts had discovered that the river was running so high that it had covered the road at the point where it turned to the west to go around the northern tip of the ridge. Determining that it would have been impossible to get the wagons between the rushing water and the northern point of the ridge, Simpson decided to climb over the ridge before they got to the river. Turning to their left near what is now the Churchill railroad crossing, the expedition made its way over what Simpson would later call the "ugly hill." The distance involved was only about a mile, but Simpson reported that it took them two and a half hours. In order to get over the steepest part, they had to double the teams on all the wagons, with the exception of one that was being driven by a teamster named Payte. After crossing the summit of the ridge, they dropped down its western slope and rejoined the wagon road in an area where it was traveling west along the south bank of the Carson River.

September 2001

During our first trip to this area, Nancy and I reached the Churchill railroad crossing by following a dirt road that leaves US 95A about two and a half miles south of the Carson River. We crossed the railroad tracks and got onto a narrow two-track that headed north, back toward the river. When we reached the end of the ridge, we turned west and followed the south bank of the river for about two and a quarter miles and came to a securely locked gate that prevented any further travel to the west. At that time I was still unaware of the actual location of the ugly hill, and we drove by both its east and west sides twice without realizing it.

September 2005

Four years after our first visit, Nancy and I returned to this area again. Now aware of the ugly hill's actual location, I parked near the railroad crossing and headed west on foot to hike over the ridge. For the first four-tenths of a mile, the route is a fairly gentle slope. The next tenth gets quite steep, and the last tenth is one of the steepest sections to be found on Simpson's entire route. After crossing the ridge, I dropped down the western slope and got back to the road near the river. From there I turned to the west, and followed the road for another two and a quarter miles to the site of Camp 35-W, climbing over the locked gate along the way. From the campsite I turned back to the east, following the road around the northern tip of the ridge, instead of retracing my steps across the ugly hill. By making this hike, I had managed

to travel on nearly half of the expedition's trail along the south bank of the Carson River. I now had to figure out a way to get to the other half.

After returning home from this trip, I spent some more time studying the maps and aerial photos of the area to the south of the river. I eventually found what appeared to be a narrow road that reached this area from the southeast, and worked its way to the river at a spot that looked like it could be beyond the fenced-in area. In late August of 2007, I decided to make one more try.

August 2007

Nancy and I drove south from Fallon on US Highway 95 until we reached Wabuska, where we left the paved road and turned to the west, following the expedition's trail to the southern end of Adrian Valley. We had been on this section of the route before, but on this day we left it when it turned north through Adrian Valley. The road we wanted turned northwest, and entered the northeastern foothills of the Pine Nut Mountains. The road was narrow and rough, and soon turned really ugly. As it climbed into the hills, it became nothing more than a barely visible track across a ten-mile boulder field. For the rest of the distance to the river, we found it impossible to go any faster than three to five miles an hour. We eventually made it over a high ridge and down the northern slope to the river at a point that, as I had hoped, was just west of the fenced-in area. And sure enough, there was another locked gate that prevented us from going east into the private property. So we headed west, which is what we really wanted to do. The road we were now on was a good two-track, and we soon found ourselves across the river from the site of Camp 36-W. I had previously hiked to this spot from the west, and I knew that the road was blocked by another locked gate about a quarter of a mile away, so we turned around and headed back along the route we had already traveled.

Simpson's map does not show it, and his report fails to mention it, but there was another wagon road just across the river. This road, along the north bank of the Carson River, was first traveled in 1848 by a small group of former Mormon Battalion members who were traveling from California to Salt Lake City. Leaving from the Placerville area, this group headed eastward into the Sierras, and opened up a new wagon road through Carson Pass. After descending the eastern slope of the Sierras, they followed the Carson River past the future sites of Genoa, Carson City, and Dayton. Just east of the Carson Plains, the river makes a major bend to the east. From this point, the Battalion members continued to follow the river, rather than taking the branch of the California Trail that follows today's US Highway 50.[31] During the years between 1848 and 1859, there had been some emigrant traffic along the north bank of the Carson River, and it may have been a better road than the one on the south bank. Regardless of whether it was, or was not, a better road, it was out of the expedition's reach, because they had no way of crossing the swollen river until they reached Pleasant Grove, which was still about eleven miles upstream.

A few months after the expedition traveled through this area, Samuel Bucklands established a ranch and built a bridge at a spot about three miles downstream from where the expedition first reached the river.[32] About a year later, the US Army established a military post on the river's northern bank. It would appear that with the construction of Buckland's toll bridge, and the establishment of Fort Churchill, most, if not all, of the wagon traffic would have shifted to the road on the northern side of the river. It seems highly unlikely that any other wagons ever followed the expedition's route across the ugly hill.

June 10, 1859

JUNE 10, CAMP No. 35, CARSON RIVER.— *Moved at quarter of 5. Continue westward along south side of Carson River as far as opposite Pleasant Grove, where at 8 o'clock A.M. we arrive. Find the raft ready, made of cottonwood-trees of an old log-house belonging to Mr. Miller, the agent of the California Mail Company at this station, and which he has pulled down for the purpose. This point a good one for ferry or ford; banks on either side low and firm. By 5½ P.M. the wagons and property were rafted across safely, except one wagon, which unfortunately capsized, causing the loss of some $31 belonging to the driver, Payte, (as he said,) and some clothing, also three sets of harness....Journey to-day, 9 miles....We have now at*

Pleasant Grove, for the first time, got into the old Humboldt River and Carson Valley emigrant-road. The California Mail Company have a station here, under the charge of Mr. Miller, who occupies quite a good, weather-boarded house. The grove of cotton-woods near it give the place its name.[33]

WILLIAM LEE DESCRIBED the crossing of the river in some detail:

It took us all day to get the wagons over. They were taken over on a raft, and unfortunately our wagon was tipped over in crossing, and we came near to losing it. All my bedding and all my clothes in my carpet bag were wet through, taking some time to dry them. The body of the wagon separated from the wheels, which sank to the bottom. But after some trouble they were hauled out. We all had to swim across, sending the animals before us.[34]

Simpson mentioned that at Pleasant Grove they got onto "the old Humboldt River and Carson Valley emigrant-road." Here he was talking about what has become known as the Carson Route, which is a branch of the California Trail. Having split away from the Truckee Route about sixty miles to the northeast, near the Humboldt Sink, this emigrant road struck the Carson River near Ragtown, then headed west. Leaving the river where it made a bend to the south, the Carson Route went through the small communities of Silver Springs and Stagecoach, and then come back to the river at Pleasant Grove. This was probably the most used variant of the Carson Route, but as mentioned previously, some emigrants remained near the river all the way to today's Dayton, passing the site of Fort Churchill along the way.

Pleasant Grove was located on the north bank of the Carson River, at the point where the river makes a bend to the east. Chorpenning had probably been using it as a mail station even before he shifted his route in late 1858. John Townley indicates that a trading post was established here in either 1849 or 1850.[35] During the time that it was being operated by Chorpenning, and then by Russell, Majors, and Waddell, the station was known as Miller's Station, presumably after the Mr. Miller who was in charge when Simpson's expedition camped here. According

Camp 35-W. On the south bank of the Carson River, about five miles west of US Highway 95 A. The river is in the cottonwood trees. *"Three miles more along and up Carson River upon its bank brought us to a good spot on the river, where we encamp in good grass."*

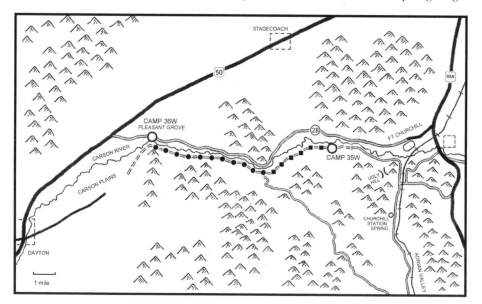

JUNE 10, 1859

to Joe Nardone, it was later called Reed's, and sometimes Ten Mile, but the official name was changed to Clugagis Station sometime after June 1861. Richard Burton mentioned that he spent a few hours here on October 19, 1860: "At Miller's Station....Whilst the rain was heavy we sat round the hot stove, eating bread and cheese, sausages and anchovies."[36]

While Simpson's party was in the process of rafting across the river, Mr. Von Beck, the expedition's artist, stood on the south bank and made a sketch. Later, John Young used this sketch to make a watercolor painting. In this watercolor, the river is in the foreground, Miller's house can be seen in the center, and a small but distinctive peak shows up in the background. During one of my visits to the Pleasant Grove site, I brought along a copy of the painting. Wading across the river, which was about a foot deep that day, I stood on the south bank, looked to the north, and compared the view with the picture. The curve of the riverbank seems to be similar, and a little peak can be seen at exactly the right place. Very little imagination is needed to figure out the place where Mr. Miller's little house once stood in the field on the north side of the river.

JUNE 11, 1859

JUNE 11, CAMP NO. 36, PLEASANT GROVE.— *Moved at quarter to 7. Immediately follow up the valley of Carson River, on its north side, the old emigrant-road, which is as well beaten as any in the States; our course, west of south.*[37]

SIMPSON'S MAP SEEMS to show that after leaving Pleasant Grove, the emigrant road remained fairly close to the river until it reached China Town, which was located somewhere near the central part of what is now the town of Dayton. The trail probably merged with today's US 50 at about a mile and a half northwest of the town.

After proceeding 7.4 miles from camp, come to China Town [Dayton], on Carson River. This is a mining town of twelve houses, and contains about fifty Chinese....At China Town we bear off somewhat from Carson River, one mile bringing us to forks of road; right leads to Johnstown, 1.5 miles off in Gold Cañon.[38]

Upon leaving China Town, the expedition turned to the west, following the emigrant road past the town's cemetery. Just west of the cemetery, the trail climbed up a short but fairly steep hill. Near the top of this hill can be found a T-rail post that notes the location of the emigrant road. The inscription on the plaque reads as follows:

CARSON TRAIL—ROCKY ASCENT
We ascend a high hill and had a very rocky road most of the way. Some places nothing but sharp angular rock. The road is not hilly. Though some hollows or ravines in two or three places.

Byron N. McKinstry Sept. 6 1850

From this marker, the route continues past a large mine dump, and after another mile and a half, crosses Nevada State Route 341 a little less than a half mile north of US 50.

Four miles from China Town, cedars 15 to 20 feet high appear on either side of the road on the mountains and in the valley—the first we have seen since leaving the Se-day-e Mountains. Seven and one-half miles farther brings us to Carson City, in Eagle Valley, where, at 5 P.M., we encamp....Journey, 19 miles.[39]

The old wagon road probably crossed US 50 near the crest of the hill near Mound House. Remaining fairly close to US 50 for another mile, it curved to the west and skirted the north bank of the Carson River near what used to be the town of Empire. From the bend in the river, the expedition traveled southwest, probably crossing diagonally through the Terrace Park subdivision and the residential areas east of Stewart Street and south of US 50, which becomes Williams Street in Carson City. When they reached the area of what is now the intersection of Stewart Street and Carson Street, they camped for the night. A small park with a stream flowing through it can be found at this location today. If there was water in this streambed in 1859, it would have been an excellent spot for a campsite.

Camp 36-W. Carson River, where the expedition made use of a raft to get the wagons across. The expedition's artist made a sketch of this scene (see facing page) which helped the author determine the location. *"This point is a good one for ferry or ford; banks on either side low and firm."*

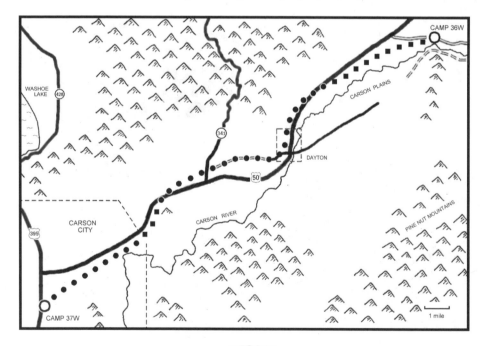

JUNE 11, 1859

Crossing the Carson River at Pleasant Grove. This Von Beckh/Young illustration
includes a view Miller's mail station.

JUNE 12, 1859

JUNE 12, CAMP NO. 37, CARSON CITY, EAGLE
VALLEY.—*Leave Carson City, at quarter past 5.
Course southwardly, continuing on the old emigrant-road between the base of the Sierra Nevada,
and Carson River. In 3¼ miles cross Clear Creek, a
beautiful stream running from the Sierra Nevada
into Carson River. Near Clear Creek approach
again Carson River, and continue along it about
10 miles to Genoa.*[40]

WHEN THEY LEFT the Carson City campsite,
the expedition traveled in a slightly east-of-south
direction, crossing Clear Creek just north of the
intersection of Bigelow Drive and Race Track
Road. After crossing the stream, the wagon road
turned to the southwest, passing the south end
of Schultz Drive. Continuing to the southwest,
the trail went through some open fields and
then began to cross the fairways of the Sunridge
Golf Course.

AUGUST 2003

There are no roads going through these
fields today so they had to be crossed on foot.
Parking at the end of Schultz Drive, I walked
across an area that appeared as if it would be
very boggy during years that are fairly wet. After
walking for about a half mile, I came to the
northern edge of the golf course. Returning to
my SUV, I drove to US 395, and headed south
until I reached the entrance to the golf course.
Now heading back toward the Clear Creek crossing, I found myself on a road that probably follows the emigrant trail. By following this road,
I was able to get back the place where I had
turned around during my earlier hike through
the open fields.

The old emigrant road and Simpson's route
crossed US Highway 395 near the entrance to the
golf course. From there it skirted the southeast
corner of the Jack's Valley Wildlife Management
Area, then turned a little more toward the southwest, entering what is now the Sierra-Nevada Golf
Ranch, where it disappears.

Camps 37-W and 2-E. The site of these two camps is now a park on the east side of Carson Street (US 395) in Carson City. *"At the east foot of the Sierra Nevada we encamp. This camp-ground beautiful; the prospect the most pleasing of any I have seen."*

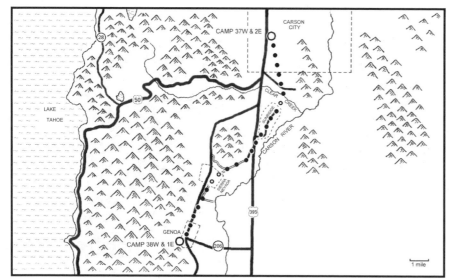

JUNE 12 AND 24, 1859

The Simpson Expedition's arrival at Genoa. A John Young watercolor from a
sketch by H. V. A. Von Beckh.

JUNE 2002

Nancy and I were able to get into this area by turning west from US 395 on Hobo Hot Springs Road. After about a mile and a half, we came to a gate with a No Trespassing sign. Stopping at the gate, I noticed a rancher unloading some hay at a feedlot a short distance away. After a brief conversation, he said that it would be okay to drive past the gate. About a quarter of a mile west of the gate is where the emigrant road turned toward the southwest, and this is where it enters the property of the Sierra-Nevada Golf Ranch. A fence now cuts off the emigrant road, so I parked and started walking. I soon found myself crossing the golf course, and the route I was following took me to the clubhouse where, in the parking lot, I struck up a conversation with a real estate agent whose office was in a small building next to the clubhouse. This gentleman knew about the emigrant road, and informed me that it had gone right through the parking lot, not far from where we were standing. He had never heard of James Simpson.

Reached Genoa at half past 9 A.M. Journey, 12.9 miles....Encamped among some giant pines at the foot of the Sierra Nevada, just upon the southern edge of the town, and on a gushing stream of pure water which courses down from the mountain. Our position is so high on the base of the mountain that we can overlook a large portion of the valley; and a beautiful one it is, fenced off, as it appears, into inclosures, and dotted with cattle. The sheen of the river (Carson), in its present high stage, discovers its course along the valley.[41]

After reaching the settlement of Genoa, the expedition continued through the town and set up camp at a spot that is now a residential neighborhood. The "gushing stream" is now a concrete-lined channel.

The expedition's arrival at Genoa did not go unnoticed. This was where John Reese lived, and it is quite likely that he had gotten there ahead of the main party. The citizens of the town were waiting, and as the expedition approached, they fired off a thirteen-gun salute and raised the US flag. Shortly after his arrival in Genoa, Simpson was visited by Major Frederick Dodge, the Indian agent for the region. Soon after that, Simpson received a telegram from Colonel Frederick Bee, the president of the Placerville and Saint Joseph Telegraph Company, asking if the new route could be used for a telegraph line.

The author's wife Nancy, at Mormon Station State Park in Genoa. The expedition was met at about this point by a crowd of local residents. *"Just as we entered town, were saluted by the citizens with thirteen guns and the running up of the national flag."*

While the other members of his command remained in camp at Genoa, Simpson made a hurried trip to San Francisco. He was accompanied by Major Dodge, and they left Genoa mounted on mules. After crossing the summit of the Sierra Nevada, they dropped down the western slope to Lake Valley, where they stopped for lunch at Chorpenning's mail station. Here Simpson became acquainted with one of the most colorful characters of the region.

At the mail-station met Mr. T. A. Thompson, the celebrated Norwegian, who carried the mail across the Sierra Nevada, on snow-shoes, from about the middle of last April to fore part of May. He represents the snow to have been, in places where he had to go, 10 feet deep.... Mr. Thompson showed me how he walked on his snow-shoes last winter.[42]

Although Simpson used the initials T. A. rather than J. A., there is little doubt that he was talking about the legendary "Snowshoe" Thompson. John Thompson had become a local hero when he began using skis, then known as snowshoes, to carry the mail across the Sierras during the winter months. Thompson must have begun to travel with Simpson and Dodge, because Simpson mentioned that after leaving Lake Valley, Thompson had pointed out several interesting sights, including Lake Bigler, which is now known as Lake Tahoe.

The party spent the night at a place Simpson called Barry's, indicating that it was on the South Fork of the American River. The next day they went through Placerville, where Simpson purchased some supplies for the expedition and arranged for them to be hauled over the mountains to Genoa. Leaving the mules in Placerville, Simpson and Dodge traveled by stagecoach to Folsom, where they boarded a railroad car for the remainder of the trip to Sacramento. From there, they found passage on the *Eclipse*, a river steamer that Simpson compared favorably to "our Mississippi boats." Reaching San Francisco on the evening of June 17, Simpson checked into the International Hotel. He spent the next day visiting a large open market and calling on a number of friends, most of whom were Army officers.

Before leaving for San Francisco, Simpson had given instructions to Lieutenants Smith and Putnam to continue making astronomical observations, and for Putnam to take a look at a couple of roads that went into the Sierra Nevada. Other than this, Simpson did not say anything about what the members of the expedition did while he was on this trip. William Lee wrote in his journal that on June 18, he and Charles McCarthy took at trip to "Lake Biljer" (Bigler). They traveled, as usual, on mule back, and followed "Daggett's Trail," which was one of the roads that Simpson had instructed Lieutenant Putnam to explore.[43]

On June 19, Simpson and Dodge left San Francisco, and began their trip back to Genoa. During this journey, they rode from Placerville to Lake Valley in an ambulance that belonged to Dodge, and the driver was Snowshoe Thompson. The ambulance was scheduled to stop overnight in Lake Valley, but Simpson was getting anxious to get back to Genoa, so he found a ride in a mail stage that left at 3:00 A.M. The driver of this stage, who Simpson identified only as "a famous whip," was still very much under the influence of a night of carousing, and this ride proved to be the most dangerous event of the entire expedition. Just before reaching the summit of Luther Pass, the inebriated driver lost control of the stage and it tipped over. Fortunately for the passengers, just minutes before the accident occurred, Simpson had suggested that it might be helpful if they all got out of the coach and walked across the steepest part of the pass. They were walking when the coach went off the road and rolled. The bad news was that the tongue of the wagon was broken, and it would not be going anywhere until it had been repaired. After about an hour, the reliable Major Dodge showed up in his ambulance and transported the stranded passengers to Genoa.[44]

Simpson arrived back at Genoa sometime during the day on June 23. The following morning the expedition began its journey back to Camp Floyd.

Seven

Genoa to Smith Creek Valley

Camps 38-W and 1-E. Near the mouth of Genoa Canyon, the campsite was probably in the grove of trees near the center of the photo. *"Encamped among some giant pines at the foot of the Sierra Nevada, just upon the southern edge of the town, and on a gushing stream of pure water."* This area is still on the southern edge of the town but the giant trees are gone and the streambed is lined with concrete.

JUNE 24, GENOA, CAMP NO. 1.—*At 7 A.M. we took up our march on our return to Camp Floyd....Mr. Reese, though a citizen of Genoa, returns with us as guide, and I have sent him, Ute Pete, and two other persons in advance, to provide for improvement of route, by taking a short cut from bend of Carson to south side of Carson Lake....Train reached Carson City early in the afternoon, and party encamped. We reached it about dark. Journey, 13.8 miles. Route the same as traveled on outward journey.*[1]

SIMPSON INDICATED that they returned to Carson City by following their earlier route, but does not specifically state whether or not they returned to the exact spot that they had used for a campsite two weeks earlier. However, since the distance was the same for both trips, it can probably be assumed that they did camp at the same place, which would mean that Camps 37-W and 2-E were both near the little park at the intersection of Carson and Stewart streets.

When the expedition left Genoa, it was accompanied by an additional passenger. While in San Francisco, Simpson had been approached by two newspaper reporters, who told him about the plight of one Walter Lowery, a fellow newspaper correspondent who was suffering from some serious health problems and wanted to return to the States. They wondered if Simpson would allow Lowery to join the expedition during its eastbound trip. Simpson was reluctant at first, but finally agreed. Lowery was suffering from what was probably tuberculosis, as Simpson described it as being "of a pulmonary character." Lowery seems to have been convinced that a "trip across the plains" would be good for him. During the return journey, Simpson must have become quite sympathetic to Lowery and his problems, because when he began his trip from Camp Floyd back to Fort Leavenworth, Lowery was traveling with him again. Unfortunately, when they reached Fort Laramie in eastern Wyoming, Lowery had to be hospitalized, and died a few days later.[2]

JUNE 25, 1859

JUNE 25, CAMP NO. 2, CARSON CITY.—*Moved at 5 A.M. In 11.7 miles reach Chinatown, about*

9.30 A.M. Here leave our old road, and immediately cross Carson River by ford, and take route along river on south side....Five miles from ford, after crossing some bad sloughs, which may be avoided by taking higher ground, reach camping place for the night. Journey, 17.2 miles.[3]

FROM CARSON CITY to Dayton, the expedition backtracked along its earlier route, but when they reached Dayton, Simpson decided to try a shortcut. Crossing the river just east of the center of town, they traveled in a northeasterly direction through an area called Carson Plains. There must have been something about this section of the route that Simpson did not care for, because the next day he commented that they should have remained on the other side of the river until they reached Pleasant Grove. The campsite was in the eastern portion of the Carson Plains, about two miles upstream from Pleasant Grove.

SEPTEMBER 2004

Nancy and I turned off US 50 near the center of Dayton, and headed east toward the area known as the Carson Plains. Parking at the northern end of Comstock Road, I hiked a quarter of a mile to the site of Camp 3-E, then headed northeast along the south bank of the river for another two miles, until I was across the river from the site of Pleasant Grove and Miller's Station.

JUNE 26, 1859

JUNE 26, CAMP NO. 3, CARSON VALLEY.—*Moved at 5 A.M. Continued along an old road on south side of Carson River for 2 miles, where we join, opposite Pleasant Grove, our old outward track, and continued on same 12.6 miles to east foot of ugly hill referred to June 9, which we found we could not, as we hoped, evade by passing between it and the river. Going east however, the hill is not bad. The difficulty, as before stated, is in the ascent from the east side.*[4]

IN HIS DESCRIPTION of the previous day's journey, Simpson failed to mention that they had been traveling on a road after crossing the river. On this day, however, he indicated that when they left camp, they "Continued along an old road on

Camp 2-E. Looking to the north from where the expedition camped on the night of June 24. This is the same place where they probably spent the night of June 11 during the outbound journey. The large structure is part of a shopping mall on the far side of Stewart Street.

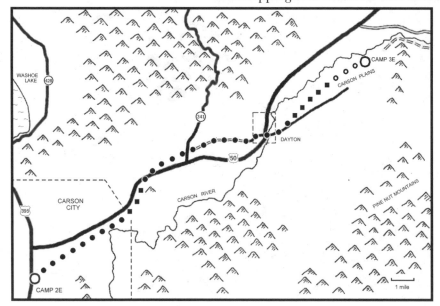

Camp 3-E. On the south bank of the Carson River, near the northern edge of the Carson Plains. The cotton-wood trees mark the course of the river.

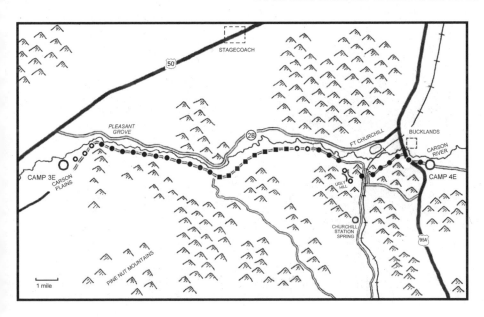

south side of Carson River." This road would have been the same one that they had followed along the south bank of the river during the outbound trip. Now traveling eastward along this road, they followed it until they were again forced to leave it to cross the ridge that Simpson called the ugly hill. In spite of their hopes, the river was still too high for them to get the wagons between the water and the northern end of the ridge.

> *After attaining valley on east side of hill, we left our outward track and old road, and turned to the left down the valley to within a few hundred yards of Carson River, and then go over another spur, and in about a mile get into valley of Carson River again, which we follow down 2 miles, and at 1.15 o'clock encamp on the river bank. Journey 18.2 miles.*[5]

At the eastern base of the ugly hill, they crossed the old wagon road, leaving their previous trail and making a turn to the north. They were now breaking new trail again, and would continue to do so until they came to their outbound trail at the southeast corner of Carson Lake.

A seldom-used road heads north from the Churchill railroad crossing along the east side of the tracks. After about three-quarters of a mile, this road makes a sharp turn to the east, and begins to climb up the ridge that lies on the eastern side of this little valley. This turn is about seven hundred yards from the normal channel of the river, but was probably only about three hundred yards from the high water level that existed in the summer of 1859, which would agree with Simpson's description of being within a few hundred yards of the river. Turning to the east, the expedition crossed the summit of this "other spur," dropped down the eastern slope, and, after another mile, came to the river again. At this point, they were across the swollen stream and about a mile east of the future site of Fort Churchill, an army post that would be established on the north bank of the river about a year later. Burton mentioned that on October 18, 1860, he could see the structures of the new army post after crossing the summit of the Dead Camel Mountains. His description of his party's travels that day begins as they leave the Carson Sink mail station.

> *Crossing a long plain bordering on the Sink, we "snaked up" painfully a high divide....From the summit, bleak with west wind, we could descry, at a distance of fifty miles, a snowy saddle-back—the Sierra Nevada. When the deep sand had fatigued our cattle, we halted for an hour to bait in a patch of land rich with bunch grass. Descending from the eminence, we saw a gladdening sight; the Carson River, winding through its avenue of dark cotton woods, and afar off, the quarters and barracks of Fort Churchill.*[6]

After following the river downstream to the east for two more miles, the expedition stopped for the night. They were now in Churchill Valley and their campsite was located a little less than a mile downstream from where US Highway 95A crosses the Carson River.

While attempting to determine the most likely location for this campsite, I had to resist the temptation to place it among the cottonwood trees that cluster along the river. Given a choice, that is where I would pitch my tent. However, this area would have been under water during the summer of 1859, and the expedition would have been forced to set up camp on the bench, about a quarter of a mile from the river's normal channel.

The talk in camp that evening must have given William Lee the idea that the expedition was going to continue to follow the Carson River all the way to Carson Lake. His journal entry for this day reads as follows:

> *Sunday, June 26th. Marched eighteen and a half miles and came to camp on Carson River. We left our old track about three miles from this camp and intend keeping down the river to Carson Lake.*[7]

Following the river all the way to the lake would have added about fifteen miles to their journey, but this route would have avoided the steep climb through the Dead Camel Mountains.

JUNE 27, 1859

JUNE 27, CAMP NO. 4, CARSON RIVER.— *Resumed march at 5. Continued down valley of Carson River eastwardly about 2 miles, when we*

The ruins of Fort Churchill, the army post that was built during the year following the Simpson expedition. On the far side of the Carson River can be seen the *"other spur"* that the eastbound expedition crossed after climbing the *"ugly hill"* for the second time.

leave it and strike for south end of Carson Lake. Low mountains, perfectly destitute of timber, and of a brownish-reddish hue, range on either side and parallel to river. Eight miles farther commence ascending a sandy ravine of slight grade.[8]

WHEN THE EXPEDITION left camp on the morning of June 27, they started out by following the river downstream for a couple of miles, but then, contrary to Lee's expectations, they left it and headed toward the Dead Camel Mountains. Simpson said that the expedition left the river, which could be taken to mean that they turned away from it. However, it was actually the river that left them. The expedition continued in a straight line in a slightly south-of-east direction and the river made a bend to the northeast.

After traveling about ten miles from camp, they passed a spot where the mail company would dig a well the following year. The well was for a Pony Express relay station, and it became known as Hooten Well. Later, the Pony Express changed its route through the Dead Camel Mountains, and built another station about a mile to the south. Just after passing the future site of Hooten Well, the expedition began to climb into the western foothills of the Dead Camel Mountains.

SEPTEMBER 2001

During our first trip to this area, Nancy and I turned off US 95A just south of the Carson River. Here we found an interpretive marker that featured a map of the area between US 95A and US 95. Extending across this entire distance was a

Camp 4-E. About two miles east of US 95A and Bucklands. The Carson River runs through the trees in the background. The campsite was probably on the bench in the foreground.

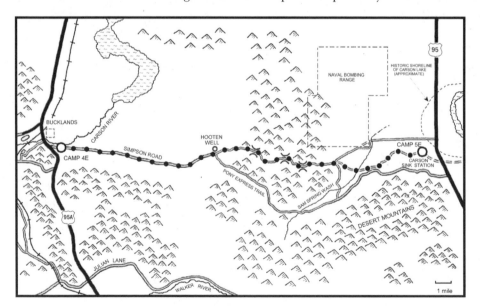

road labeled "Simpson's Road." This was something of a surprise to me, but I later learned that the USGS 7.5-minute maps also use this designation. We found that although it is drivable in a high-clearance vehicle, the road through the Dead Camel Mountains is very rough and rocky, and, in many places, the top speed that could be tolerated was something less than five miles an hour. There is a certain amount of irony in the fact that the only section of Simpson's route that bears his name is by far the very worst of all the sections that can be driven today.

In 3 miles, attain summit of low range, from which, looking back, Carson River can be seen, well marked by the trees which line its banks. At intervals of 2.5 and 1.7 miles cross other low ridges, the last tolerably steep on east side; and 7½ miles farther, at half past 5, reach south end of Carson Lake where we encamp. Journey, 25.1 miles.[9]

The road across the Dead Camel Mountains crosses three separate and distinct ridges, and Simpson noted the distance measurements for each of them. After crossing the third ridge, the trail drops down the eastern slope of the mountains and comes to a three-way fork. From this fork, the branch that is called Simpson's Road veers to the northeast toward the city of Fallon. There is a little more irony here, because Simpson's expedition did not travel the eastern section of Simpson's Road. The expedition continued almost due east, following the center branch of the fork. This was the route that was later used by Chorpenning, then the Overland Stage and the Pony Express. Today, this trail can be driven in a high-clearance vehicle for a couple of miles beyond the fork, but at that point it comes to an ungated fence.

It appears that the spot that Simpson chose for that night's campsite was later used by Chorpenning's mail company, and then by the Pony Express, and was known as the Carson Sink Station. Although the camp would have been a short distance from the shore of Carson Lake, young William Lee said that for drinking water they had "nothing but the alkali slough water."[10] According to John Townley, there was a good spring "within a few feet" of the station,[11] but I have been unable to find anything that looks like a spring in this area. However, I have noticed large numbers of freshwater clamshells in the sandy flats just east of the station site, where the shore of the lake would have been at that time.

SEPTEMBER 2006

During my earlier trips to the area, I had been unable to find a way to get a vehicle onto the last three-mile section of this day's journey. On the west, the trail is blocked by the fence, and on the east it is bordered by a large, but presently dry, canal. There is a narrow road on the east side of this canal, and I was able to follow it until I was about a quarter of a mile east of the Carson Sink Pony Express station. Leaving my SUV on the east bank of the canal, I began hiking to the west. I soon passed the station site and continued on across the flats, following a very shallow but clearly discernable swale. After about two miles, I came to the western edge of the flats and began a gradual climb up a gravely bench. After another mile, I came to the fence that had previously stopped me from following the trail in my vehicle. The USGS 7.5-minute quad shows that there is a Pony Express "monument" at this location. I found that it is one of the small concrete posts that were erected by the BLM many years ago to mark the trail. Between driving and walking, I had now covered the entire route between Fort Churchill and the Carson Sink station. It had taken the expedition one day to negotiate the straight-line shortcut between Churchill Valley and Carson Lake. Three weeks earlier, it had taken them four days to travel between these same points.

JUNE 28, 1859

JUNE 28, CAMP NO. 5, SOUTH END OF CARSON LAKE.—*Moved at 5 minutes after 5. Continue along shore of Carson Lake, at foot of point of low range or spur [White Throne Mountains], being sometimes, on account of marsh, forced on first bench; and after crossing an alkali flat, 7.5 miles from last camp, join our outward route, which we follow along the lake shore 4.5 miles farther and encamp. Journey 12.2 miles. Road good....Our old road along the lake is at present overflowed by the water of the lake.*[11]

Camp 5-E. Near what was then the southwest corner of Carson Lake, probably at the same location as the Carson Sink Pony Express station, now marked with both a Trails West T-rail post and a stainless steel marker.
"At half past 5, reach south end of Carson Lake, where we encamp."

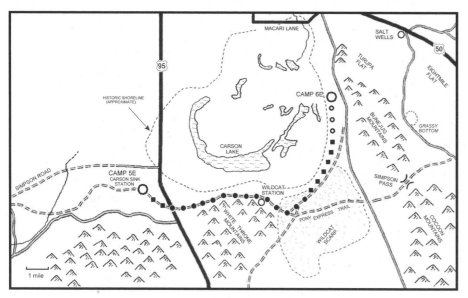

JUNE 28, 1859

SEPTEMBER 2003

Leaving US 95 about fifteen miles south of the city of Fallon, I got onto a very difficult two-track that follows the Pony Express Trail along the northern base of the White Throne Mountains. Much of this road is in deep sand, and the rest of it is on a bench that is frequently cut by steep-sided ravines. Travel through this area definitely requires a vehicle equipped with a good four-wheel drive. Sometimes the trail virtually disappears because of washouts, and on a few occasions I had to get out of my SUV and search ahead on foot to find the trail. About four miles east of US 95, I came across the ruins of an old rock building, in front of which has been erected an interpretive sign:

WILDCAT FREIGHT STATION
(ALLEN'S STATION)

THESE RUINS ARE THE REMAINS OF THE WILDCAT FREIGHT STATION. FOUNDED IN 1863 BY LEMUEL ALLEN THIS STATION WAS A WATERINGSTOP ON A TURNPIKE WHICH ORIGINATED WEST OF FORT CHURCHILL AND EXTENDED PAST SAND MOUNTAIN. THE TURNPIKE CLOSELY FOLLOWED A ROUTE EXPLORED BY CAPTAIN JAMES SIMPSON IN 1859 AND USED BY THE PONY EXPRESS IN 1860–1861.

Although the sign says that the turnpike closely followed Simpson's Route, it actually followed the Pony Express Trail through Simpson's Pass, rather than the expedition's route along the eastern shore of Carson Lake. A little over a mile east of the freight station's ruins, the road drops down off the rocky bench onto Wildcat Scarp, which Nancy and I had previously crossed while following the outbound trail. Near the eastern edge of the scarp, Simpson's return trail joined his outbound route, and turned to the north along the eastern edge of the lake. Simpson's comment about their old road now being under water indicates that the route they had to follow on this day was just slightly east of the trail they made through this area during their outbound trip. Although Simpson's map shows only a single track, this is presumably due to the scale of the map.

It was my intention to proceed farther along the lake, but Wilson Lambert, of the guide's party, meeting us here, and informing me that Mr. Reese had not, as was hoped, been able to find a practicable route for wagons through the mountain-range immediately to the east of the sink or more northern lake of Carson River, I am obliged to give up the idea of shortening my route in that direction, and strike eastwardly and cut off the angle or cusp, caused on my outward route by the mistake of my guide, mentioned in my journal of June 5. There is an Indian trail, it appears, east from the sink of Carson, which is practicable for pack animals, but it would require considerable work to make it so for wagons.[12]

The camp for this night was midway along the east shore of the lake, about four miles south of the outlet, where the expedition had spent the night of June 5. Simpson explained that they had traveled this far to the north because he wanted to return to the east on a route that would be somewhere north of their outbound trail. Although the report contains no previous mention of this plan, Simpson now indicates that he had sent Reese and a small party to look for such a route. He was obviously disappointed when the guide reported that they had been unable to find a satisfactory route for the wagons in this direction. Acting on this new information, Simpson reluctantly decided to turn back to the south along their outbound route. Once again, Simpson's plans were thwarted, and once again he found himself near the northern end of Carson Lake when it would have been better to be south of it.

JUNE 29, 1859

JUNE 29, CAMP No. 6, EAST SIDE OF CARSON LAKE.—*In consequence of laying over at this camp for the benefit of the water and feed, and not wishing to tarry any longer than necessary at our next, where the water and grass are said to be very scant, and the latter alkaline, we did not move till 2 o'clock.... The nearest direction for the road would be from south end of Carson Lake directly across eastwardly to Alkaline Valley [Salt Wells Basin]. But though there is a low pass [Simpson Pass] to admit of a pack-route, Mr. Reese has reported it too full of sand to allow the passage of wagons.*[13]

Camp 6-E. On what was then the eastern shore of Carson Lake. In 1859 the water would have covered the light area in the center of the photo.

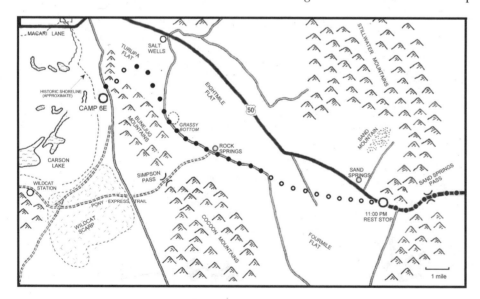

Wagon ruts on the west slope of the ridge east of Camp 6-E. *"We cross a low rocky ridge, 1 mile to the east of camp."*

THE LOW PASS that Simpson refers to here is Simpson Pass, which they had unknowingly bypassed during their outbound journey. This time they did know about it, but did not use it because Reese said it was too sandy. As mentioned previously, within a year this route was being used on a regular basis by mail coaches and the Pony Express.

We cross a low rocky ridge, 1 mile to the east of camp, and gradually bear to the right, and pass east of south along west edge of Alkaline Valley.[14]

The Bunejug Mountains run north and south, just to the east of Carson Lake. Near the northern tip of this range is a rather sizeable knoll.

During the outbound journey, the expedition had passed just north of this knoll on its way to the outlet of Carson Lake. On the south side of the knoll, between it and the main body of the hills, can be found the "low rocky ridge" that the expedition used as a shortcut.

In the May 2002 edition of *News from the Plains*, the newsletter of the Oregon-California Trails Association, I noticed a photograph of Dave Hollecker of Reno, Nevada. Hollecker was standing in some ruts, and the caption indicated that they had been made by the Simpson expedition. I was able to make contact with Hollecker, who told me that Don Wiggins, also of Reno, was the one who had found the ruts and had more information about them than he did. I made contact with

Rock Springs, near the western edge of Eightmile Flat in Salt Wells Basin. *"Two and a half miles farther brought us to a spring, which is sulphurous, but not unpalatable. There is a small patch of rushes in the vicinity, but no grass."*

Wiggins, who provided me with detailed information on how to find the ridge and the ruts.

SEPTEMBER 2003

I drove to the area east of Carson Lake, and hiked up the ridge and found the ruts without difficulty. They are not really ruts, in the normal sense of deep depressions that have been worn into the ground. The ridge is densely covered with volcanic rocks measuring from one to two feet in diameter. The ruts were made when large numbers of the boulders were moved to the sides of a swath that heads up the slope at an angle to the southeast. This swath is now filled with sand, and is quite visible as it climbs up the slope and across the top of the ridge. On the eastern slope, which is not as steep and is not nearly as rocky, there are a large number of visible tracks, and it appears that most of them have been made by rubber-tired vehicles in fairly recent years. Wiggins also told me about the emigrant journal written by Edward Mathews, which indicated that he crossed this ridge while traveling from the east. Sometime later, I was able to obtain a copy of this journal, and learned that Mathews had spent a few days at Camp Floyd, arriving there on August 10, just six days after Simpson had returned from the expedition. Leaving Camp Floyd on the August 13 or 14, the Mathews party reached the Carson Lake area on September 8. The journal entry for the previous day indicates that his party had camped at Sand Springs during the night of September 7. Mathews describes their travels on the eighth as follows:

Sep. 8th. Fine day. Started out at eight o'clock. Felt very tired. Got to Carson Lake at eleven o'clock. Rested. No feed. Carson Lake and junction of outward road. Warm Springs. Camped on east shore of Carson Lake.[15]

While this description of the route leaves something to be desired, it does seem to indicate that Mathews was traveling westward on Simpson's return trail, and came to where it joined Simpson's outbound route. It seems reasonable to assume that if he had been traveling on Simpson's outbound route, he would have said that he came to its junction with the return road. If this is the correct interpretation, it follows that the wagons of the Mathews party crossed the rocky ridge and helped to make the ruts.

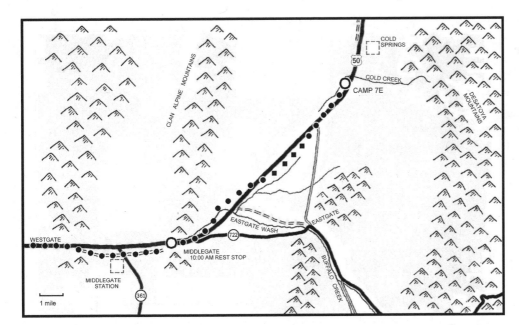

After reaching the summit of the low ridge, the expedition continued in a slightly north-of-east direction, and dropped down onto Turupa Flat. Once on the flat, the route began to bend to the south and soon joined the present-day road that comes south from Salt Wells.

Five and a half miles from camp come to grassy bottom, where there is some tolerable grass, and water probably within a foot of the surface. To the west of this place in the flat is a very small warm spring of pretty good water. The efflorescence around it is not alkali, but pure salt.[16]

The grassy bottom is easily recognized. A well-traveled dirt road leaves US 50 at Salt Wells and, after traveling four miles, comes to a flat area where numerous grass-covered hummocks protrude above the swampy ground. I have been unable to find the small warm spring.

Two and a half miles farther brought us to a spring 6 feet long, 2 deep, and 1½ wide, which is sulphurous, but not unpalatable. There is a small patch of rushes in the vicinity, but no grass. This was the locality intended by our guide as our camping-ground for the night, but the water and grass proving insufficient we only water the animals scantily and then push on.[17]

This was what is now known as Rock Springs. Reese had planned for the expedition to spend the night at these springs, but after taking a look at the area, Simpson did not feel that there was enough feed for the livestock and decided to keep going, even if it meant that they would have to travel through the night. Rock Springs is located in Salt Wells Basin, near the southwest edge of Eightmile Flat. Immediately to the west of this road, the terrain begins to rise toward the foothills of the Bunejug Mountains. The springs are out in the flats, about a city block from the road. In order to get to the springs, it is necessary to drive across an area that seems to remain fairly wet most of the time.

SEPTEMBER 2003

After finding the ruts on the west side of the Bunejug ridge, I made my way around the northern tip of the ridge, then turned south along its eastern base. When I came to the place where the expedition's trail came down from the ridge, I parked and hiked to the top of the ridge from the east. Returning to my SUV, I headed in a southeasterly direction across Turupa Flat and down the western sides of Eightmile and Fourmile Flats. When I reached Rock Springs, I got myself into a little trouble. The spring is located out in the mud flats, about a hundred yards away from the road. I decided to drive to the springs, and I got there without a problem. But on the way back to the road I got stuck. Thankfully, I was prepared for such an emergency, and it only took me a couple of hours to get out. My SUV was not equipped with a winch, but I was in the habit of carrying a good rope, a manually operated come-along, a four-foot steel bar, a sledgehammer, and a shovel. Making full use of all this equipment, I was finally able to get out of the mud. I was covered head-to-toe with sticky mud, but it could have been much worse.

Leave spring at 17 minutes after 5, and in 7.5 miles after crossing Alkaline Valley [Salt Wells Basin] join our outward route, near point of mountain, not far from our old camp, No. 30. Here we halt to take some coffee and feed the draught mules with some of the forage we have brought with us.[18]

This section of Simpson's trail crosses Four-mile Flat, which is a totally barren area with no indication of a trail along the route that the expedition traveled. The Pony Express and the Overland Stage also crossed these flats, but I have been unable to find any visible trace of the route they used.

SEPTEMBER 2003

After getting out of the mud at Rock Springs, I continued along the west edge of Fourmile Flat in a southeast direction for three more miles to where I believe the expedition began to cross the mud flats. Leaving my mud-covered SUV on the western edge of the flats, I set off on foot, and walked until I came to US 50 near Sand Springs. Even though this part of the country was in the midst of a several-year drought, I found that much of the trail across the flats was muddy. It is difficult to imagine how teams and wagons could have made it across this area. When the expedition reached the eastern edge of the flats, they were just a short distance south of where the road to Sand Mountain leaves US 50. Here they stopped, had a cup of coffee, and fed the animals.

Leave at half past 11 P.M....Proceeding on in advance of train, I arrived at old camp (No. 29), Middle Gate, 23.4 miles from halting place of last

evening, at 7 A.M. June 30; but unfortunately found the water, which was running before, was now to be got only by digging, and that scantily. The train did not get in till 10. We shall turn out our mules to graze and let them drink what water they can in the dug wells.[19]

By the time the main party reached Middlegate, they had been on the road for twenty hours, and had traveled thirty-nine miles, but they were not finished yet. After getting some breakfast and letting the animals graze for about three hours, they moved out again.

Resumed march at half past 1. In 1.7 miles cross an arroyo where the water yesterday, according to Mr. Reese, was running, but now exists in small pools....After crossing an arroyo, or creek, immediately leave old road, and bearing off to the left or northwardly, pass up valley, bounded by the Se-day-e Mountains [Desatoya Range] on our right and a range of high mountains [Clan Alpine Mountains] on our left.[20]

After leaving the Middlegate gap, the expedition traveled in a slightly north-of-east direction, following its outbound trail for about one and three-quarters of a mile. Then, almost certainly using the same crossing that they had used during the outbound journey, they crossed to the north side of Eastgate Wash. Shortly after they had gotten across the wash, they left their old trail and headed in a northeasterly direction up the valley. For the second time during the return journey, they were now traveling a route that was to the north of their outbound trail.

Ten miles from Middle Gate reach, near base of Se-day-e Mountain [Desatoya Mountains] a small running brook of icy-cold, pure water, which I call Cold Spring, and which after running few hundred yards, sinks. A more refreshing drink than I obtained from this brook, after the parched, wearisome travel of last night, I believe I never had. The men all seemed equally eager for the cold draft, and were equally delighted. But we have felt most for the poor animals, which have had but about a pailful apiece since yesterday afternoon. They are so fagged, they failed to get up with the wagons to the stream, and we are forced, therefore, to go into camp a mile from the water. The animals are driven to the water, and find an abundance of grass at the head of the creek....Journey, since 2 P.M. yesterday, 49.9 miles. Road good.[21]

Simpson and some others must have been traveling some distance ahead of the wagons when they came to Cold Creek. After getting a good drink from the flowing stream, Simpson decided to make camp at that spot. But when the teamsters attempted to bring the wagons to that location, the mules were unable to do it. The grade that they had been climbing for the last few miles was not very steep, but the animals were so worn out they were unable to pull the wagons all the way to the water. Simpson changed his mind about the campsite, and they stopped the wagons about a mile from the water. Immediately after stopping the wagons at the new campsite, the teamsters unhitched the mules and drove them up the streambed to where the water was still running.

Cold Creek flows in a westerly direction out of the Desatoya Mountains, crosses US 50, and immediately makes a bend to the south. Simpson's map clearly shows that the campsite was on the inside of this bend. A few years later, the Overland Telegraph Company built a large station at this same location. The ruins of this rock structure can be seen here today. About a half mile farther south, there is a similar-looking set of ruins, but these are the remains of an Overland Stage station. The Cold Springs Pony Express station is about a mile and a half to the southeast from the telegraph station ruins. Vehicles are not allowed in this area, and visitors must walk from a trailhead on the east side of US 50. However, this one of the best-preserved stations, and is well worth the walk.

JULY 1, 1859

JULY 1, CAMP NO. 7, COLD SPRING.—*At 9 A.M. Mr. Thompson, the Norwegian, before spoken of, arrived and brought our mail from Genoa.*[22]

AS THEY WERE PREPARING to leave on the morning of July 1, the mailman arrived. This was in the person of Snowshoe Thompson,

the Chorpenning employee that Simpson had become acquainted with during his trip to San Francisco. Apparently, some mail intended for the expedition had arrived at Genoa after the expedition departed. Whether by prior arrangement, or simply because Thompson thought it was the thing to do, he had packed up the mail and headed east, intending to catch up with the expedition. Thompson left Genoa three days after the expedition, but instead of following the expedition's route past Fort Churchill and across the Dead Camel Mountains, he stayed on the emigrant road until he reached Ragtown. Heading south from there, he passed by the western shore of Carson Lake, getting onto Simpson's trail somewhere near Carson Sink Station. Then, following the expedition's eastbound route, he caught up with them at Cold Springs. Thompson delivered the mail, and then traveled with the expedition throughout the day and camped with them that night.[23]

Party and train decamped at 1 P.M., and continue northwardly up valley. After proceeding 11 miles come to rapid stream of pure water [Edwards Creek], 2 feet wide, ¾ deep, flowing from the Se-day-e Range [Desatoya mountains]. On this we encamp. Willows fringe it, and grass is to be found higher up in the cañon. I call the stream after one of my assistants, Mr. Edward Jagiello, a Polish gentleman; his surname being difficult of pronunciation, I have preferred his Christian name as the appellation....Opposite our camp, in the range of mountains lying to the west of us, is a deep pass, in which can be plainly seen an extensive bottom of grass, and a creek running down from it into the valley in which we have been traveling. This creek, and the valley [Edwards Creek Valley] into which it flows, I propose calling after Major Frederick Dodge, the Indian agent of the Pi-Utes and Washos, who was so courteous to my party, and myself, at Genoa.[24]

North of Cold Springs, and a short distance west of US 50, can be found the traces of an abandoned road that is designated as "Old Overland Road" on the USGS 7.5-minute map of the area. It is almost certain that this old road follows the route that Simpson's party used as they traveled

Camp 7-E. The ruins of this old telegraph station near Cold Springs are probably found at the same spot as the expedition's campsite: *"reach, near base of Se-day-e Mountain, a small running brook of icy-cold, pure water, which I call Cold Spring."*

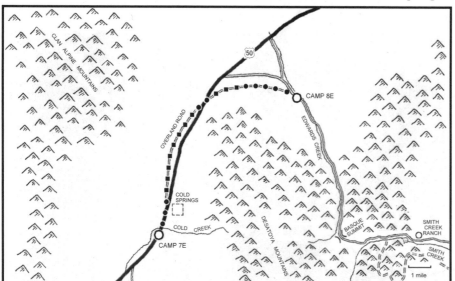

Camp 8-E. Edwards Creek, near the northern base of the Desatoya Mountains: *"come to a rapid stream of pure water, flowing from the Se-day-e range. On this we encamp."*

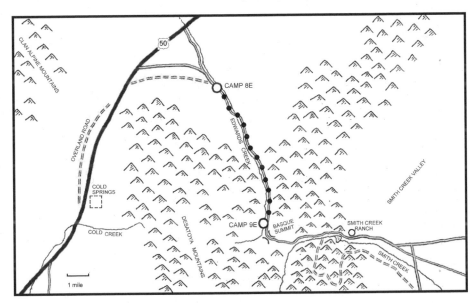

north. As they neared the northern end of the Desatoya Mountains, they left this road, made a turn to the east, and began climbing into some low foothills. The Pony Express followed Simpson's route in this area, and it is marked with signs erected by the BLM. I have driven the eastern part of this section of the trail, but the western two miles has been so deeply cut by so many washouts that I had to give up on it.

The expedition's camp for this night was on Edwards Creek, near the northern base of the Desatoya Mountains, and about three miles south from where the creek crosses US 50. Simpson gave the name Dodge to the valley. Today it bears the name of the stream that he named after his civilian assistant.

JULY 2, 1859

JULY 2, CAMP NO. 8, EDWARD CREEK, DODGE VALLEY.—*Mr. Thompson left us at half past 7 for Genoa, and intends going by the way of North Carson Lake [Carson Sink]. We at the same time decamp, our course being southeast up the cañon of Edward Creek, the purpose being to cross the Se-day-e range. After traveling 7 miles, at half past 1 go into camp in superior grass, and on the babbling Edward Creek, three-fourths of a mile short of summit of pass [Basque Summit].*[25]

WHEN THEY BROKE CAMP that morning, Snowshoe Thompson left them, intending to return to the Carson Lake area by a route that was farther to the north. Thompson was going to attempt to follow the route that Simpson had wanted to use as his return route from Carson Lake. Thompson must have seriously believed that Simpson was still interested in this northern route, because on July 28 he sent him a letter describing the country. He reported that the terrain would not allow him to turn to the west where he had hoped to, and had forced him to continue in a northerly direction until he reached the southern edge of the Forty-Mile Desert about seventeen miles east of Ragtown. Thompson closed his letter by saying, "I did not see any route north of yours that is practicable, and I think yours is the only route in that vicinity that can be made passable."[26]

During this day's travel, the expedition followed Edwards Creek upstream, in a southerly direction, into the interior of the Desatoya Mountains. The camp was set up in a small level area, about a half mile below Basque Summit.

The camp near the top of Edwards Creek was a pleasant one, with plenty of grass and water. Because of this, and because the next day was a Sunday, Simpson decided to remain here for an additional day. Lieutenants Murry and Putnam, along with Charles McCarthy, the expedition's specimen collector and taxidermist, reconnoitered the route that the expedition would be following the next day. They reported that it would take "but little work" to get the wagons over the pass and down into what Simpson had decided to call Woodruff Valley.

JULY 4, 1859

JULY 4, CAMP NO. 9, EDWARD CREEK CAÑON.— *Move at 5.15 o'clock. Continue three-fourths of a mile up cañon to summit of pass, and then turning eastwardly, in 1.5 miles, by branch ravine, reach Kirby Smith's Creek, the cañon of which we follow down, 3.25 miles, to where it debouches into Woodruff Valley [Smith Creek Valley], and, continuing along creek 3.3 miles farther, encamp on it....Journey, 8.5 miles.*[27]

AUGUST 2001

During my first long trip on Simpson's route in 1999, I had taken a look at Edwards Creek Canyon from US 50, but had not had time to explore it at all. Returning to this area a couple of years later, I made my way to Edwards Creek and found the site of Camp 8-E. From there, I continued to follow Edwards Creek to the site of Camp 9-E. At that point the stream and the road separate, and I followed the road to the ridge, which is now known as Basque Summit. Turning to the east at the summit, I followed a narrow two-track down Smith Creek Canyon. At the lower end of Smith Creek Canyon, Simpson's return route, the Overland Stage Road, and the Pony Express Trail all go through the Smith Creek Ranch. In *The Traveler's Guide To The Pony Express Trail*, which was published in 1995, author Joe Bensen warns his readers that the owners of the ranch have

Camp 9-E. Near the upper end of Edwards Creek. *"After traveling 7 miles, go into camp in superior grass, and on the babbling Edward Creek, three-fourths of a mile short of summit of pass."*

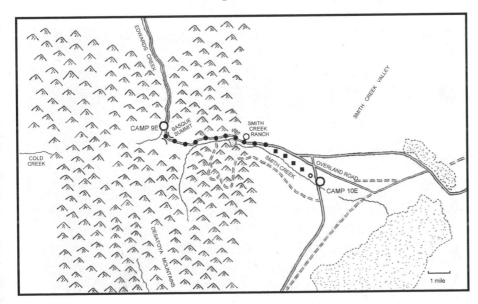

Smith Creek Pony Express Station, located on property belonging to the Smith Creek Ranch, is one of the best preserved Pony Express stations that the author has seen. The expedition's trail would have passed the far side of the station.

locked the gate to this section of the trail. Bensen expressed his hope that "Perhaps this situation will be changed in the future."[28] As I traveled down Smith Creek Canyon, I was hoping that the situation had changed. I soon discovered that it had not. About a mile above the mouth of the canyon, I came to the gate and found that it was still securely padlocked. Reluctantly, I turned around at the gate and started back up the canyon, thinking that my only option was to backtrack the entire distance to US 50 in Edwards Creek Valley. However, after traveling back up the canyon for about a half mile, I noticed a faint two-track trail leaving the road and climbing up the steep slope of the south side of the canyon. I decided to give this trail a try, and after a couple of hours of fairly serious four-wheel-drive travel, I had worked my way around the ranch and had managed to find my way into Smith Creek Valley. Taking a look at my map, I was happy to see that I was not very far from the site of Camp 10-E, where the expedition had spent the night of the Fourth of July. On the

other hand, I was disappointed by the fact that by being forced to take the roundabout route through the hills, I had missed about five miles of the expedition's route. But since it was late in the day, I decided that I would have to leave and come back some other time.

JULY 2002

On the same day that I had driven across Smith Creek Summit and had gotten the flat tire while turning around in the sagebrush, I drove to the Smith Creek Ranch and spent some time talking to the manager. When I explained what I was doing, he offered to unlock the gate for me, but I told him that I had already been on the other side of the gate, and all I wanted to do during this trip was to cover the section of the trail that I had missed during my previous trip. He said that would be fine, and I headed up the canyon until I came to the gate. On my way back out of the canyon, I stopped to visit the Smith Creek Pony Express station, which is just a few yards from today's road. This rock structure may very well be the best-preserved Pony Express station in existence today. The outside walls are all intact, and it even has a roof. The expedition's campsite for this night was on the north bank of Smith Creek, about a half mile south of the old Overland Stage Road. William Lee mentioned that this campsite was about two miles from where they had camped on this same stream during the outbound journey.[29] He would have been referring to Camp 26-W, the site of which is almost exactly two miles from where I believe Camp 10-E was located. Thus, Lee's journal entry helps to confirm the location of these two campsites.

As previously noted, for the past two days the expedition had been traveling on a route that was to the north of their outbound route. While at this camp, Simpson made a few comments comparing the two routes across the Desatoya Mountains.

There is a great deal of grass in Smith's Cañon and the adjoining ravines, and some little clover in the former; but the south pass; or that of our outward route, is still better in respect to pasture. The distance, also, is about 4 miles in favor of the more southern route; but in grade the more northern is much the best. I think it also probable, on account of the bottom of Smith's Creek being moist and, therefore, miry early in the season, that until about the middle of June the route through the southern pass would be preferable for wagons; after that, however, the most northern route will be found the best. The truth is, both branches of the route should be made perfectly practicable when the road is perfected, so that either can be taken at any time.[30]

As it turned out, the northern route was the one that developed into a well-used road, becoming the route of the Overland Stage, the Pony Express, and many emigrant parties. On the other hand, I have found no evidence that anyone other than the Simpson expedition ever used the southern route. When I hiked Simpson's southern route through these mountains, I came across several places where even a minimum amount of wagon travel would be expected to produce some ruts, but I found nothing other than the modern two-track that travels a short distance through the upper end of Skull Canyon.

Eight

Smith Creek Valley to Steptoe Valley

Camp 10-E. Near the western edge of Smith Creek Valley: *"reach Kirby Smith's Creek, which we follow into Woodruff Valley, and continuing along creek 3.3 miles farther, encamp on it."*

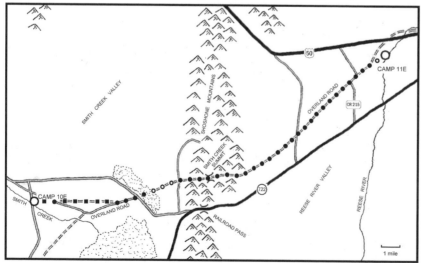

JULY 5, CAMP No. 10, SMITH'S CREEK.—
Decamped at 20 minutes after 5. Course north of east, directly toward our old pass between Woodruff and Reese Valleys [Smith Creek Summit]. In 3.7 miles get into our outward route, and follow it till near Reese's River, where we leave it to the left, and encamp on river, about 2 miles above old Camp No. 25....Day's travel, 20.8 miles.[1]

ALTHOUGH SIMPSON REPORTED that they started out by heading somewhat north of east, they probably traveled almost due east at first. This would have had them coming to their outbound route at about three and a half miles. Today there is no evidence of a trail for the first part of this route, but at about a mile from camp, their route may have joined a faint trail that can be seen on aerial photos of this area. This route would have crossed Old Overland Road, which is heading southeast at this point but which soon turns to the northeast. The expedition's route would have cut across the angle and come back to the road about two miles northeast of Camp 26-W. This would be where they rejoined their outbound route. Backtracking along the outbound route, the expedition crossed the dry lakebed, climbed over Smith Creek Summit, and dropped down into Reese River Valley. Leaving their earlier trail when it neared the river, they set up camp on the river's west bank, about three-quarters of a mile south of US 50. Simpson mentioned that this camp was about two miles from where they had camped on the river during the outbound trip. When I measure between Camp 11-E and Camp 25-W, I get 2.4 miles.

JULY 6, 1859

JULY 6, CAMP No. 11, REESE RIVER.—*Move at 5 A.M....About a mile below camp cross Reese's River; ford, miry; not near so good as that used on outward route. In 5 miles more join outward route and continue on it through Simpson's Pass [Emigrant Pass] and park in the P-er-re-ah Mountains [Toiyabe Range] to about a mile below the lake, where we encamp in the cañon on Won-a-ho-no-pe Creek [Willow Creek]. Journey, 16.5 miles.*[2]

SIX WEEKS EARLIER, the expedition had crossed the Reese River Valley while traveling almost due west. Then, after fording the river, they turned to the south along its western bank. During the return trip, Simpson must have decided that they could save some distance by cutting off the angle that the outbound trail had made while traveling across the valley. On this day, after leaving camp, the expedition followed the river in a northerly direction along its western bank for about a mile, then crossed to its eastern side. This crossing was about a quarter mile south of today's US 50 bridge. Heading northeast from the ford, they crossed today's highway about a quarter mile east of the bridge.

There is no way to drive to the site of Camp 11-E, but I have walked to this area once from the Pony Express Trail to the west of the campsite, and twice from US 50. During the first two trips, I had not yet begun to use my GPS, nor was I very certain about the site's exact location. The last time I hiked to this area was in 2005. I had my GPS receiver, and I was able to go directly to the location of the campsite. During this hike, I left US 50 near the bridge and walked upstream along the west bank of the river. On my way back I crossed the stream where the expedition made its eastbound ford. I then followed the expedition's route until it crosses US 50.

At six miles from camp, the expedition rejoined its outbound trail and turned almost due east toward the Toiyabe Mountains. Backtracking along their previous route, they crossed Emigrant Pass and dropped down into Simpson Park. After crossing the length of the park, they made camp for the night near the upper end of Simpson Park Canyon.

Simpson's map shows only one campsite symbol in the Simpson Park area, and it is labeled with the numbers 24 and 12. This makes it appear that the expedition camped at the same spot during both the outbound and the return trips, but other items of information indicate that the camps were at different locations. During the outbound trip, Simpson stated in a couple of places that Camp 24-W was on the shore of the lake. On the return trip, he indicated that Camp 12-E was about a mile below the lake. The table of distances indicates that the

Camp 11-E. On the west bank of the Reese River, about a mile south of US Highway 50: *"get onto our outward route, and follow it till near Reese's River, where we leave it to the left, and encamp on river, about 2 miles above old Camp No. 25."*

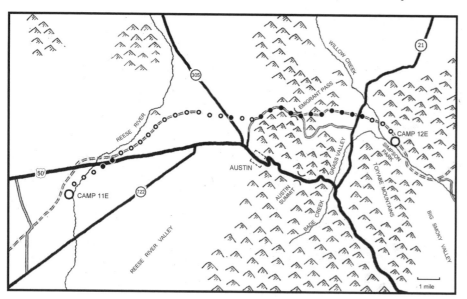

JULY 6, 1859

Camp 12-E. In Simpson Park, looking south toward the upper end of Simpson Park Canyon. The campsite was probably on the creek bank, near the center of the photo: *"join outward route and continue on it . . . to about a mile below the lake, where we encamp in the cañon on Won-a-ho-no-pe Creek."*

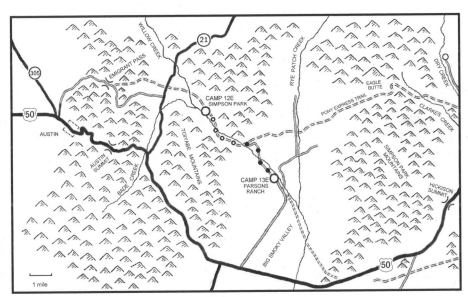

JULY 7, 1859

westbound camp was 4.7 miles from the summit of Emigrant Pass, while it shows the eastbound camp as being 5.3 miles from the pass. William Lee indicated that the camps were separated by at least some distance when he said the eastbound campsite was "on Simpson's River near our camp of May 27th."[3] After taking all of this into consideration, I have placed the eastbound campsite near the southern edge of Simpson Park, just before the trail enters the upper end of Simpson Park Canyon. Townley believes that this was the location of the Simpson Park Pony Express and Overland Stage stations.[4] The apparent discrepancy between the map and the other information about the locations of the two campsites is clearly due to the scale of the map. The mapmaker must have decided that it would be better to show one symbol rather than to crowd two symbols next to each other.

JULY 7, 1859

JULY 7, CAMP NO. 12, WON-A-HO-NO-PE CREEK CAÑON.—*Decamped at 6.15 o'clock. Continue down the Won-a-ho-no-pe Cañon [Simpson Park Canyon].... After journeying 4.8 miles, at 9 A.M. encamp at spring near mouth of cañon and sink of creek. Make only this short march so as to be enabled to reach Wons-in-dam-me Creek [the Willow Creek of Kobeh Valley] to-morrow.*[5]

IN THE TEXT of the report, Simpson does not say whether the campsite was on the east or the west side of the stream. On his map, the symbol for the camp is on the west bank, but that needs to be scrutinized carefully, because the map also has the symbol for Camp 23-W on the east bank, which it very clearly was not. In his description of the expedition's travels on May 26, Simpson indicated that they were traveling in a northwesterly direction along the east bank of the creek. When they came to the mouth of the canyon, they crossed the stream, went about a quarter of a mile farther, and set up camp on the west bank.[6] He did say, however, that the eastbound camp was in the mouth of the canyon, and near a spring. Today, there is only one spring in this area, and it is on the west bank of the creek, just below Wes Parson's ranch house. Because of the nature of

the terrain, it appears to me that as the expedition approached the mouth of the canyon, they were probably traveling along the west bank of the stream, which would have taken them right past Camp 23-W. Another tenth of a mile would have brought them to the spring where they set up their camp for the night. William Lee's journal indicates that during this day they "Marched four and twelve-thirteenths miles and came to camp at mouth of canyon near our camp of May 26th."[7]

JULY 8, 1859

JULY 8, CAMP NO. 13, MOUTH OF WON-A-HO-NO-PE CAÑON [SIMPSON PARK CANYON].— *Leave outward track, and taking a short cut, join it again in 3.1 miles. Continue on it 1.3 miles, and then leaving it and taking another short cut through a good pass in the Pah-re-ah range [Toquima Mountains], join it again in 18 miles, within 1.3 miles of our old Camp 21, on Wons-in-dam-me Creek [Willow Creek, Kobeh Valley] where we again encamp. Journey 25.4 miles.*[8]

THE FIRST OF THE TWO shortcuts that the expedition took this day served only to cut off a bend in the creek. This route took them in a straight line toward Cape Horn, rather than following the creek, which they had done during the outbound journey. After traveling three miles, they crossed to the east side of the creek, and after another mile, they rejoined their outbound route. Later on, the stage road would follow this shortcut. It appears that Simpson made a mileage error when he said they rejoined their outbound route after 3.1 miles; the actual distance would have been closer to 4.5 miles.

The second shortcut involved a much longer distance, and by taking it, they bypassed Hickison Summit and crossed the Toquima Mountains through a pass that is located about three miles farther to the south.

AUGUST 2000

I spent almost a full day in my efforts to travel the route of this second shortcut. I arrived in this area late in the evening, and camped overnight near the ruins of the Cape Horn stage station. When morning came, I spent a couple of hours

Camp 13-E. Just below Wes Parson's ranch house in the mouth of Simpson Park Canyon. *"After journeying 4.8 miles, encamp at spring near mouth of cañon and sink of creek."*

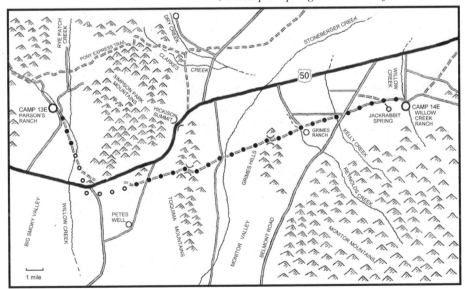

searching for indications of the trail in the area just south of US 50, but was unable to find anything. Deciding to try another area, I headed east on US 50 for about four miles, then turned south on a fairly well-traveled dirt road that leads to a place called Pete's Well. About a mile south of US 50, I came to an abandoned two-track trail that is marked as "jeep trail" on my map. Although the map shows that this trail only goes eastward from the Pete's Well road, I found that it actually crosses the road and continues to the west. I decided to follow it in that direction first. After traveling about a mile and a half, I came to the top of a low ridge, from which I could see the faint track continuing into the valley and heading toward Cape Horn. Making my way down off the ridge, I continued to the west for about a mile before a dense growth of sagebrush prevented me from driving any farther.

Returning to the road that leads to Pete's Well, I crossed it and continued eastward along the seldom-used two-track. This road turned out to be a real challenge. Not that it was dangerous in any way, but it did require a great deal of patience. I eventually made it over the summit of the Toquima Mountains and down the eastern slope into Monitor Valley. As I was heading down the slope, I could see that the road continued in an easterly direction across the valley, but I soon found that I could not follow it. At the point where the old road crosses Stoneberger Creek, a deep wash has made it impassable for vehicles. Turning back from this wash, I got onto a well-traveled dirt road and headed north, reaching US 50 near the eastern base of Hickison Summit. Upon reaching the highway, I drove east for about four miles, then turned south again on the Grimes Ranch Road. When I reached the deserted ranch site, I was back on Simpson's route again. I was hoping to be able to follow the old road back to Stoneberger Creek, but found that a new, and ungated, fence has been built across the old road. Heading to the east instead, I was able to follow the old road to the Willow Creek Ranch, where the expedition camped for the night. This camp was at the same location as Camp 21-W, where they had spent the night of May 24.

At the time that I was traveling this section of Simpson's return trail, I was completely unaware

that it was also the route of the early Lincoln Highway. It was some time later that I found that the 1924 edition of *The Complete Official Road Guide of the Lincoln Highway* lists "The Willows Ranch" and "Floyd Grimes Ranch" as checkpoints.[9] There is also some evidence that seems to indicate that it was this route over the Toquima Mountains that earned the nickname of "Ford's Defeat." In 1925, construction began on a new section of the Lincoln Highway farther to the north. This new road crossed Hickison Summit at the same place that the Simpson expedition crossed it during the outbound journey. A caption on a photograph of the new road at Hickison Summit states that it had been constructed to replace Ford's Defeat,[10] which, it follows, means that Ford's Defeat was somewhere other than Hickison Summit, and it can probably be safe to conclude that it was on the ridge of the Toquima Mountains, about three miles to the south. The new Lincoln Highway route would become US 50, and the old road was essentially abandoned.

MAY 2003

The washout at Stoneberger Creek, and the new fence at Grimes Ranch, meant that a stretch of about five miles could not be accessed in a vehicle, so three years later I was back in Monitor Valley, prepared for a long walk. Leaving my SUV on the west side of the dry streambed of Stoneberger Creek, I crossed the wash on foot and headed eastward toward Grimes Ranch. For the entire distance, I found myself walking along a road that could be easily driven if only I could have gotten past the wash or the fence. As I was going through a low pass in the Grimes Hills, I found one of the metal signposts that had been used to mark the route of the Lincoln Highway during the early 1920s.

JULY 9, 1859

JULY 9, CAMP NO. 14, WONS-IN-DAM-ME (OR ANTELOPE) CREEK [WILLOW CREEK].— *Moved at 7....After proceeding on outward route 1.6 miles, we diverge to left slightly around some foot-hills [Twin Spring Hills], and in 5.1 miles come to a couple of springs, which I call Twin Springs.*[11]

Looking east from the road to Pete's Well toward the Toquima Mountains. The expedition went through the pass near the center of the photo. This route was later used by the early Lincoln Highway, and the pass earned the nickname of "Ford's Defeat."

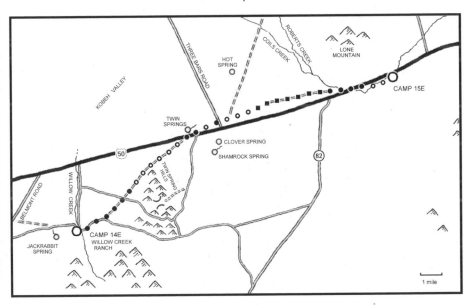

AS THEY LEFT camp that morning, the expedition headed in a northeasterly direction, backtracking along their outbound trail. A well-traveled two-track follows this route today, but at about one mile from the ranch, it begins to turn toward the southeast. The older route, now nothing more than a faint track, continues straight ahead for another half mile, then begins to turn toward the north. After traveling 1.6 miles from the campsite, the expedition left the outbound trail and veered off in a more northerly direction. Continuing along the western base of the Twin Spring Hills, the expedition crossed the route of US 50 and came to Twin Springs.

AUGUST 2000

During my first visit to this area, I drove right by the first fork without noticing it. After following the well-used road for a couple more miles, I realized that it was leading me too far to the south so I stopped and turned around. As I was heading back toward Willow Creek Ranch, I found the abandoned road and began to follow it. After about a mile, I came to an ungated fence and was forced to turn around again and return to the ranch. From there I headed north for a couple of miles and got onto another well-traveled road that headed east. I followed that road for two miles and found where the abandoned road that was the expedition's route crossed it. Turning north onto the abandoned road, I followed it for about a mile, but because I did not know if it would take me all the way to US 50, and because it was getting quite late in the day, I turned around once more and left the area.

MAY 2003

Three years after finding the southern end of the section of the trail that skirts the western base of Twin Springs Hills, I came back to cover the northern section. Since I had been unable to find a way to drive into this area from the north, I parked on the side of US 50 near Twin Springs, and hiked the four miles of the old road to the spot where I had been in 2000. As I hiked along the abandoned road, it was very apparent that it had seen a lot of traffic in the past. In some places, the roadbed is from two to three feet lower than the surrounding terrain. In many places the sides of the road are littered with rusty cans and broken glass.

Two miles further we cross our old road, and leave it, not to get into it again, probably, until near Camp Floyd. One mile further reach a spring, which I call Fountain Spring, on account of its welling up like a fountain. Here is an abundance of water of good quality, but the grass is scant and alkaline. There are, however, two or three acres of rush-grass about it, which would answer for a small party....Six and three-tenths miles further across the valley (Ko-bah) we come to a creek, which, on account of the color of the water, I call Clay Creek [Slough Creek]. The water exists in holes, but is pronounced constant by the Indians. There is a great deal of grass on different portions of it. Train got into camp at half past 2....Journey 16.1 miles.[12]

At Twin Springs, the expedition turned to the east and began paralleling US 50 across the southern end of Kobeh Valley. The place where they crossed their outbound trail was probably just a little less than two miles from Twin Springs, and it is only another half mile to where two artesian wells can be found today. Simpson's Fountain Spring was probably somewhere near these wells. For the next several miles, their trail was never more than a half mile from today's highway. Continuing east from Fountain Springs, the expedition's route followed an abandoned roadbed that was used for a time by the Lincoln Highway. Re-crossing US 50 near the southern base of Lone Mountain, the expedition made camp on the north bank of Slough Creek, a short distance upstream from where it enters a bend to the north. Lone Mountain is a very large knoll located near the southeast corner of Kobeh Valley. Simpson named it Mount Lowery, in honor of Walter Lowery, the consumptive newspaper correspondent who had joined the expedition at Genoa.

JULY 10, 1859

JULY 10, CAMP NO. 15, CLAY CREEK, KO-BAH VALLEY.—*Intending to travel only about 5 miles to reach a better camp-ground, we did not move till half past 6....Immediately at camp, cross Clay Creek by an excellent crossing, and traveling in a northeasterly direction, a range of mountains lying off to our right about 2 miles [Mahogany Hills], in 5.2 reach some fine springs (three or four in number), which I call after Mr. William Lee, one of my assistants.*[13]

THE EXPEDITION BEGAN this day's march by fording Slough Creek at a point just east of the campsite. From the ford, they moved toward the northeast, climbed to the top of the hill, and merged with US 50. There is good evidence of an abandoned road leading from the campsite to the top of the hill, and it is quite probable that it was used by the early Lincoln Highway. After traveling a little over five miles, they came to a small group of springs, which Simpson called Lee's Springs after his young assistant, William Lee. During the Lincoln Highway period, this place was known as the Hay Ranch. When the expedition reached these springs, they found two members of the scouting party who, much to Simpson's displeasure, reported that they had been unable to find a passable route to the east.

The guides persist in representing the mountain range ahead impracticable, and it would seem that I am after all forced to join my old route, and go through Cho-kup's Pass [Telegraph Canyon], which, on account of its steepness, is not so good as I could like. To strike off from these springs would make the turn in the road too abrupt. I have, therefore, ordered the party to return immediately to our old camp ground of last night, on Clay Creek, so as to make the divergence to old road as slight as possible. Train reached old camp at 15 minutes to 11 P.M.[14]

This decision to go back to the previous night's campsite illustrates once again that Simpson's objective was not simply to travel through the area, but to establish the best route for future travelers to follow. When he made his decision to go back to the previous campsite, he was thinking that the road would be turning to the north, probably along the eastern base of Lone Mountain, rather than going west to Lee's Springs. He took the expedition back to the Slough Creek campsite so

that when they started toward Telegraph Canyon, they would be taking the most direct route across Kobeh Valley. But Simpson was not the sort of person who gave up easily, and even after making the decision to return to their previous campsite, he was still thinking about his plan to return to Camp Floyd by a route that would be well south of his outbound route.

After returning to camp, I called Stevenson again, and had another talk with him and Mr. Reese about the prospect ahead. He (Stevenson) is not so decided about the new pass in the We-a-bah Mountains [Diamond Mountains] being so impracticable as he this morning represented it. I have, therefore, some little hope that we may yet, by a more thorough examination, get through the mountains ahead of us, without being forced to take our old road through Cho-kup's Pass. I have accordingly ordered Mr. Reese, Stevenson, Lambert, and Private Collamer, with two pack-animals and 10 day's provisions, to go again forward and make a more thorough and conclusive examination of the passes. If a practicable pass is found Collamer is immediately to return and report the fact.[15]

One has to wonder about what was said during this late-night discussion. Earlier that morning, Stevenson and the other guides seemed to be quite convinced that there was no way to get the wagons through the mountains that were directly to the east. But before this discussion was over, probably sometime around midnight, Stevenson had changed his mind and was ready to concede that there just might be a useable pass in the southern part of the Diamond Mountains. In other words, he had waffled. So what was this whole situation really about? Could it have been that the guides simply did not like the idea of returning by a different route? Were they attempting to manipulate Simpson into getting back onto the outbound trail? If so, their scheme did not work, because Simpson remained steadfast in his determination to find a southern route.

Whatever the reason for the guides' apparent reluctance to find a new route, Simpson did persuade them to look again. They left early the next morning, with two pack mules and provisions for ten days. The other members of the expedition

Camp 15-E. On the north bank of Slough Creek, about one hundred yards south of US 50. The stream is marked by the lighter horizontal line across the center of the photo. *"We come to a creek, which, on account of the color of the water, I call Clay Creek."*

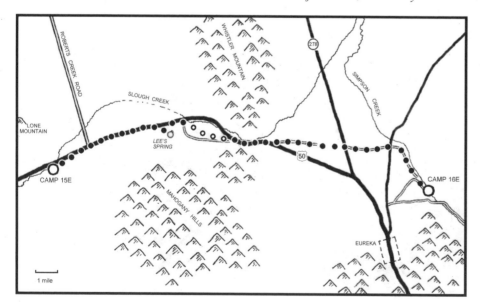

spent that day in camp. Simpson spent the day making a number of astronomical observations and waiting impatiently for some word from the scouts. None came during the day, but probably well after he had turned in for the night, he was rousted out with some good news.

JULY 12, 1859

JULY 12, CAMP NO. 15, CLAY CREEK [SLOUGH CREEK].—*Private Collamer came in just after 12 o'clock, (midnight,) and reported to our joy, a practicable pass in the range ahead of us, on the proposed course of our new return-route. The pass had been found by Ute Pete, who, though he had been four days and three nights without food except roots, yet had been the instrument of finding us a pass, and thus enabling us to keep on our course.*[16]

A few hours later, shortly after daybreak, Simpson had the expedition headed east again.

Retrace our steps to Lee's Springs, 5.2 miles, and turning to the right around the point of some low rolling hills, and threading a narrow valley thickly clothed with different kinds of grass of luxuriant growth, in 2.5 miles get into a plain cañon or pass [Devil's Gate] of Colonel Cooper's range which in 1.5 miles, leads us into Pah-hun-nu-pe Valley [Diamond Valley]. The rocks of this cañon are quite fine, on account of their abrupt height and well-defined stratification....In consequence of the number of swallows which build their nests in its walls, I call it Swallow Cañon.[17]

The expedition returned to Lee's Springs along the same trail they had used two days earlier. After passing the springs, they came to Slough Creek again and followed it through what Simpson called Swallow Canyon, but is now known as Devil's Gate.

Leaving this cañon we cross Pah-hun-nu-pe Valley [Diamond Valley], the cross range of mountains closing it at the south being about 5 miles distant....Six miles from mouth of Swallow Cañon brings us to the sink of a fine creek [Simpson Creek], which comes from the pass through the

We-a-bah Mountains [Diamond Mountains] to which we are tending, which creek I call after Mr. Charles S. McCarthy, the indefatigable taxidermist of the party. We turn southwestwardly up along this creek, and in 2.1 miles, at 1.15, reach a locality where, amid excellent and super abundant hill and bottom grass and good wood fuel, we encamp....Road, to-day, excellent; journey 17.3 miles.[18]

After passing through Devil's Gate, the expedition continued in a straight line in an easterly direction across the southern end of Diamond Valley. Today's US 50 veers to the southeast from Devil's Gate, but the early Lincoln Highway traveled the same straight line that the expedition followed. Aerial photos from the late 1990s show the trace of an old road cutting through the sagebrush in the western portion of the valley, but in 2002, this old trail was destroyed when this area was plowed for farmland expansion. Near the center of the valley, the old road can still be seen, but it has been abandoned.

Nearing the eastern side of the valley, the expedition came to a small creek that was flowing in a slightly west-of-north direction. Here they turned and began to follow the creek upstream. Although Simpson reported that they followed the creek in a "southwestwardly" direction, they were actually heading a little to the east of south. After following the stream for a couple of miles, they made camp for the night at a point about three miles northeast of the town of Eureka. Simpson named the stream after the expedition's taxidermist, but within a few years it had become known as Simpson Creek.

JULY 13, 1859

JULY 13, CAMP NO. 16, MCCARTHY'S CREEK [SIMPSON CREEK], WE-A-BAH MOUNTAINS.— *Decamped at 5 minutes of 5. Continue up McCarthy's Creek....The creek continues to within a mile of summit, which is 6.2 miles from last camp. Pass rocky near summit; grade all the way up very good....We find the descent from pass to valley, east side of We-a-bah range, steeper than we have just come up.*[19]

Camp 16-E. On Simpson Creek, northeast of the town of Eureka. *"We turn southwestwardly up along this creek, and . . . reach a locality where, amid excellent and super-abundant hill and bottom grass and good wood fuel, we encamp."*

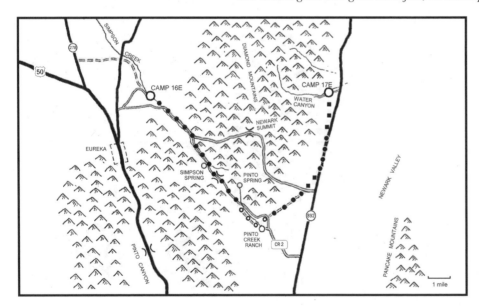

AUGUST 2001

When I made my first attempt to follow the expedition's trail across the south end of the Diamond Mountains, I missed it completely. I started into the mountains on a well-traveled dirt road, and was well over halfway to the top of the ridge before I realized that I had been traveling in the wrong direction for several miles. Turning around and heading back down the mountain, I was still unable to find the correct canyon. After a while I gave up and went back up the mountain, crossing Newark Summit, and dropping down into Newark Valley. I later learned that my problem was that I had not started looking soon enough. During my next trip to the Eureka side of the mountains, I discovered that the canyon I was looking for begins before the road I had been traveling on even enters the mountains.

JULY 2002

During this trip, I approached the Diamond Mountains from the east. This time I was equipped with my new GPS receiver, and I had decided to see if I could locate the pass from the eastern side. I found a road that led toward the correct pass, and was doing just fine until I ran into a securely locked gate about a mile short of the summit. As it was late in the afternoon and I needed to get home that night, I left the area without doing any additional exploring.

AUGUST 2002

Nancy was with me on this trip, and we approached the Diamond Mountains from the western side. With the aid of my GPS receiver, I was able to locate the mouth of the correct canyon this time. It was at the very bottom of the mountain, where the main road turns to the east to go over the summit, but once again we were stopped by a locked gate. We drove back to Eureka and stopped at the county courthouse and made some inquires. I learned that the western gate was under the control of a rancher named James Baumann, whose residence was near the mouth of the canyon. We had already driven by the Baumann place twice, and when we went back, there was no answer to my knock on the door.

After returning home, I made a telephone call and talked to Mr. Baumann's wife, Vera. I explained a little about my research and told her what I was trying to do. She seemed very interested and said she would talk to her husband about it. I followed up on the phone call with a letter, but time went by and I received no response. About a year later, I called again and Mrs. Baumann apologized for not getting back to me, explaining that there had been a couple of deaths in their families, and they had simply not gotten around to it. She hastened to add that there would be no problem in letting me travel up the canyon, and, as a matter of fact, the gates were all unlocked at that time because of a big power-line construction project that was taking place in the canyon.

OCTOBER 2003

Two days after my telephone call, Nancy and I made another trip to Eureka. After checking into the motel, we drove past the Baumann ranch to Simpson Canyon, and got onto the dirt road that follows Simpson's route across the Diamond Mountains. Part of the time we were traveling on an essentially abandoned two-track, and part of the time on a well-used construction road. We made it over the summit and down the eastern slope to the Pinto Creek Ranch, where we turned around and returned to Eureka.

About a mile from summit strike a small, swift mountain stream [Pinto Creek]; 3 feet wide, ¼ deep, which we follow down into main valley [Newark Valley], which I call after Maj. Don Carlos Buell, assistant adjutant general.... The stream I call after Capt. Thomas H. Neill, Fifth Infantry. Grass continues abundant in the cañon of this stream. At mouth of cañon, about 1.25 miles from summit, turn northwardly up west side of Buell Valley.[20]

There appears to be a minor discrepancy between Simpson's description of the route down the eastern side of the mountain and what is shown on his map. In the report, he stated that at about a mile below the summit they came to a stream, and then followed it until they reached the valley. But his map shows his trail crossing the stream at a right angle. Modern maps show a stream called Pinto Creek in this area, and there can be little doubt that Pinto Creek and Simpson's Neill's Creek are one and the same. It also appears to me that the expedition would have no choice but to follow the creek down the canyon for close to a mile before being able to leave it at the mouth of the canyon. This would have been just above today's Pinto Creek Ranch, where, after crossing the creek, they could have made a turn to the northeast. Today a utility road for the power line crosses Pinto Creek at about the spot where the expedition reached the stream.

JULY 2005

I wanted to check out some additional information that I had noticed while studying aerial photos of the Pinto Creek area. Nancy and I drove to the Pinto Creek Ranch, and then followed the utility road until we came to the creek about a mile above the ranch. Parking at this spot, I began hiking downstream. I crossed the creek and immediately found myself on an abandoned roadbed. This old road follows the west bank of the creek until it reaches the mouth of the canyon just above the ranch. This was exactly the route that I felt the expedition would have used. It would be my guess that the old road was abandoned when the power company cut the utility road into the north side of the canyon.

Turn northwardly up west side of Buell Valley through an extensive grove of cedars, and in 7.9 miles reach a small stream which I call Bluff Creek on account of the imposing bluffs of the cañon through which it debouches from the We-a-bah range [Diamond Mountains] into the valley. We encamp on this creek at quarter of 1 o'clock, after a journey of 15.5 miles.[21]

The stream that Simpson called Bluff Creek must have been the stream that flows out of Water Canyon, which is located on the eastern side of the Diamond Mountains, about twelve miles north of US 50. The campsite was probably about a quarter mile east of State Route 892, on the south bank of the usually dry streambed. Simpson also remarked that there was another small stream about three-quarters of a mile to the north of the camp, which may have been the stream that flows out of Sadler Canyon.

JULY 14, 1859

JULY 14, CAMP NO. 17, BLUFF CREEK [WATER CREEK].—*Raised camp at 10 minutes of 5. Strike eastward across Buell Valley [Newark Valley].... In 6.4 miles reach a point in mid-valley, where I put a ☞ pointing to mouth of Neill's Cañon, as follows:*

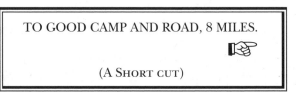

TO GOOD CAMP AND ROAD, 8 MILES.

(A SHORT CUT)

By this cut-off about 6 miles can be saved.[22]

ALTHOUGH SIMPSON SAID they began the day's march by heading eastwardly, his map shows that they actually started out by traveling in more of a southeasterly direction. His placement of the sign along the trail once again makes it clear that he was fully expecting that westbound travelers would soon be following his route. His purpose in erecting the sign was to let these travelers know that they would be better off to ignore the trail he had made from Water Canyon, and head straight to Pinto Creek. This raises a question however. If the lower end of Pinto Creek was such a good place to camp, why had Simpson taken the expedition all the way north to Water Canyon?

The journal of Charles Tuttle, one of the few emigrants known to have traveled Simpson's return route through western Utah and eastern Nevada, indicates that his party reached "Niell's Creek" on August 21, 1869. He mentioned nothing about the sign, but it seems quite likely that the small group that he was with passed by it and took the shortcut to the Pinto Creek area.[23] On the other hand, a few days later, on August 26, the Edward James Mathews party passed the place where the sign had been erected and either failed to see it, or simply ignored it. Instead of taking the shortcut to Pinto Creek, this group of emigrants turned northwest and followed the expedition's trail to Water Canyon. Mathews called this stream Bluff Creek, the name that Simpson had used.[24]

Camp 17-E. Water Canyon, on the east side of the Diamond Mountains: *"reach a small stream, which I call Bluff Creek, on account of the imposing bluffs of the cañon, through which it debouches from the We-a-bah range."*

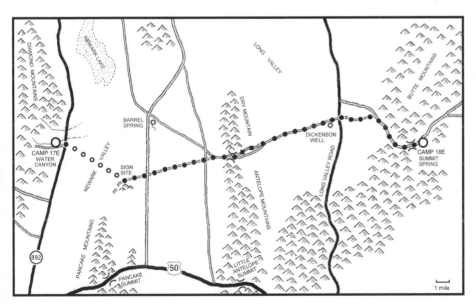

Looking west toward the Diamond Mountains from the spot where Simpson erected a sign for future travelers: *"reach a point in mid-valley where I put up a (sign) pointing to mouth of Neill's Cañon."* Water Canyon is the cleft in the mountain slightly to the right of center.

OCTOBER 2002

By plotting what seemed to be the most likely route across Newark Valley, I was able to determine the approximate latitude and longitude of the place where the sign had been erected. On a brisk October morning, I left US 50 at the western base of Little Antelope Summit and headed north on a well-traveled dirt road. At nine miles from the highway, I came to a seldom-used two-track and turned to the southwest. I was now on Simpson's route. After driving six miles in a perfectly straight line, I came to the spot that I felt was the site where the sign had been erected. It turned out to be near the northwest corner of a good-sized knoll that rises abruptly from the valley floor. From this spot, the two-track turned to the south, heading in a direction that I did not want to go. I did a little scouting around, but was unable to find any road or trail heading toward Water Canyon, so I put on my hiking boots and set off on foot across the western part of Newark Valley. When I reached State Route

892 near the mouth of Water Canyon, I turned around and retraced my steps to where I had left my SUV. This is fairly level country, and it would have presented no difficulties for the wagons. The only exception to this may have been a fairly deep wash, about a mile west of the sign site. However, the soil in this area is all lakebed silt, and is very soft. A few minutes of pick-and-shovel work by the troopers would have gotten the wagons across this wash. After erecting the sign, the expedition turned to the northeast and continued across Newark Valley toward a pass in a low ridge known as Dry Mountain.

Proceeding 6.7 miles farther, we commence going up pass over a low ridge dividing Buell Valley from the adjoining valley lying east of it which I call Phelps Valley [Long Valley], after Capt. John W. Phelps, Fourth Artillery. In 1.8 miles reach summit by a gentle grade, and in 1 mile east foot, also by an easy descent. Then striking northeastwardly, 8.1 miles across Phelps Valley, brings us

to the west foot of the Too-muntz range of mountains [Butte Mountains], dividing Phelps Valley
from Butte Valley.[25]

JULY 2001

A little over a year before making the hike
from the sign site to Water Canyon, I had driven
the expedition's route going east from the eastern side of Newark Valley. Just as I had done on
my way to the sign site in October of 2002, I drove
north on the well-traveled dirt road that leaves
US 50 at the western base of Little Antelope
Summit. After driving the same nine miles, I
came to where the expedition's route crosses the
road. Turning to the east this time, I soon began
to climb into the foothills of Dry Mountain.
After dropping down the eastern side of this low
mountain, the road continues in a slightly north-
of-east direction across the southern end of Long
Valley. Near the eastern side of the valley the old
trail crosses White Pine County Road Number 3,
which leads from US 50 to Ruby Valley.

*Ascending this range [Butte Mountains] 8.3 miles,
by an excellent grade through a winding cañon,
we attained the summit of the pass, a quarter of a
mile below which, on east side, we encamp, at the
foot of a conspicuous bluff called by the Indians,
on account of its dark basaltic color, Black Head,
or Too-muntz Mountain [Sugarloaf]. Here is
an icy-cold spring, and about half a mile farther down, or to the east, a small stream to which
we drive our stock. Good grass in vicinity. The
spring I call Summit Spring.... The journey has
been 32.8 miles, too long a day's travel, but necessary to get water. Road good. Train reached camp
at 8.30 P.M.[26]*

The expedition continued almost due east
from the county road, got into Long Valley
Canyon, climbed up and over the summit, and
made camp at Summit Spring. They remained at
this campsite for an extra day while the guides
went ahead to look for water. While they were
waiting, Simpson hiked to the tops of two nearby
peaks to make observations. One of these hikes
probably took him to the top of the bluff that
the local Indians called Black Head, and which is
now known as Sugarloaf.

JULY 16, 1859

JULY 16, CAMP NO. 18, SUMMIT SPRING,
TOO-MUNTZ MOUNTAIN RANGE [BUTTE
MOUNTAINS].—*Move at 5, and continue eastwardly down cañon to Butte Valley. In 1 mile from
camp pass a fine gushing spring, which gives rise
to the small stream referred to before, which after
running a third of a mile, sinks. This spring,
creek, and cañon [Thirty-Mile Wash] I call after
Pete, the Ute Indian, who has been of so much service to us in our explorations.... In three-quarters
of a mile from Pete's Spring reach mouth of cañon
by gentle descent, and in 10.9 miles more cross
Butte Valley, with low range of mountains, 5 miles
off, limiting it at the south, and strike a stream of
pure cold water [Combs Creek] which I call after
Dr. Garland Hurt, the late accomplished Indian
agent for the Ute Indians.[27]*

TODAY A WELL-TRAVELED dirt road goes past
Summit Spring, heading northeast, then drops
into the southern end of Butte Valley. In a little less than a mile, the road passes Thirty-Mile
Ranch, where the spring that Simpson named
for the Indian guide can be seen at the bottom
of a steep hill. After another mile, the road forks
and Simpson's route turns to the east. In another
three-quarters of a mile, the main road begins a
turn to the southeast, while the expedition's trail
continues to the east on a seldom-used two-track
that skirts the southern base of an isolated knoll
known as Red Pepper Butte. When the expedition reached the eastern side of this knoll, they
turned slightly to the south and headed across
the sagebrush flats of the southern part of Butte
Valley. Reaching the eastern side of the valley,
they came to Combs Creek, which Simpson called
Hurt's Creek, and began following it upstream
into the Egan Mountains.

AUGUST 2001

I left US 50 near the western edge of Jake's
Valley and headed north on Long Valley Road.
After driving about sixteen miles, I turned east
on Simpson's trail, and followed it past Summit
Spring and the south side of Red Pepper Butte.
I then spent the better part of an afternoon in a

Camp 18-E. Summit Spring, near the southern end of the Butte Mountains. *"Here is an icy-cold spring, and about half a mile farther down. . . a small stream to which we drive our stock. . . . The spring I call Summit Spring."*

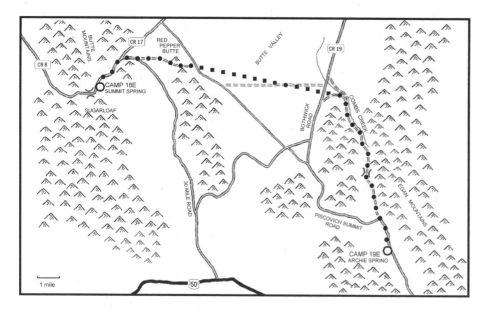

fruitless attempt to find where the trail crossed the valley. I did find a very faint two-track that crosses the valley in a due east-west direction, but as I was quite certain it was not Simpson's route, I did not spend any time trying to follow it. I finally managed to get to the eastern side of the valley by following a good dirt road that loops down to the south end of the valley, then turns back to the north. I found the mouth of Combs Canyon, but because it was getting late in the evening, I did not try to follow the creek into the mountains. Turning back to the south, I made by way back to US 50 and left the area.

July 2002

I returned about a year after my first trip into the southern end of Butte Valley, but this time I followed the expedition's route in the reverse direction, traveling north from Ely and over the Egan Mountains. After leaving the mouth of Combs Canyon, I spent some time looking for the expedition's trail across Butte Valley, but once again, I was unable to find it. I finally gave up and decided to cross the valley on the seldom-used, east-west two-track that I had noticed during my first trip. Although this abandoned trail does not follow the route of the expedition, it is never far from it. In fact, it appears to me that the routes cross each other near the center of the valley.

Ascending the cañon [Combs Canyon] by a good grade, albeit in some places a little sidling and rocky, 3.2 miles brought us to the summit of the pass of the Mon-tim range [Egan Mountains] dividing Butte and Steptoe valleys.... There is an old beaten trail down this cañon, about the largest we have seen on the trip. The Indians say it is the trail of the To-sa-witch band of the Sho-sho-nees, living about the Humboldt River, who yearly take this route, to trade horses with the Pahvant Indians about Fillmore.[28]

In his report, Simpson states that he named the stream after Garland Hurt, but on his map, he shows the canyon through which it flows as "Horse Cañon." Obviously, this name came from the well-worn horse trail that they followed through this area.

Descending the eastern slope by a winding cañon of pretty steep grade for 200 or 300 yards, near summit, 3 miles more in a south direction brought us to a spring [Archie Spring], where we encamped.... The guide also reports four more springs within the compass of half a mile from camp. I have therefore called this cañon Spring Cañon.... Journey, 19.1 miles.[29]

What Simpson called Spring Canyon is the upper end of today's Smith Valley, where a number of springs are located. There is something of a problem here, because none of the springs are exactly three miles from the summit. However, it appears to me that the most likely spot for the campsite would have been Archie Spring. Although this spring is about four miles from the summit, it is the most accessible of all the springs due to its location in the bottom of the canyon. In addition, the area around Archie Spring is relatively level and would make a good campsite, while the others are all located higher up on the slope of the canyon.

July 17, 1859

July 17, Camp No. 19, Spring Cañon.— *Decamped at 25 minutes of 6; continued in an east of south direction down Spring Cañon, the grade of which, except near summit, is exceedingly slight. This cañon gradually opens to 2.5 miles wide as you descend to Steptoe Valley, and the cedar on either side is almost inexhaustible.... Just at outlet of Spring Cañon into Steptoe Valley, 8.2 miles from camp on north side of cañon, there is a spur from the north wall or mountain of the cañon, through which there is a gap, gate, or cañon, which for sulimity, on account of its confining walls, equals, probably, anything we have seen on the route.... I call the place the Gate of Hercules [Hercules Gap], on account of its stupendous walls. The echo in it is very fine, and our fire-arms have startled a great number of swallows and hawks.*[30]

Near the south end of Smith Valley, a state prison facility has been built directly on top of an abandoned road, and today's road passes the prison about a hundred yards to the east. It is

Camp 19-E. Archie Spring, at the upper end of Smith Valley, north of Ely. *"3 miles more in a south direction brought us to a spring where we encamped."*

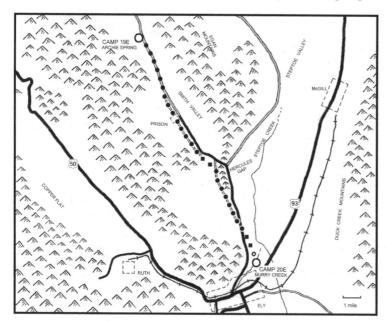

Hercules Gap, about seven miles north of Ely: *"there is a spur. . . through which there is a gap, gate, or cañon, which for sublimity. . . equals, probably, anything we have seen on the route. . . . I call the place the Gate of Hercules, on account of its stupendous walls."*

my assumption that the expedition followed the route of the abandoned road.

About seven miles north of the city of Ely, the expedition came to a gap that cuts through the low ridge that extends southward from the foothills of the Egan Mountains. Simpson called this gap the Gate of Hercules, but today it is known as Hercules Gap.

Although the wagons passed by the gap about a half mile to the west, some members of the party, including Simpson himself, rode over to it and fired off a few rounds from their rifles or sidearms. Today a paved highway, State Route 490, goes through the gap,

The road leaves this gate to the left about 0.5 mile, and 1.7 miles further down Spring Cañon brings us to Steptoe Valley, which we follow, on its western side, for 4 miles, in a southeasterly direction, and encamp on a noble creek, which I call after Lieut. Alexander Murry, the energetic officer in command of the escort of my party. This stream heads some 12 miles off in the mountain range, is rapid, and after running in a northeasterly direction, sinks 2 miles below camp.[31]

The expedition continued in a southerly direction along the west side of the ridge, crossing SR 490 about a mile and a half north of Lackawanna Spring, then dropping down to the floor of Steptoe Valley. It appears to me that the campsite for that night was located on the east bank of Murry Creek, near the northern end of the White Pine County Golf Course.

SEPTEMBER 2006

After spending a night in Ely, Nancy and I drove to the pro shop of the White Pine County Golf Course, where I contacted the manager and asked for permission to walk across the course. He was reluctant at first because it was a frosty morning, and he was concerned that I might do some damage to the putting greens. I assured him that I had no reason to get onto the greens, and would stay on the cart trails until I got the far side of the course. He finally agreed to my request and I set off, following the probable route of the expedition as closely as I could while staying on the cart paths. At the western side of the golf course, between Hole Number Six and the perimeter fence, I found the dry streambed of Murry Creek and the spot where I believe the expedition camped. Although there is some water in the creekbed about a mile to the southwest, it no longer flows past the campsite area.

Nine

Steptoe Valley to Swasey Mountain

Camp 20-E. The Sixth Hole of the White Pine County Golf Course now occupies the campsite. The old channel of Murry Creek is just beyond the trees, but the stream is now diverted before it reaches this point.
"Encamp on a noble creek, which I call after Lt. Alexander Murry, the energetic officer in command of my party."

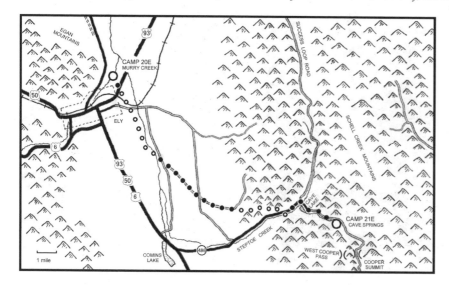

JULY 18, 1859

JULY 18, CAMP NO. 20, MURRY'S CREEK, STEPTOE VALLEY.—*Moved at 20 minutes after 5; course, southeastwardly, across Steptoe Valley. Two miles and eight-tenths from camp get into and follow a wagon-road, which, an Indian who lives in this valley says, was made by the Mormons in the spring of last year.*[1]

As MENTIONED PREVIOUSLY, Simpson had first heard about this wagon road just two months earlier, when the expedition was still westbound, and was camped in the northern end of Butte Valley. Lot Huntington, the Chorpenning agent, told him that the trail had been made by a group of emigrants from the town of Fillmore, who were on their way to California.[2] At that time, Simpson may have been somewhat skeptical about its actual existence, but now he was seeing it for himself. He was very interested in the origin of this road, and he wanted to know what it was doing in a part of the country that the army still regarded as unexplored territory. Simpson seems to have discounted some parts of Huntington's story after talking with the Indian who lived here in the lower part of Steptoe Valley. This unidentified Indian told Simpson that a group of Mormons had made the road just a little more than a year earlier, and that there had been about fifty wagons that had traveled northward through this area. After continuing up the valley a few miles, they turned back and returned to the Mormon settlements. Simpson's conclusion was that this wagon train was probably made up of Mormons who were fleeing from the approach of the Utah Expedition. This was a fairly good guess, although the party that made the trail was not actually fleeing. It was a scouting party, looking for a place where other Mormons could find refuge if it became necessary for survival. Shortly after his return to Camp Floyd, Simpson received information that confirmed his conclusion. He also learned that he was very well acquainted with one of the group's leaders.

On August 10, a week after getting back to Camp Floyd, Simpson had an opportunity to talk to George Washington Bean, who had been his guide during his October reconnaissance trip. Bean told Simpson that he had been a member of a group that Brigham Young had sent to explore the area west of Fillmore during the early part of 1858. The purpose of this exploration was to find a place that could be used as a refuge if the residents of Salt Lake City should be forced to flee from the city.[3]

A thorough account of the exploration that Bean had been involved in can be found in Clifford L. Stott's *Search For Sanctuary; Brigham Young and the White Mountain Expedition.* Bean and a group of about twenty men left Fillmore and headed west across the Sevier Desert. Somewhere near the present Utah-Nevada border, the group split into two smaller groups. Bean's contingent headed south. The other group, led by Orson B. Adams, turned northwest, crossing Sacramento Pass and the Schell Creek Mountains. In Steptoe Valley, they turned to the north and passed the site of present-day Ely, which is where Simpson picked up their trail. Some distance north of Ely, probably near Duck Creek, Adams's party turned around and headed back to the south, retracing their trail to the mouth of Steptoe Canyon, then continuing south for another forty miles to Cave Valley, where they rejoined Bean's party of explorers.[4]

Stott's account of this exploration is well researched and well written, and it solves the mystery of the Mormon road, but he did get one important fact wrong. The paragraph below shows that Stott was under the mistaken impression that Bean was traveling with Simpson in 1859.

Indeed, Capt. James H. Simpson, the army engineer who explored the Great Basin in 1859 in search of a wagon route to Carson Valley, could not, at first, account for a portion of the White Mountain trail he discovered in Steptoe Valley. Ironically, Simpson had hired George W. Bean to guide him, and although Bean was leading the engineers over a segment of his own trail from the previous year, Bean told the captain nothing about its origin until after their return to the settlements, allowing Simpson to believe a story concocted by a Mormon mail agent in Ruby Valley that the trail had been forged by a California-bound emigrant train which had not been heard from since leaving Fillmore. Until he was enlightened by an Indian in Steptoe Valley who had witnessed the White Mountain Expedition, and Bean later confirmed the story after their return, Simpson was as ignorant as was the rest of the world concerning the Mormons' efforts to explore the Great Basin's interior in 1858. Bean's lack of candor with Simpson and the mail agent's outright falsehood is clear evidence of the covert nature of the expedition.[5]

This clearly indicates Stott's mistaken belief that Bean was with the expedition as it traveled the Mormon road in July of 1859. And he suggests that Bean was consciously withholding information about it from Simpson. The facts are, however, that although Bean had been with Simpson in October of 1858, he was not with the 1859 expedition, and therefore could not have been with Simpson when he was attempting to figure out the origin of the Mormon road. On the other hand, the mail agent that Stott refers to was Lot Huntington, who probably did attempt to mislead Simpson about the identity of the travelers.

As will be seen, Simpson's expedition followed the trail made by the White Mountain Expedition all the way from Ely to the eastern base of the House Mountains.

About a mile from where we struck the Mormon road, we cross a fine creek [Steptoe Creek] which I call after Capt. Carter L. Stevenson, of the Fifth Regiment of Infantry. This stream comes from the Un-go-we-ah [Schell Creek] range, and after getting into Steptoe Valley, runs northwardly in it for 3 or 4 miles below where we crossed it and sinks....After crossing Stevenson Creek we left the Mormon road (which goes around by the way of the mouth of the cañon, through which the creek flows,) and cut across some short and rather steep hills, crossing the river again 7.5 miles from last crossing, up in the cañon, and joining again and following the Mormon road up the cañon from this point.[6]

It appears that the Mormon road remained fairly close to the stream all the way into the canyon, while the expedition took a shortcut across the southeastern part of the valley and through the foothills of the Schell Creek Mountains. Because of this shortcut, Simpson failed to discover that there was another branch of the Mormon road that continued in a southerly direction past the mouth of Steptoe Canyon. This branch was the route that Adams and his group of Mormon explorers had followed to the White Mountain area where they rejoined the group that was being led by Bean.

MAY 2002

Nancy and I made our way into the area to the east of Steptoe Creek, and attempted to find the route that the expedition followed across the "short and rather steep hills." A short distance from the crossing, we located an old road that seemed to be heading in the right direction. Following this seldom-used two-track in a southeasterly direction for about three miles, we came to an area that is crisscrossed by a veritable maze of old mining roads. I was satisfied that we had located the expedition's route from the creek to the mining area, but its trail through the mining area eluded me during this trip.

JULY 2004

After spending more time studying maps and aerial photos, we made another trip to the mining area and Steptoe Canyon. This time we were able to work our way through the mining area and down a shallow canyon to where the creek flows through Steptoe Canyon. But I still did not feel that I had the route exactly right, because it was reaching the stream too soon. According to Simpson's mileage figures, they reached the creek after traveling seven and a half miles from where they had first crossed it near Ely. The route that I had traveled came to the creek at six and a half miles.

After returning home, I spent some more time studying the maps and aerial photographs of this area, and found what appeared to be a more likely route between the mining area and the stream. On the photos, I was able to make out a faint trace of a trail that crossed another ridge before dropping down to the creek at the correct distance. If this was their route, it would mean that the expedition had skirted the northern edge of the mining area, had crossed two low ridges, and then dropped down to today's paved road near what is now a developed camping area. It was also evident that this section of the route would not be drivable.

The arch in the ridge above Cave Creek. *"On right side of cañon, high up, I noticed a very pretty arch, through which I could see the blue sky."*

AUGUST 2005

Returning to the mining area once again, I parked the SUV and hiked eastward through the low hills until I reached the campground. During this hike, I found abandoned trails all through this area, and it does not appear to me that this route would have presented any serious difficulties for the wagons. I was finally confident that I had located and traveled the correct trail through the hills between the mining area and the creek.

The stream at this last crossing was so miry as to make it necessary to take the teams over by hand. In one-half mile we crossed it twice again.... This cañon discovers some splendid rocks of the most massive character, some of them being isolated and looking like castles. In one instance, on right side of cañon, high up, I noticed a very pretty arch, through which I could see the blue sky.... A mile and a quarter from where we last struck Stevenson's Creek, we again leave it and take up a branch ravine, which we follow for 2

miles, and encamp at a fine spring, the source of the branch, among good luxuriant grass and timber.... Journey 14.5 miles.[7]

Today the Cave Lake Recreation Area, which includes a small man-made lake, occupies the mouth of the branch ravine. The pretty arch that Simpson mentioned is very easy to see on the skyline as you drive south from the lake.

Simpson did not mention it, but at the base of the ridge below the arch there is a large cave, presumably the source of the names Cave Springs, Cave Creek, and Cave Lake. The expedition made camp in the area just below Cave Springs.

JULY 19, 1859

JULY 19, CAMP NO. 21, STEVENSON'S CAÑON, UN-GO-WE-AH RANGE.—*Sent out guide-party early this morning, with particular instructions to send back a man daily to inform me of the country ahead. We are approaching, doubtless, the most*

Camp 21-E. Cave Springs, near the southern end of the Schell Creek Mountains. *"We take up a branch ravine, which we follow for 2 miles, and encamp at a fine spring, the source of the branch, among good luxuriant grass and timber."*

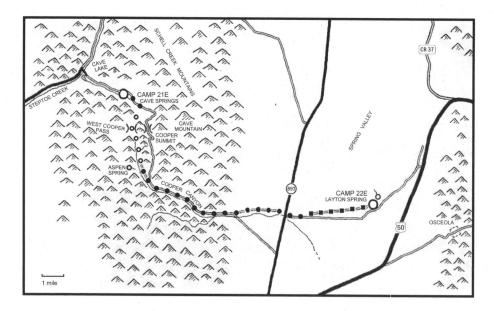

difficult portion of our route, and I feel anxious that there shall be no faux pas. The party goes out with ten days' provisions, and, besides the usual persons (Reese, Stevenson, and Lambert), I have ordered three soldiers to accompany them. Pete also accompanies them for a distance, and then is to push on with all dispatch with my report to General Johnston, at Camp Floyd.[8]

AT THIS POINT, Simpson did not provide an explanation of why he felt that the next part would be the most difficult part of the journey. He knew, of course, that except for the mysterious wagon road, this territory was essentially unexplored, and what little was known about it indicated that there would be several mountain ranges to cross, and that there were serious questions about the availability of water. He was attempting to leave nothing to chance, but as it turned out, the guides did not follow his instructions very well, and a few days later the party did become involved in what Simpson felt was a serious *faux pax*.

Main party moved at 5.45. Course eastwardly up branch of Stevenson's Cañon, 1.7 miles to summit of Un-go-we-ah or Pine range [Schell Creek Mountains], and thence down a cañon [Cooper Canyon] I call after Capt. Henry Little, Seventh Infantry, 7.4 miles to its debouchment into Antelope Valley.[9]

The most prominent peak in this part of the Schell Creek Range is Cave Mountain, which is located to the southeast from Cave Springs. A slightly lower peak, known as Cooper Summit, lies about a mile and a quarter to the west of Cave Mountain. A fairly well-used mountain road crosses the ridge at the western base of Cooper Summit, and since I have been unable to find an official name for this spot, I call it Cooper Pass. The mountain road continues south from Cooper Pass, then drops down the eastern slope of the Schell Creek Range through Cooper Canyon. Just west of Cooper Pass is another, but much lower and apparently unnamed peak, and then another pass. And because I have been unable to find a name for this second pass, I have decided to refer to it as West Cooper Pass. West

Cooper Pass is seven tenths of a mile due west from Cooper Pass and today's road.

JULY 1999

As the last leg of my first major trip on Simpson's route, I drove up Steptoe Canyon, over Cooper Pass, and down the east side of the Schell Creek Mountains. At that time, I was assuming that the expedition's route followed today's road. Later, after additional study of Simpson's map and the distances given in his text and the table of distances, I became convinced that the expedition did not follow today's road across Cooper Pass. It is my conclusion that the expedition and the Mormon road crossed the mountain by going across West Cooper Pass.

The most significant factor involved in reaching this conclusion is Simpson's figure of 1.7 miles for the distance between the campsite at Cave Springs and the summit of the pass. According to my measurements, it is 2.4 miles from Cave Springs to Cooper Pass, but from Cave Springs to West Cooper Pass it is almost exactly 1.7 miles. If this was the only factor involved, I would be tempted to pass it off as simply another mileage error, but there are some other persuasive arguments, one of which is the altitude of the two passes. Simpson listed the altitude at the summit he crossed as 8,140 feet above sea level. My GPS receiver gave me altitude readings of 8,680 at Cooper Pass, and 8,280 at West Cooper Pass. It must be kept in mind that Simpson's altitude readings were never exactly right, but the difference of 540 feet between Simpson's reading and the elevation at Cooper Pass is well beyond his average range of error. On the other hand, the difference between Simpson's reading and the elevation at West Cooper Pass is only 140 feet, which is within the normal range of Simpson's errors.

Simpson also mentioned that one of the men, a Sergeant Barr, who must have been doing a little scouting, ran across a couple of springs after crossing the summit.

A spring and fine grass are reported by Sergeant Barr, 1.5 miles down the cañon and a quarter of a mile to right, in a branch cañon, and another spring about 3 miles down the cañon to the right, also in a branch cañon.[10]

Maps of this area show springs that could fit this description. If you begin at West Cooper Pass and head south for a mile and a half, then turn to the right and go up a shallow side canyon, in just a little less than a half mile you will come to Aspen Spring. This fits very well with Sergeant Barr's description of the first spring. On the other hand, at 1.5 miles south of Cooper Pass, there is no branch canyon and no spring. At three miles from the summit, Sergeant Barr's second spring would have been in the Cooper Meadows area, which is reached after the two routes come back together, so its location has no bearing on which of the two possible routes is the correct one.

JULY 2003

Today there is no road across West Cooper Pass, and I calculated that the roundtrip hike would be about five miles, but I had no clue as to how steep or rugged the trail might prove to be. After staying overnight in Ely, I drove to the Cave Spring area, reaching it just as the sun was coming up. Leaving the road at a point about a half mile south of the springs, I began hiking up the shallow side canyon that leads to West Cooper Pass. It was immediately apparent that the first quarter-mile of this small canyon would have been impassable for wagons. In addition to being very steep, the bottom of the canyon is simply too narrow and choked with boulders for the wagons to have gotten through it. This was not an auspicious beginning. However, after looking around a little more, I noticed that the ridge on the eastern side of the canyon might have offered another possibility. It appeared to me that by utilizing one or two switchbacks, it might have been possible for the wagons to bypass the mouth of the canyon. By leaving today's road at some point a short distance to the south of the mouth of the canyon, the trail could have climbed up the eastern side of the ridge that forms the eastern side of the canyon, and then dropped into the canyon somewhere above the problem area. Later in the day, as I was returning to my vehicle, I followed the top of this ridge, and it looked to me as if it would have been possible for the wagons to have followed such a route. It may not have been easy, but I think it could have been done.

After passing the problem area, I continued up the canyon and soon found myself on a trail that has the appearance of having been made by wheeled vehicles. Although they were extremely faint, I could make out two parallel tracks that were the correct distance apart for wagon tracks. This trail begins to show up at about a half mile from the mouth of the canyon, and continues for about a mile, with the tracks being most evident in the area of the summit of the pass. At about three-quarters of a mile beyond the summit they start getting faint, and then fade out entirely.

After crossing the summit of the pass, I continued down the south slope of the mountain for another mile, and came to the upper end of a jeep trail. At that point, I turned around, retraced my steps back over the summit, and returned to my SUV. I then drove over Cooper Pass and dropped down the south slope of the mountain until I came to where the jeep trail I had encountered during my hike leaves the main road. Turning onto this trail, I followed it for about a mile to its upper end, where I had first encountered it. I had now traveled the entire route across West Cooper Pass, and I was convinced that it would have been a practical route for the wagons. I am quite certain that the White Mountain explorers and the Simpson expedition used West Cooper Pass to surmount the Schell Creek Range.

A couple of years after this hike, I came across another item that seems to support the idea of the West Cooper Pass route. On August 17, 1859, just a month after the Simpson expedition had crossed the Schell Creek Mountains, emigrant Charles Tuttle made the following entry in his journal:

> *Wednesday Aug 17. We came today about 23 miles and encamped in about a mile of the summit of Ungo-we-ah or Pine Range.... The road to day has been very good considering the newness of it.*[11]

Since these were the names that Simpson used for the Schell Creek Mountains, it is clear that Tuttle was relying on information that came from Simpson. A couple of days after returning to Camp Floyd, Simpson gave a written itinerary of his return trail to a small group of emigrants,

Wheeler Peak, which Simpson called Union Peak, from Cooper Canyon on the eastern slope of the Schell Creek Range. *"As you descend Little's Cañon, the Go-shoot, or Tots-arrh range, looms toweringly in front of you, the most conspicuous portion being Union Peak."*

which included Tuttle. During my hike through this area, when I was about a mile south of West Cooper Pass, I found a small stream flowing through a level area that would make a very good place for a camp. On the other hand, on today's road, at a mile south of Cooper Pass, you are in a very narrow and steep-sided canyon, where there is no water and no level areas. This would be a terrible place to make a camp.

After passing Cooper Meadows and the second spring that had been reported by Sergeant Barr, the expedition made its way down the eastern slope of the Schell Creek Mountains through Cooper Canyon. Simpson noted that as they were moving down this canyon, the mountain that he called Union Peak could be seen directly in front of them. I have driven down Cooper Canyon three times, and have found the view of Wheeler Peak to be spectacular.

Thence 6.6 miles, or about two-thirds of the way across Antelope Valley, to some springs [Layton Spring], which, by being opened, may be made to serve a large command. We encamp at these springs at 2.15....Journey 15.7 miles.[12]

APRIL 2002

During my first trip across the Schell Creek Mountains in July of 1999, when I reached the lower end of Cooper Canyon, I left Simpson's trail and turned to the southeast until I reached State Route 893, where I turned south to US 50 and left the area. Three years later, I returned to this spot and found the place where the expedition had crossed SR 893. Turning to the east, I got onto a power line service road and followed it across Spring Valley to Layton Spring. A couple of years later, while examining aerial photos of

Camp 22-E. Layton Spring, in Spring Valley: *"about two-thirds of the way across Antelope Valley, to some springs, which, by being opened, may be made to serve a large command."*

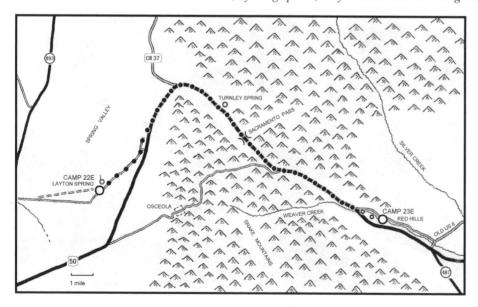

JULY 20, 1859

the area, I discovered the faint trace of an old trail that leaves the utility road about a quarter mile east of the highway, and follows a straight line to Layton Spring. Convinced that this faint trace was the expedition's route, in 2005 Nancy and I took a trip to the area with the intention of driving the old trail. Leaving SR 893, we turned east and made our way to the spot where the trail leaves the service road. We found that the trail is clearly visible, but we also found that it has become so overgrown with greasewood that it is impassable. I had to be satisfied with having crossed the valley on the service road, which in most places is no more than a quarter of a mile away from the trail.

William Lee described the Layton Spring area as "a fine spring; with good grass but no wood." He also mentioned that John Reese left the expedition at that point, intending to travel ahead of them all the way to Camp Floyd.[13] Lee either misunderstood the plan, or circumstances intervened, because the main party caught up with Reese eight days later at Chapin's Spring, in the interior of the House Range.

JULY 20, 1859

JULY 20, CAMP NO. 22, SPRINGS, ANTELOPE VALLEY.—*Decamped at 20 minutes past 5. Course east of north, 5.8 miles up Antelope Valley [Spring Valley], to mouth of cañon, which I call after Capt. P. T. Turnley, assistant quartermaster at Camp Floyd, and which leads us to the pass over the Go-shoot or Tots-arrh range.*[14]

SIMPSON EVIDENTLY FELT that Spring Valley was the southern end of Antelope Valley, which the expedition had crossed on May 11 during its westbound journey. When the expedition left Layton Spring, they turned north and merged with US 50 at a point about three miles south of the bend that takes the highway into Turnley Canyon.

Our road turns up this cañon southwestwardly, and 2.2 miles from mouth we find some fine copious cold springs, which I call also after Captain Turnley. Grass and wood-fuel found in vicinity. Persons traveling our route will find a road to the north of ours, and move direct from near the mouth

of Little's Cañon to the mouth of Turnley's Cañon, which will cut off several miles. In that case they will make their encampment at these springs, and not where we did in Antelope Valley.[15]

Here Simpson is advising future travelers to take a direct line between the mouth of Turnley's Canyon and the mouth of Cooper Canyon, which would bypass Layton Spring. He added that if they follow this shortcut they "will find a road to the north of ours." This probably means that the Mormons' wagons had taken this shortcut the previous year, leaving a discernable trail. If this is true, it also means that as the expedition traveled from the mouth of Cooper Canyon to Layton Spring, and from there to the mouth of Turnley Canyon, they were breaking their own trail and not following the Mormon road. Simpson's map shows the Mormon road as a dotted line, and indicates that it is "Practicable for wagons."

Proceeding up Turnley's Cañon 1.8 miles by a remarkably easy grade, the cañon being amply wide, we reach summit of pass [Sacramento Pass] of the Go-shoot or Tots-arrh range [Snake Mountains], whence we had toward the east a fine view of some distant mountains, Union Peak [Wheeler Peak] of the Tots-arrh range [Snake Mountains] to the east of the summit towering far above every other height, and showing a great deal of snow and apparently depending icicles in its recesses. Indeed, I think this peak the highest we have seen on either of our routes.[16]

Simpson erred when he said that his Union Peak was east of the summit of Sacramento Pass. It actually lies almost due south from the pass.

Descending from pass on east side, by a cañon of very easy inclination, in 7.2 miles reach a fine spring of flowing water, where we encamp. This cañon I call Red Cañon, on account of its red-colored rocks. The spring is called by the Indians Un-go-pah or Red Spring. Plenty of grass exists near and in vicinity, and I notice also some springs to the south of us, in the cañon, about 2 miles off. Union Peak, which lies some 10 or 15 miles to the west of south of us, the Indians call Too-bur-rit;

Camp 23-E. Strawberry Creek Ranch, on Weaver Creek, about nine miles west of the Utah-Nevada border.
"Descending from pass on east side. . . in 7.2 miles we reach a fine spring of flowing water, where we encamp."

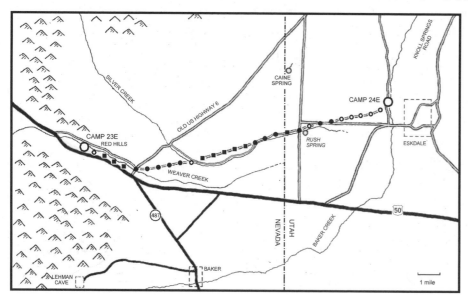

but I cannot learn its meaning....Journey 17.1 miles. Train got into camp at 12.45.[17]

This time, the direction to Wheeler Peak is exactly right. This campsite was located on the south bank of Weaver Creek, about three miles west of the junction of State Route 487 and US 50. Today this site is occupied by the Strawberry Ranch.

JULY 21, 1859

JULY 21, CAMP NO. 23, UN-GO-PAH OR RED SPRINGS. — *Resumed journey at 25 minutes after 4. Course eastwardly. Continue to descend Red Cañon to valley on east side of Tot-arr range [Snake Mountains], which valley I call after Deputy Quartermaster-General George H. Crosman, stationed at headquarters Department of Utah. The road we are following, and have been since we left Steptoe Valley, is the Mormon road referred to July 18. The indications are that some fifty wagons have been over it. The tracks of the cattle are still visible, and the dung yet remains on the road. About 3 miles from camp we leave the road, to cut off a bend of it. About 2.5 miles farther cross a dry branch [Silver Creek] just below its sink. Cottonwood at crossing.*[18]

IN THE AREA below the Strawberry Ranch, Weaver Creek flows in a fairly deep ravine along the southern base of some low hills. As the expedition left the campsite, they were following the south bank of the stream. At about three miles from Strawberry Ranch, the ravine disappears and the hills on the north side of the stream flatten out. A well-maintained graveled road comes from the northeast, crosses Weaver Creek, and joins US 50 a short distance south of the stream. At one time, this graveled road was designated as US Highway 6, but it lost that designation in the mid-1950s when the paved highway that is now US 50 and 6 was completed between the town of Hinckley and the Nevada border. At this point, the expedition crossed to the north side of Weaver Creek and started across Snake Valley, heading in a slightly north-of-east direction.

It would appear that the Mormon road continued to follow the south bank of Weaver Creek for some distance, then turned north to follow Baker Creek toward the town of Eskdale. Simpson decided to take a shortcut by cutting diagonally across the valley. The dry branch that they crossed at five and a half miles from camp was Silver Creek, a small stream that flows in an easterly direction out of the Snake Mountains. An irrigated alfalfa field now occupies the creek bottom in the area where the expedition crossed the dry streambed.

Five and a half miles farther brings us to a rush spring of tolerable water, which, by excavation, could be made to serve a pretty large command. There is a great deal of grass about it, and in the vicinity.[19]

About five and a half miles northeast of Silver Creek Reservoir, lying directly on the Utah-Nevada border, and surrounded on all sides by sagebrush flats, is a pleasant little oasis known as Caine Spring. When I first started looking at this section of Simpson's route, I assumed that this would have been the spring that Simpson described as a "rush spring." Acting on this assumption, I hiked the four miles between Caine Spring and Baker Creek, thinking that I was following the expedition's route. Sometime later, after obtaining a better copy of Simpson's map, I discovered that the expedition's trail followed a perfectly straight line all the way across Snake Valley, passing about three miles south of Caine Spring. This meant that I had to look for another spring, one that was on a straight line between the Weaver Creek crossing and Eskdale. While studying aerial photos of the area, I located what appeared to be a vegetated area at about the correct distance. Although this spot is not marked as a spring on the USGS maps of the area, it does have the appearance of a spring on the aerial photos. As I continued to study the photos, I noticed a faint trail extending both east and west from the spring. This turned out to be an important discovery. I soon found that I could trace this line in an absolutely straight line all the way from the Weaver Creek crossing to a point just a short distance north of Eskdale.

Three and a half miles farther we join and follow again the Mormon road. Half a mile farther we

Camp 24-E. The campsite was in the middle of this alfalfa field. Baker Creek once flowed through here but the water has been diverted and the streambed plowed and leveled: *"we come to a creek. . . which comes from the south, and sinks a quarter of a mile below camp."*

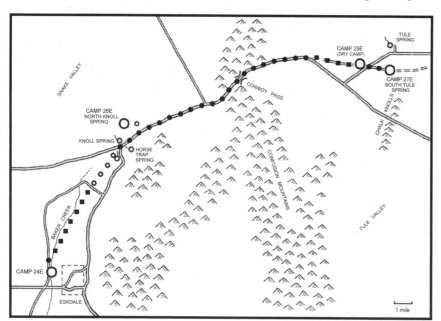

come to a creek [Baker Creek], 3 feet wide, 1 deep, which comes from the south, and sinks a quarter of a mile below camp. In places it is lined with rushes and willows. On this creek, which I also call after Colonel Crosman, we encamp at half past 12, amid abundance of grass....Journey, 14.8 miles. [20]

About a mile northwest of the small community of Eskdale, aerial photos show a bend in the trail that comes from the spring, and the faint trace of another trail coming from the south. This fork in the abandoned trail could very well be where the expedition rejoined the Mormon road. A short distance from the fork, the old trail joins a modern ranch road. This road goes past a cluster of ranch houses and sheds, and at a half mile northeast of the fork, it reaches the edge of an irrigated alfalfa field, which now covers the old Baker Creek streambed. It was at this point that the expedition made camp for the night. The campsite was on the west bank of Baker Creek, about five miles north of US 50, and about a mile and a quarter northwest of Eskdale.

MAY 2005

Nancy and I spent the better part of a day attempting to follow the abandoned trail across Snake Valley. Between the Weaver Creek crossing and the old Silver Creek crossing, we found that we could drive on the old roadbed. The junk that we noticed on the sides of the old trail in this area seems to indicate that it had been used for some time by people traveling in automobiles. When we reached Silver Creek, we could find no way to cross it anywhere near the old trail, so we headed northwest and crossed it on the old US 6 bridge. From there we were able to drive down the east side of the stream and pick up the trail again. However, we soon found that in the area east of Silver Creek, the trail was so overgrown with greasewood that we were unable to drive on it. We backtracked to old US 6, and found a power line service road that seemed to be going in the right direction. Three miles to the east we found where the old trail crossed the utility road. It was still not drivable. Another three miles to the east brought us to the Utah-Nevada border

and a gated fence that was clearly marked with prominent No Trespassing signs. Reluctantly, we turned around and retraced our path all the way back to US 50, then returned to the east until we came to a graveled road that goes north to Gandy, Trout Creek, and Callao. Three miles north of US 50, we reached the spot where the old trail crosses the road at a point that is only about a half mile east of where we had turned around at the No Trespassing signs. A short distance to the east of the road, we could see the spring that I had discovered on the aerial photos. Simpson called it a "rush spring," but today it is surrounded by a thick growth of willows. A fence prevented us from driving on this section of the old trail, so I started walking. I found some traces of the trail, but also found that it is impassable for vehicles due to the greasewood that has invaded it. After walking about a mile and a half, I returned to the SUV and we drove north for a short distance, then headed east on a road that leads to Eskdale. When we came to where the trail crosses this road, I parked again and hiked another two and a half miles to where the old trail meets the well-used ranch road. Turning around at that point, I hiked back to the SUV, and we drove to the ranch and the site of Simpson's eastbound camp number 24.

I am quite certain that Simpson's expedition was the first to travel the trail that I found across Snake Valley, but it is very apparent that a significant number of other travelers used it later, and did so for many years.

JULY 22, 1859

JULY 22, CAMP NO. 24, CROSMAN CREEK.— *Moved at 5, and continue on Mormon road. Course, northwardly in valley for 10.2 miles, when we come to a number of small springs [Knoll Springs], which I call after Lieut. Peter V. L. Plympton, Seventh Infantry.* [21]

WHEN THE EXPEDITION began this day's march, they headed almost due north along the west bank of Baker Creek. At about a quarter of a mile they passed the creek's sink, then crossed the dry streambed and began bearing a little to the east. Simpson said that when they were

10.2 miles from camp, they came to the first of a group of springs. Some of these springs have formed large mounds on the otherwise level valley floor. Although they are scattered over a fairly large area, it appears that Simpson referred to the entire group as Plympton Springs. The most prominent of the springs have since been renamed as Knoll Springs, North Knoll Spring, and Horse Trap Springs, but the name Plympton survives as the name of a low ridge that lies to the northeast of the springs.

JUNE 2002

Maps of the area north of Eskdale show a dirt road that follows the Baker Creek streambed for some distance. Although this road does not follow what I believe to be the expedition's route, it appeared that it would be as close as I could get to it in a vehicle. When I attempted to get onto the road, I found that I would have to go right through a group of ranch buildings. I drove into the yard and knocked on the door of the ranch house to see if I could get permission to drive through the property. I was a little apprehensive, being well aware that, undeserved or not, the folks who live in this area have a reputation for being antagonistic toward strangers. My apprehension proved to be groundless. As soon as the rancher was satisfied that my reason for being there had nothing to do with either law enforcement or the news media, he made me quite welcome. After a brief conversation, we got into his pickup truck and headed north on the old road for a couple of miles as he showed me the unmapped side roads that I should avoid. Returning to the ranch house, I got back in my SUV and headed north again. By following the map and the rancher's instructions, I drove up the valley, paralleling the dry creek bed until it disappeared completely. Although I was not directly on the expedition's route, I was never more than a half mile from it. At about seven and a half miles from the ranch, the road made an abrupt turn and left Simpson's route altogether. Heading in an easterly direction, the road soon began to climb out of the bottomland, and came to the main road that traverses the east side of Snake Valley. Turning north again, I drove to Knoll Spring, where I parked my SUV and hiked back along the last three-mile section of the trail.

Although Simpson says nothing about stopping at Plympton Spring, one can assume that the expedition spent enough time there to allow the animals to drink their fill. But because Simpson believed that there would be more water a short distance ahead, the party soon pushed on. As things turned out, it would have been much better for them if they had remained here for the night. The remainder of this day, and the next couple of days, would turn out to be difficult and confusing.

The soldier who last joined us at Un-go-pah Springs [Red Springs] was directed by the guide to conduct us to a spring 12 miles distant from our last camp, but as these are only 10 miles distant, and the soldier has not been to the place, we continued on in the hope of seeing the springs referred to within about a couple of miles and camping at it.[22]

This statement shows that when they were at Knoll Springs, Simpson believed that they would come to another spring after traveling about two more miles. Later, he was to learn, much to his displeasure, that they were already at the spot where Reese intended for them to camp.

It proved, however, that at this distance there were no springs, so I was lured on in hope of finding them a little farther on. At 13, 14, and 15 miles from camp we saw none, and then, according to the notes of the guide, which he had shown me, feeling confident that they were beyond, in striking distance, I continued on till, at quarter to 5 o'clock, we had traveled 30.1 miles, when we were obliged to encamp near some puddles of water, which had been made by the rain, just before we reached the spot.[23]

They were relying on a guide who had never been anywhere near the spot to which he was supposed to guide them, and Simpson was obviously very unhappy about it. It becomes apparent that Reese had simply told the soldier who was acting as the guide that there would be some springs at about twelve miles from the previous night's camp. Reese must have been talking about Knoll Springs. But because they had traveled only ten miles to get to Knoll Springs, Simpson was certain that the springs Reese was talking about were another two miles ahead. After leaving Knoll Springs, they traveled another twenty miles, all the time expecting that they would soon come to some other springs. Late in the afternoon, Simpson finally gave up on finding these other springs, and they stopped and set up camp for the night. This camp was located near the center of Tule Valley, where there was neither water nor any decent forage for the animals.

William Lee described this day's journey as follows:

Friday, July 22nd. Marched thirty-one miles and came to camp on the desert, miles from any water; but fortunately for us it rained all day (a very rare thing by the way in this country) and the water lay in pools on the ground so that we secured enough for cooking.[24]

Lee was wrong when he said they were miles from water. If they had continued on for only another mile and a half, they would have come to South Tule Spring, where there was plenty of water and grass. Simpson must have been exasperated, indeed, two days later, when he learned that this spring was such a short distance from where they had stopped for the night of the twenty-second.

Before he concluded his writing for the day, Simpson added a more detailed description of the day's journey.

After reaching, as above stated, Plympton's Springs, our route lay eastwardly 6.7 miles to foot of pass, across a low, thirsty mountain-ridge, which I call Perry Range [Confusion Mountains]; thence 3.1 miles by a good grade up a broad cañon to summit [Cowboy Pass], the rocks on the left side being buttress or bluff like; and thence, by gentle descent 10.1 miles to camp....From the summit of the pass, could be seen, some 25 or 30 miles off, on west side of range of mountains, quite remarkable on account of its well-defined stratification and the resemblance of portions of its outline to domes, minarets, houses, and other structures. On this account I call it the House range. Between it and the ridge forming our point of view is a very extensive valley [Tule Valley], very generally white with

alkaline efflorescence, and I have therefore called it White Valley....It is in the middle of this valley we have encamped, and on account of the guides having neglected to send back a man, as he was wont, according to orders, to point to me a camp of which he was personally cognizant, the party is in its present uncomfortable situation.[25]

The expedition now found itself right in the middle of the faux pax that Simpson had earlier emphasized that he wanted to avoid. They had gone right by a good source of water, and after an extra long march, they had been forced to go into a dry camp. Simpson was not at all pleased with his guide. He would become even less pleased during the next few days.

JULY 23, 1859

JULY 23, CAMP NO. 25, WHITE VALLEY.— *Koenig, the dragoon, did not come in from the guide party in the night as was anticipated. I do not understand the guide's movements. It was enjoined upon him over and over again to send us back a man daily, to guide the party with certainty to water and grass, and he has still Pete, Lambert, Stevenson, and Private Koenig with him. It will be hazarding too much to persist in going forward at a venture, though Sanchez, who was with the guide when he examined to the northeast of the House range, on our outward trip, says there is water on the east side of the House Mountains. The route to the water, however, is not known to be practicable, and it would consume nearly the whole day to have it examined, and in the meantime the animals are without grass and water, and we cannot afford to give them another feed of forage, it being necessary for the desert stretch, which we may possibly have to pass before reaching Rush Valley. I have, therefore, determined to fall back to Plympton's Springs, where we can get grass and water, and await there the arrival of some one from the guide's party. Leave at 7 A.M., and retrace our steps to Plympton's Springs, where, at 2, we encamp. Journey 18.7 miles.*[26]

BECAUSE OF HIS lack of information about conditions in the country ahead of them, Simpson decided to return to the last place that he knew for certain that there was an adequate supply

Camp 25-E. Near the center of Tule Valley. The road to the right leads to South Tule Spring, which, not yet known to Simpson, was only another mile and a half away. *"we were obliged to encamp near some puddles of water, which had been made by the rain, just before we reached the spot."*

of water. Accordingly, they turned around and headed west again, crossing back over the Confusion Mountains and Cowboy Pass, and made camp at North Knoll Spring. This retreat explains how camp number 26 got to be to the rear of camp number 25.

Cowboy Pass is located near the center of the Confusion Range. Some people say that these mountains got their name from the area's rugged topography, but I have to believe that it has something to do with Simpson's experiences in this region. In *Utah Place Names*, John Van Cott gives this area a Simpson connection when he says that the name of the Disappointment Hills, which are located about ten miles to the north, is "associated with the frustrations and disappointments endured by Captain Simpson and his party during the 1850s while surveying and exploring the region."[27] That could very well be, but it seems more logical that the name of the

Confusion Mountains was a result of Simpson's problems in this area.

The expedition remained camped at North Knoll Spring the following day, waiting for some word from the guides. Sometime during that day, Simpson sent Sergeant Barr and two soldiers, Privates Collamer and Sanchez, eastward again in an attempt to locate some water and the missing guides.

JULY 25, 1859

JULY 25, CAMP 26, PLYMPTON'S SPRINGS.— *Sergeant Barr came in at 11 last night, having ridden 40 miles, and reports that 2 miles beyond our rain-puddle camp (No. 25) he found a note from the guide to me stuck in a cleft-stick near a rush pond, informing me that the Indian with him says there are water and grass 10 miles beyond that locality. This mode of guiding me by notes stuck up, depending upon the contingency of my reaching or getting them, is a new feature introduced by the guide since I have approached the desert, and is entirely unauthorized. It is true that he sent word by Private Nune, the last man he sent in, that I could continue to follow the Mormon road, and that if anything was wrong he would send back a man to notify me. But this is placing me entirely at his mercy, and this I do not choose to sanction. I must know what lies before me. The sergeant alone came back. Collamer and Sanchez continued on to examine the water and grass ahead, and are to return to us at Rush Pond, where the note was found. I have concluded, therefore, to again move forward. Started at 5.45 and retraced our track to our old camp-ground, No. 25. A mile and a half farther brought us, at 1 o'clock, to the Rush Pond reported yesterday by Sergeant Barr. Journey 20.3 miles.*[28]

WHEN I BEGAN looking at this section of the route, I started out by assuming that the expedition had followed today's well-traveled road across this section of Tule Valley. This, in turn, led me to assume that this evening's campsite was located at Tule Spring. Later, after making more accurate distance measurements and re-examining Simpson's description of the route and his map, I changed my mind and concluded that the camp was at South Tule Spring, about a mile to the south of Tule Spring and some distance off the main road.

The mileage figures reported by Simpson for the distances the expedition traveled during the three trips between Snake Valley and Tule Valley deserve some detailed explanation. At first glance, these figures appear to be as confusing as everything else about this part of the journey. However, these numbers do provide clues that help to determine the location of the three campsites involved. First, it should be noted that in the area to the west of Cowboy Pass, there are several groups of springs, which are scattered over a fairly large area, and it appears that Simpson considered them all to be a part of what he called Plympton's Springs. The most prominent of these are now known as Knoll Springs and North Knoll Spring. Knoll Springs is found just slightly north of old US 6, and North Knoll Spring is 1.3 miles north-northeast of Knoll Spring. Simpson reported that

on July 22, the expedition left the camp on Baker Creek, and after traveling 10.2 miles, they came to Plympton Springs. At this point, they would have been at Knoll Springs. As they traveled east from here, they went past North Knoll Spring, which would have been about a half mile to their left. From Knoll Springs, they traveled 6.7 miles to the base of the Confusion Mountains, 3.1 miles to the summit of Cowboy Pass, and then 10.1 miles to Camp 25-E, which Simpson called the "rain-puddle" camp. All of this adds up to the 30.1 miles that Simpson gave as the total distance traveled that day. Using Simpson's figures, the distance from Knoll Springs to Camp 25-E would be 19.9 miles. However, the next day Simpson stated that they traveled only 18.7 miles to get back to Plympton's Springs. This apparent discrepancy of 1.2 miles would be explained if they had returned only as far as North Knoll Spring. I have visited this spring a couple of times, and have found plenty of water. There seems to be no good reason for the expedition to have gone past it and all the way back to Knoll Springs. Finally, when they headed east again on July 25, Simpson reported that the distance from Camp 26-E to Camp 27-E was 20.3 miles, which is almost exactly the distance between North Knoll Spring and South Tule Spring. All of this leads me to the conclusion that Camp 26-E was at North Knoll Spring.

SEPTEMBER 1998

The first time that I ever traveled any section of Simpson's route with the conscious intent of exploring a part of his trail was in September of 1998. Phil Miller, a fellow Lincoln Highway enthusiast, and I had stopped at Knoll Springs after having spent part of a day exploring the route of old US Highway 6. This was shortly after I had obtained a copy of Simpson's report, and I had studied it only enough to know that his expedition had traveled through this part of the country. We picked up the trail at Knoll Springs and began to follow it toward the east. Staying on today's well-traveled road, we unknowingly bypassed the section of Simpson's route that goes past South Tule Spring, but we soon got back on the actual trail and followed it through Dome Canyon and down the east side of the House Mountains.

Camp 26-E. North Knoll Spring. Failing to find water in Tule Valley, the expedition returned to Snake Valley and set up camp here. Like a number of springs in this area, the water flows out of the top of the mound.

On the morning of July 25, the expedition headed east again, traveling the 18.7 miles back to the spot where they had camped during the night of the twenty-second. After passing this spot, they continued to the east for another mile and a half, then came to South Tule Spring, where they set up camp for the coming night. The past few days had been difficult and discouraging, and it would seem that Simpson might have been getting more than a little irritated with the performance of his guide and the scouts. But his problems were not over; even more difficult days were coming.

JULY 26, 1859

JULY 26, CAMP No. 27, RUSH POND [SOUTH TULE SPRING], WHITE VALLEY.—*Decamped at 5.30 o'clock. Continue on old Mormon road, north of east to mouth of cañon, leading to pass through House range. To get to it, cross an alkali flat, 3 miles wide, which in wet weather, must cut up very much....After crossing flat, pass through a mile of sand knolls, where pulling is difficult. Reach foot of cañon, 8 miles from camp.*[29]

THE EXPEDITION'S ROUTE rejoins the main valley road about three and a half miles east of Tule Spring. About five miles east of the spring, there are a number of sand dunes, many of them ten to fifteen feet high. After passing the dunes, the road begins to climb into the foothills of the House Mountains, and enters Dome Canyon, which on some maps and road signs is identified as Death Canyon.

APRIL 2002

Nancy and I drove to South Tule Spring, reaching it by following old US 6 to Tule Valley, then getting onto a narrow two-track that leaves the main valley road at a point that is very close to the site of the expedition's "rain-puddle" camp. The road appeared to stop at the spring, so we parked and I began hiking to the east. After a short distance, I began to see indications that a well-traveled road had once continued to the east from the spring. The road is not drivable now, but I found myself walking in a definite swale, which would occasionally appear and then disappear in the sagebrush. About a mile from the spring, I came to the edge of a large playa, and at about a hundred yards into this flat I began to notice what looked like the marks of wagon wheels.

I have visited the mudflats of the Great Salt Lake Desert near the Silver Island Mountains, and have seen the tracks made by the wagons that had traveled the Hastings Road. The marks that I found in Tule Valley look very much like those that can be seen near Floating Island and Pilot Peak. Because Nancy was waiting for me at the spring, I was unable to spend much time examining these tracks, but a few weeks later, I returned by myself and spent several hours taking photographs and obtaining GPS readings at various places where the tracks can be seen. There are so many tracks in this area that it is quite certain that this route had been used for a long time before being abandoned in favor of today's road, which goes past Tule Spring.

...and 4.1 miles further, by a good grade, except near summit, where for about 100 yards it is rather steep, we reach the culminating point of pass. The bluffs at the entrance of this cañon are tremendously high and massive; that on the right very high, probably 1,500 feet, and like a dome. Call the cañon, therefore, Dome Cañon. Ascended a high point to right of pass to get an extensive view. To the south, some 20 miles off, lies a lake of sky-blue color, apparently some 10 or 15 miles long, and less broad. This is doubtless Sevier Lake, the sink of the Sevier River, on which Captain Gunnison and party were massacred in 1853, and to which he was tending for the purpose of examining it when the catastrophe occurred. The valley lying to the north of this lake exhibits one extended low, flat, desert plain, showing many spots of a whitish alkaline character.[30]

In 1998, when Phil Miller and I reached the Dome Canyon summit we parked next to a small sign that was fastened to a wooden post.

> UTAH
> HISTORICAL TRAIL
>
> SIMPSON'S RETURN TRAIL
> 1859
>
> Carson City, Nevada
> To
> Camp Floyd, Utah
>
> BSA HISTORICAL TRAILS
> TROOP 340
> 3-20-88

According to the date on the sign, it had been ten years since it had been placed at the summit by a Boy Scout troop. When Phil and I saw it, there were perhaps a dozen bullet holes in it. I have driven past it several times since, and each time there have been another ten to fifteen holes added. At this rate, in another four or five years, this scout project will be completely obliterated.

While Phil and I were parked at the summit, I took off on foot and hiked a short distance to the south in an effort to duplicate the hike that Simpson had taken. While it is doubtful that I was at the exact viewpoint that Simpson found, I did get to a spot where I had an excellent view of Sevier Lake.

After descending from summit on east side, about two miles, met Collamer, who conducted us up a cañon to the left about half a mile, when we came to a fine cold spring of good water, where, at 12.45, we encamp.... Animals driven to the creek, up the cañon about a mile from camp, where there is a considerable quantity of fine grass and a growth of pines. Journey 14.5 miles. This spring, creek, and cañon I call after Lieut. Gurden Chapin, Seventh Infantry.[31]

About one and a half miles east of the Dome Canyon summit, the road begins a sweeping loop that takes it around the north side of a prominent, steep-sided knoll. This knoll is located in the lower part of a large cove, known as Wheeler Amphiteater, in the southwest side of Swasey Mountain. About halfway into this loop, the expedition came upon Private Collamer, one of the dragoons who had been sent ahead

Camp 27-E. South Tule Spring. Returning to Tule Valley, Simpson found this spring a mile and a half to the east of where they had camped two nights before. *"Retraced our track to our old camp-ground, No. 25. A mile and a half farther brought us. . . to the Rush Pond reported yesterday by Sergeant Barr."*

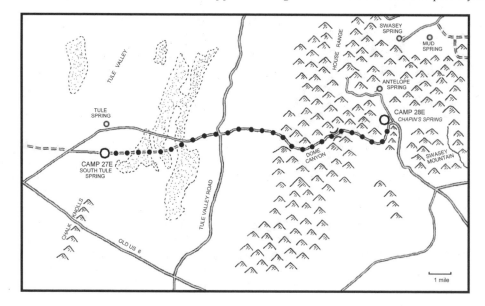

Wagon ruts in the flats east of South Tule Spring. *"Cross an alkali flat, 3 miles wide, in which wet weather, must cut up very much."*

when they were camped at North Knoll Spring. Collamer led them to a small spring that was located a short distance to the north of the road. Their camp for the night was next to the spring, which Simpson named after Lieutenant Chapin, who had been in command of the escort that had accompanied Simpson during his reconnaissance the previous October.

In an article that appeared in the *Utah Historical Quarterly* in 1984, Dr. Owen Bennion, then an associate professor at Brigham Young University, suggested that Chapin Spring was probably the same as the Antelope Spring that is located on the southwest side of Swasey Mountain.[32] However, according to Simpson's description of the location, and what he shows on his map, it is quite apparent that Chapin Spring was just a short distance off the main road, while Antelope Spring is a mile and a half from the main road and higher up in the canyon.

During one of my first trips to this area, I located a small spring that was a little less than a quarter mile off the road, at the foot of a skinny poplar tree. Since then I have visited it several times. On two or three occasions, I have observed a meager flow of water coming out of the ground and running down the slope, but most of the time it is just a damp seep. I have been unable to find a modern name for this spring, and I think it is quite possible that Bennion was unaware of its existence.

There are several factors involved in my conclusion that the small spring near the road is Chapin's Spring. According to Simpson, the expedition had traveled two miles from the Dome Canyon summit when they found Private Collamer. He also stated that it was a half mile from that point to the spring, which would make it two and a half miles from the summit to the spring. My measurements indicate that this is the exact distance from the summit to the little spring by the tree. On the other hand, it is slightly over four miles from the summit to Antelope Spring. Another factor is Simpson's comment that after they reached the campsite, the animals were "driven to the creek, up the cañon about a mile from camp."[33] All of the water from Antelope Spring now goes into a pipe, but there is a dry streambed extending down the canyon from the spring area. This would have been the creek to which the animals were driven. An additional factor is the altitude. Simpson obtained a reading of 6,530 feet above sea level at the Chapin's Spring campsite. My reading at the small spring near the poplar tree is 6,637 feet; 107 feet higher than Simpson's reading. The altitude of Antelope Spring is 7,480 feet, which is 950 feet higher than Simpson's reading, well outside the range of Simpson's average error.

William Lee made a short entry in his journal that evening.

Tuesday, July 26th. Marched fifteen miles and came to camp at a spring of fine water with plenty of wood and grass. There is a fine view of Lake Sevier from the mountains near camp. Met Reese here, his mules having given out.[34]

John Reese had not made it back to Camp Floyd as had been planned. He was waiting for the expedition at Chapin's Spring. The guide reported that he had found water and grass at a spot about fifteen miles ahead. This was Simpson's first meeting with Reese since the fiasco of the Tule Valley camps, but he remains silent about whether or not he mentioned his displeasure with Reese's actions during the last few days.

Ten

SWASEY MOUNTAIN TO TRIPLE PEAKS

Camp 28-E. A small spring bubbles up at the foot of this poplar tree near the southwest base of Swasey Mountain. Simpson called it Chapin's Spring. *"Collamer conducted up a cañon to the left about half a mile, when we came to a fine cold spring."*

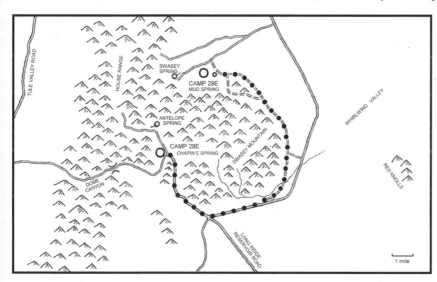

JULY 27, 1859

JULY 27, CAMP NO. 28, CHAPIN'S SPRING.—
*Marched at 20 minutes past 5. Retraced our steps
one-fourth of a mile to old Mormon road, and
then leave it and cut off an unnecessary detour, by
winding in the cañon to the left.*[1]

UPON LEAVING CAMP that morning, the expedition followed its earlier track back to the Mormon road, then turned to the left and began to follow it down the southeast slope of Swasey Mountain. Simpson's description makes it sound as though they left the road almost immediately after getting onto it, but it is more likely that they stayed on it for about two miles before taking the shortcut. When Simpson said they were "winding in the canyon to the left," he seems to have meant that they took a route that went somewhere to the east of the Mormon road. At two miles from the spring, today's road makes a sharp turn and goes past the eastern side of a small knoll. Traces of an abandoned road can be found on the west side of the knoll. It appears to me that today's road probably follows Simpson's shortcut.

Three and a half miles further get into it again, in Sevier Valley, and after following it a few yards, leave it entirely, we turning to the left around a southeast spur of the House range, and the Mormon road continuing in an easterly direction to Fillmore and crossing the Sevier, it is said, at the Government bridge on the main southern road to Los Angeles.[2]

When the expedition reached the valley, they came to what is now a four-way intersection. One of the branches heads southwest to join old US 6, which soon enters Marjum Pass. The branch in the center continues in a southeasterly direction, crosses old US 6, and hits today's US 50 and 6 near the north shore of Sevier Lake. This was the route of the Mormon road, and it eventually led to the city of Fillmore. The third branch heads east, then turns north to go through Whirlwind Valley and Swasey Bottom. The expedition began to follow this route. When Simpson mentioned the "main southern road to Los Angeles," he was referring to the old Mormon Corridor that is now followed by Interstate 15, but I have been unable to determine the location of the "government bridge."

After following the route of today's well-traveled road for about a mile and a half, the expedition left it and began to veer a little to the north, staying closer to the base of the mountain. The faint remains of an abandoned road can be found in this area, but after another two and a half miles, it is cut by a deep washout that cannot be crossed in a vehicle. In order to get to the far side of the washout, it is necessary to approach it from the north.

Continuing around along the east base of House range our route, after proceeding northwardly up the valley about 11 miles, turns to the left up a cañon a quarter of a mile, where we reached some good springs, and at 12 meridian, encamped. In this vicinity there are other springs, and about half a mile further up toward the mountain, there is a small creek, 4 feet wide, 1 deep, which after running a short distance, sinks. The springs, creek, and canyon I call after Lieut. Charles H. Tyler, Second Dragoons. To this creek, along which there is an abundance of grass, we drive our mules....Journey to-day 15.5 miles.[3]

After passing the washed out area, the expedition continued along the base of the mountain by following what is now an almost totally abandoned trail. When this trail reaches the northeast corner of Swasey Mountain, it turns to the west and comes to the area of Mud Spring, where the expedition set up camp for the night.

APRIL 2002

While exploring the area near the southeast base of Swasey Mountain, I discovered a narrow two-track that leaves the Whirlwind Valley Road about two miles north of where it makes its major bend. Following this two-track toward the mountain, I came to where it intersects the abandoned road and the expedition's trail near the base of the mountain. Turning south on the abandoned road, I was able to make my way back to the washed-out section. Turning around again, I followed the abandoned road northward along the eastern base of Swasey Mountain until I reached Mud Spring and the expedition's campsite.

In the article that appeared in the *Utah Historical Quarterly*, Owen Bennion speculated that this camp was located at Swasey Spring, which is about a mile and a half farther to the west and a lot higher on the mountainside.[4] Several factors have convinced me that the camp was at Mud Spring instead. The first, and most important, consideration is distance. In Simpson's table, the distance between what he called Chapin's Spring and what he called Tyler's Spring is listed as 15.5 miles. When I use the Google Earth map program to measure between these two springs, along what I believe was the expedition's route, I get the same distance. But it is another mile and a half to Swasey Spring. A second factor is Simpson's statement that to get to the spring, they turned to the left and went up a canyon a quarter of a mile. This is a reasonably good description of the route to Mud Spring, but a route to Swasey Spring would not have made a turn. Simpson also mentioned that there was a flowing stream about a half mile up the mountain from the campsite. Most of the water flowing out of Swasey Spring now goes into a pipe, but it previously flowed down a streambed that passes about a half mile above Mud Spring. There appears to be no significant streambed above Swasey Spring. A final factor is the altitude. Swasey Spring is probably too high. Simpson's reading at the campsite was 5,992 feet above sea level. Using my GPS receiver, I obtained a reading of 6,060 feet at Mud Spring, which is only 68 feet higher than Simpson's figure. Swasey Spring is about 6,640 feet above sea level, 648 feet higher than Simpson's reading.

July 28, 1859

July 28, Camp No. 29, Tyler's Spring.— *Remained in camp till 2.30 P.M. for the purpose of recruiting the animals, preparatory to crossing the desert, and traveling all night.*[5]

GETTING A LITTLE EXTRA rest for the men and animals was a very good idea, because the next forty-eight hours were going to be the most difficult of the entire journey. And Simpson's description of the route through this region proved to be the most difficult for me to understand.

There is little doubt that Simpson's return route is even less well known than his outbound route, and it is also quite certain that the trail the expedition followed between Swasey Mountain and Rush Valley has been the least understood section of all. Virtually all of the maps of Simpson's route that I have been able to examine show that the return route in this area follows a generally northeasterly direction, with little or no regard for actual geographical features. Even Dale Morgan's otherwise excellent trails map ignores the existence of Keg Mountain, which had a significant effect on the route. The most probable explanation for this lack of accurate detail is the fact that no long-lasting or well-traveled roads were ever established along Simpson's route through this area. Simpson himself dismissed a forty-mile section of the trail the expedition traveled as having been the wrong route for a wagon road. Furthermore, Simpson's descriptions of the route were becoming increasingly difficult to follow. It seems that he may have been getting tired of traveling, tired of dealing with his unpredictable guide, and tired of making detailed journal entries.

Take a course northwardly for about 15.6 miles up a branch of arm of Sevier Lake Valley [Whirlwind Valley], where we, about 11 o'clock, stopped to take supper and bait the animals with some grass we had brought with us.[6]

During the first leg of this part of its journey, the expedition traveled in a slightly east-of-north direction, slanting across Whirlwind Valley, then turning a little closer to due north as they crossed Swasey Bottom, which lies to the northeast of the House Range. No road or trail of any description follows the first sixteen and a half miles of this day's journey today. It is doubtful that anyone ever used this section of the trail again. The few emigrant journals that have been found all indicate that they traveled the route that Simpson recommended, not the one he actually followed.

After studying this area for some time, it became apparent that if I wanted to follow the expedition's exact route, I would have to do it on foot. This was going to be an extra long hike, and I decided to get some help.

July 2003

It did not take much to persuade Lou Dunyon to make a trip to Whirlwind Valley with me. We

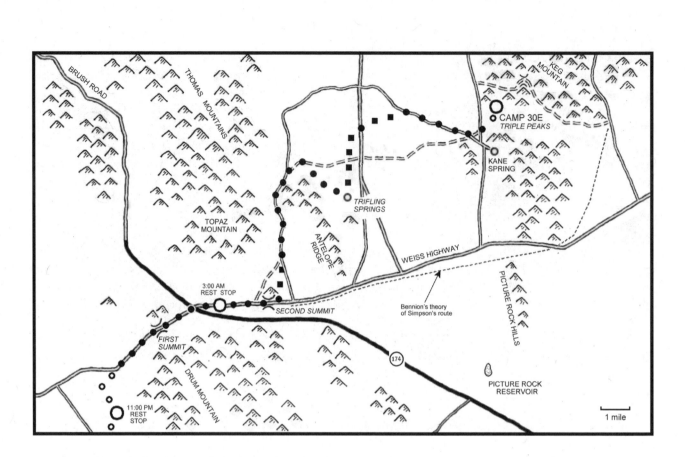

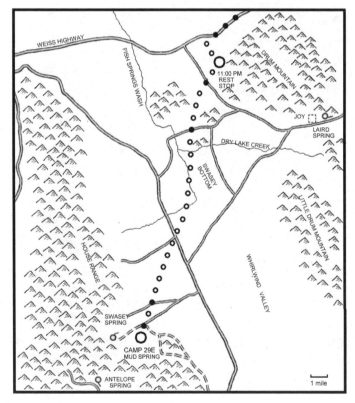

traveled to the area in his pickup truck, and he dropped me off at a spot where a narrow two-track crosses the expedition's trail at the northern end of Swasey Bottom. He then continued along the two-track until it joined the main valley road, and turned south to wait for me at the road that leads to Mud Spring. I headed south on foot, traveling the expedition's route in reverse. I covered about ten miles of the route during this hike. It was a long day, but for once, I did not have to hike the same trail twice.

Simpson did not mention it in the text of his report, but the table of distances lists a "summit of Thomas's range" at 14.6 miles from the camp. This summit is on a ridge that is not a part of what is known as the Thomas Mountains today. The ridge in question runs east and west between Drum Mountain and the north end of the House Mountains, dividing Whirlwind Valley from Fish Springs Flat. On a greater scale, this relatively low ridge is the division between the Sevier Lake basin and the Great Salt Lake basin.

At 11:00 P.M., when the expedition had reached a point one mile beyond the summit of the low ridge, they stopped for a short time to have some supper and give the animals some of the grass they had cut while camped at Mud Spring. Simpson did not say how long they remained at this location, but due to the fact that they fixed some supper and fed the animals, it is probably safe to assume that they were there for about an hour.

From this point we bore off northeastwardly to a pass through Colonel Lorenzo Thomas's range, 3 miles, by an easy grade, bringing us to the summit.[7]

After driving through this area several times, and spending a considerable amount of time studying the maps, I finally concluded that the site of their supper break was about a mile and a half from the nearest road, which called for a short cross-country hike. I also noticed that in this area there seems to be a slight discrepancy between Simpson's description of the route and what is shown on his map. In the text of the report, Simpson states that when they left the site of their supper break, they went in a northeasterly direction, but an examination of his map shows that at about this point the trail turns to the northwest for a short distance, possibly about a mile, before turning again and heading northeast. I needed to find out why there was a difference between the map and the text.

JULY 2005

My friend Jim Hall decided to take another desert trip with me, and we drove to the low ridge near the base of Drum Mountain. Leaving his SUV near the road, we hiked to the spot where I believe the expedition had stopped for supper. We approached this location from the southwest, following what I believe to be the expedition's route. When we reached the site, the reason for the turn to the northwest became obvious. We found ourselves on the western edge of a deep wash with almost perpendicular banks, and could see that it would have been very difficult, if not impossible, to continue to the northeast from that point. To make matters even more difficult, on the far side of the gully they would have been forced to begin climbing into some steep hills that make up the northern tip of Drum Mountain. By turning to the northwest, the trail could remain on fairly even terrain, with a gradual downhill slope. After traveling in this direction for about a mile, they would have reached the bottom of the slope, where it would become possible to turn to the northeast again. From there they began to climb up a gentle slope as they approached the south end of the Thomas Mountains. It would appear that when Simpson said they went northeast from where they had stopped for supper, he was speaking in broad, rather than specific, terms. I was now satisfied that the puzzle of the kink on the map had been solved.

I was also able to determine that the place where they made their turn back to the northeast was the same point that is listed in the table as the "base of Thomas's range." For quite some time I had a question about why Simpson had described this point as the base of a mountain range. Although during my first few visits to the area I had not determined the exact location, I had noted that it was nowhere near any sharply rising mountain slopes. When I did discover the location of this point, the answer became clear. From this particular spot, the terrain begins to slope upwards toward the north. Although the slope is quite gradual for the next few miles, it is continuous. Simpson's statement that they were at the base of the mountain now made sense. It should be kept in mind that the expedition traveled through this area during the night, and that particular night was darker than usual. Simpson mentioned that there was no moon, and to make matters even worse, there was a cloud cover that even blocked out the starlight. It is a wonder that he was able to provide any description of the country at all.

The spot that Simpson called the base of the Thomas Range is located in the bottom of a shallow drainage, a little less than a mile east of an old government well. The well is just south of a graveled and well-maintained road that is known as the Weiss Highway. This road leaves US Highway 6 near Jericho, then heads west across the desert all the way to the Deep Creek Mountains. After making the turn to the northeast, the expedition started up the slope, and after traveling a little less than a half mile, they joined the Weiss Highway. After another mile and a half, they came to the summit of what Simpson described as "a pass through Colonel Lorenzo Thomas's range," where they paused long enough for someone to take an altitude reading. Whoever did this may have been hampered by the darkness, because the reading was more inaccurate than usual, being about 400 feet higher than the actual elevation of this summit. Because of this error, I spent quite a bit of time attempting to find a higher spot that could have been crossed by the expedition, but I finally concluded that this summit is the only place that fits Simpson's description of the route. Although Simpson said the pass was in the Thomas Range, it actually lies southwest of those mountains, and northwest of Drum Mountain. It is the highest point on a very low ridge, and I doubt that many people would describe it as a pass. But once again, it must be remembered that Simpson never did see this area in daylight.

Descending on east side by a good grade, 2.2 miles more, we halted, at 3 o'clock in the morning, to take breakfast, and feed the animals with barley.[8]

East of the low summit, the Weiss Highway slopes slightly downward for about a half mile, then begins to head upslope again. At a mile and a half from the summit, the expedition's trail crosses today's State Route 174, sometimes called Brush Road. This paved highway leaves US 6 a few miles south of Lynndyl, and leads to some beryllium mines that are located on the southwest side of the Thomas Mountains. Turning to the east near this intersection, the expedition continued to follow the future route of the Weiss Highway. The site of the 3:00 A.M. breakfast stop was about three-quarters of a mile east of the intersection.

While the expedition was stopped for breakfast, Simpson inserted some comments into the report about the route they had just traveled and his feelings about Reese's recent actions;

The route we have come from Tyler's Springs, evidently a crooked one, in Colonel Thomas range; and besides, it makes too great a detour to the north. The true route should evidently pass the range 4 or 5 miles to the south of us, and the indications are, there would be no difficulty. The guide, though he has examined these passes twice, has bungled a great deal to-day.[9]

This route that Simpson decided they should have followed, and which he referred to as the "true" route, would have taken them farther to the east. Leaving Mud Spring, the other route would have gone northeast, rather than north-northeast. After crossing Whirlwind Valley, it would have gone through a pass that is located near the center of the Drum Mountains. This route would have taken them past the deserted mining town of Joy, and then past the northwest side of Mount Laird. Evidently someone, possibly Reese, told Simpson that there was water along this route. Without ever traveling this route himself, Simpson decided to add it to his map. Immediately after the expedition returned to Camp Floyd, Simpson sent Lt. Smith back to this area, instructing him to travel this other route, and to find and develop Marmaduke Spring, which was supposed to be somewhere along this route. Smith, who also referred to this spring as Big Horn Spring, reported that he had found no flowing water. There was some water, but it was in a small basin where a small amount of runoff water had collected. Attempts to dig a well were fruitless.[10] Charles Tuttle's emigrant journal indicates that his party was traveling just behind Lt. Smith's detail through this area, and he and other members of his party had assisted the soldiers in their futile attempts to excavate the spring.[11]

Ironically, there is a good spring not far from where they were digging. It is known as Laird Spring, and is located at the southern base of Mount Laird. On the day that I had hiked across Whirlwind Valley, Lou Dunyon and I drove by it on our way back home. For some time I wondered if it might be the same as Marmaduke Spring, but after making some careful measurements and comparing them to the distance figures in Smith's report, I have concluded that Laird Spring would be too far away from his route. In order to get to Laird Spring, Smith's detail would have had to have gone around the south side of Mount Laird, and an analysis of his distance figures show that his route passed at least a mile and a half to the north of this mountain. Another argument against Laird Spring is that it has too much water. Although it could have been different in 1859, today there is a large pool surrounded by a lush growth of reeds and rushes.

When Phil Miller and I traveled through Whirlwind Valley in 1998, we knew next to nothing about the expedition's route. We simply stayed on the better-traveled road, and unwittingly followed the route that Simpson decided would have been the better one. Crossing the valley in a northeasterly direction, we passed the abandoned mining camp of Joy and entered the canyon that leads to the base of Mount Laird.[12]

At 4.15 A.M., July 29, we left our place of bivouac, and in 2 miles reached second summit of range, whence, bearing magnetically north 25 E., could be seen the Champlin Mountains [Simpson Mountains], for the water in which we were aiming.[13]

In the text of his report, Simpson said they came to a "second summit." The table lists this spot as "Summit east of Thomas's range." This second summit is so slight that it is difficult to be

certain about its highest point, but it is located on the Weiss Highway, a little east of the southeastern base of Topaz Mountain, which makes up the southern tip of the Thomas Range. Looking a little to the north of east from this summit, one can see Keg Mountain and, beyond that, the upper peaks of the Simpson Range. The members of the expedition could see the place they wanted to get to, a place where they knew they could find water. But they still had to find a route that would take them past Keg Mountain, and they still had a long way to go. They were beginning to realize that if they did not find some water soon, the livestock, and perhaps even some of the men, might start dying from thirst.

From the base of Topaz Mountain, the Weiss Highway continues toward the east, and it appears to me that it is at this point that trails researchers have lost Simpson's route. The maps that I have seen do not show very much detail, but they all seem to indicate that the trail continued in an easterly direction until reaching the area of the Sheeprock Mountains. (There is one exception to this, and there will be more about it later.) I have become convinced that this concept of the route is wrong, and the main reason that this error has occurred is because Simpson failed to mention a critical change in the expedition's direction of travel.

I have become quite certain that when Simpson left the second summit, he made an abrupt turn to the north in an attempt to get back to his outbound route. Although he probably did not know exactly where he was, he must have been aware that he was getting relatively close to the expedition's outbound trail, and I think he now wanted to get back to it as soon as possible. If the expedition had not been so desperate to find water, they may have followed the eastern base of the Thomas Range for fourteen miles, where they would have intersected the outbound trail a few miles east of Dugway Pass.

When Simpson left the second summit, he decided to leave the wagons behind and do a little scouting on his own. This may be an indication of how desperate he was getting, because it is one of only two instances in the entire report where he mentions that he did his own scouting. Turning to the north, he headed up the valley toward what he described as a pass. Simpson failed to mention this change in direction, and not being aware of this turn, trails researchers have assumed that the expedition simply continued in an easterly direction along the Weiss Highway. Although this turn in the trail is shown on Simpson's map, without any mention of it in the text of the report, it seems to have gone unnoticed.

> At half past 9 A.M., being about 5 miles in advance of column, hurrying on alone over the desert to the east of Thomas range to examine a pass ahead, I heard a halloa from some one in rear, whom I found to be Mr. McCarthy.[14]

Simpson had traveled about five miles from where he left the wagons, and would have been near the northern tip of Antelope Ridge, when McCarthy caught up with him. At this point Simpson was only about nine miles from the outbound trail, but his plan for getting back to it was quickly discarded when he learned that there was water to be found back toward the south and in the mountains to the east.

> He brought me the intelligence that Stevenson had returned and reported a small spring and some grass to the right of the route we were pursuing, and about 6 miles from the train; also another spring, or rather a couple of springs, 6 miles beyond that again, in the mountains. In consequence of this, I immediately sent word to Lieutenant Murry to divert the train to the first mentioned spring, going there also myself. I found, however at the locality two trifling springs of no value, the water even by digging not being sufficient for half a dozen men. Besides, it had a very poor taste.[15]

Acting on the information brought to him by McCarthy, Simpson altered his direction of travel and headed southeast until he came to two small springs. As it turned out, these springs were not very important to Simpson, and he did not bother to give them a name or even list them as springs in the table of distances. He realized right away that these meager seeps would never provide enough water to be of any use to future travelers, and it would serve no purpose to tell anyone how to find them. Not only did he fail

to describe their location, he did not even mark them on his map. However, it was important for me to know where they were. As valueless as they were to the expedition, they were nevertheless an important turning point on the trail, and the actual alignment of the trail could not be determined until the location of the springs had been identified.

Simpson said the springs were to the right of his position when McCarthy overtook him, but he neglected to say how far away they were. However, his map shows that the trail made a little open-topped loop that drops to the south, turns back to the north, and then turns to the east again. It seems reasonable to assume that Simpson was at the top of the western leg of the loop when McCarthy arrived. After learning about the springs, he would have turned to his right and traveled in something of a southeasterly direction until he reached them. Upon determining that the springs were inadequate for the expedition's needs, he changed directions again and headed back to the north, thus forming a loop with the springs located at its lowest point. This scenario seemed to explain the general alignment of the route, but it did not provide an accurate location for either the loop or the springs. For reasons that will be described shortly, I was confident that I had already determined the location of the next campsite, and I was also aware that Simpson said it was three miles from the trifling springs to this camp. I therefore felt that I should be able to find the site of the springs by working back from the campsite.

MARCH 2002

I traveled to the west side of Keg Mountain, left my SUV near Kane Spring, and, relying on my new GPS receiver to tell me where it was, hiked to a spot that I had calculated to be three miles southwest of Camp 30-E. Then I spent almost an entire day wandering around in ever-expanding circles, working my way outward from where I thought the springs should have been. This was the first time that I had an opportunity to use my GPS, and it was good practice for that, but I found nothing that looked like a spring. By the end of this day, I had concluded that there was something seriously wrong with the information

I was relying on, and finally concluded that it was Simpson's three-mile figure that was the problem. Although I later learned that Simpson made several other fairly serious errors in his distance figures, this was the first time that I had discovered one, and I expended a great deal of effort in making certain that it was Simpson's error rather than mine. After failing to find the springs from the east, I began to examine the western approach again. I started by going all the way back to where Simpson made his turn to the north, and soon decided that I had been looking at the wrong side of Antelope Ridge. Up until this time, I had assumed that after Simpson made this turn he began traveling along the eastern side of Antelope Ridge. He said that he was east of the Thomas Mountains, and I had assumed that he was also east of Antelope Ridge. But as I was taking another look at the maps of this area, I noticed a faint road traveling through the small valley that lies between the Thomas Range and Antelope Ridge. After reaching the northern tip of Antelope Ridge, this faint road turns to the southeast along its eastern base. As I studied it further, I began to realize that the alignment of this road is very similar to the alignment of the trail on Simpson's map. It occurred to me that if Simpson had gone through this valley, he would have been very close to the northern tip of the ridge when McCarthy caught up with him. This scenario would also fit better with Simpson's statement that he was going to examine a pass. The valley becomes quite narrow at its northern end, and can clearly be described as a pass. There is nothing to the east of Antelope Ridge that can be described as a pass.

Assuming that Simpson had been at the northern tip of Antelope Ridge when McCarthy reached him, and had then turned to his right, he would have been traveling in a southeasterly direction, along the eastern base of Antelope Ridge. Looking at Simpson's map, I attempted to estimate the distance from the beginning of the loop to its lowest point, and came up with about a mile and a half. Now going back to my USGS 7.5-minute map, I plotted a line that resembled the first half of Simpson's loop, and marked a spot that was 1.5 miles from the northern tip of Antelope Ridge. I felt that this

was as close as I was going to get. I found that this spot is in a low area, a little less that a half mile north of an unnamed and isolated knoll that lies about midway along the eastern side of Antelope Ridge. My next step was to recheck the distances between the various segments of the day's journey. To my surprise, I discovered that the distance between Simpson's second summit and the possible location of the springs was 6.7 miles. I was surprised because I recognized that this was the figure that appears in the table of distances as the distance between the second summit and the spot that Simpson designated as "In the valley." This could hardly have been a coincidence, and everything fell into place. The trifling springs and the "In the valley" site were the same. Simpson did not think the springs were important enough to be mentioned in the table, but they were at a spot that could be used as one of his "in the valley" locations.

The next thing that I needed to do was to locate the route between the trifling springs and the next campsite. Working on my USGS map and referring to Simpson's map, I plotted a line that resembled the second half of his loop, and then continued on to the location of Camp 30-E. I found that part of the probable route corresponded to a well-traveled dirt road that crosses the valley between the Thomas Range and Keg Mountain. I also found that the distance along this segment of the trail is 7.2 miles, which is the figure that is listed in the table as the distance between the "in the valley" site and the next camp. This was the clincher for the location of the trifling springs. I was now certain that I had found the location of the springs, and just as certain that when Simpson said it was three miles from the springs to the campsite, he should have said 7.2 miles.

AUGUST 2003

Nancy and I took a trip to the area between Topaz Mountain and Keg Mountain to take a look at the section of the route that I now believed the expedition had followed during the late morning and early afternoon of July 29. We found the two-track that leaves the Weiss Highway near Simpson's second summit, and headed north on it as it traveled through the valley following a narrow two-track between Topaz Mountain and Antelope Ridge. After circling the northern tip of Antelope Ridge, we turned to the southeast until we reached the northern base of the isolated knoll. We were unable to find any springs, but we did see two or three grassy areas, which usually indicate the existence of some subsurface moisture.

These springs proving of no value, after resting the mules and putting in fresh ones for those broken down, we attempted to reach with our wagons the springs reported by Stevenson, 6 miles farther on. The teams, however, were too much fagged out to accomplish it, and the consequence was that late in the afternoon, after proceeding 3 miles, we were obliged to halt and encamp for the night in a locality near some triple peaks, where there was neither grass nor water.[16]

In the text of the report, Simpson again fails to indicate the direction they took after leaving the trifling springs, but the map clearly shows that the trail went north for a short distance, then began a sweeping turn that had them heading slightly north of east until they reached the western base of Keg Mountain. In order to understand the expedition's movements through the interior of Keg Mountain, it helps to realize that when looking down from above, the mountain resembles the shape of the letter H. There are two main ridges, nearly equal in size, running north and south, and they are connected near their centers by a ridge that runs east and west. After crossing the valley between Antelope Ridge and Keg Mountain, the expedition reached the base of the western ridge at a point about midway along its length.

November 1998

I drove to the west side of Keg Mountain, and spent the best part of a day exploring the area. I was specifically looking for the triple peaks that Simpson mentioned in his report. I had approached this area by driving north from the Weiss Highway, skirting the western base of the mountain. I was taking my time, driving slowly along the narrow road, looking for a formation that included three separate peaks. After driving

the entire length of the ridge and seeing nothing that would fit that description, I turned around and headed back to the south, intending to get back on the Weiss Highway and leave the area. When I was about halfway back to the highway, the road topped a small rise and there they were, three tipi-shaped peaks, rising up from a common base, and standing in a row. It surprised me to realize that I had driven right by this formation while on my way north. Driving back and forth a couple times to view the peaks from different angles, I soon realized that it is very easy to miss them when facing to the north, but equally difficult to miss them when looking south.

This formation is very distinct, the peaks are of nearly equal size, and they are spaced equal distances apart. But is it truly the formation that Simpson called the Triple Peaks? I am quite certain that it is. I will readily concede that three mountain peaks, in fairly close proximity to each other, is not a rare occurrence, and I am sure that there might be any number of places in Keg Mountain itself where one might look around and see three peaks. However, I am just as certain that anyone who has seen this particular formation would agree that it could have inspired the name "triple peaks." I made no effort to determine the exact location of the campsite during this trip, but since then I have been back to this area several times. After doing a lot more measuring and trail plotting, I have concluded that the campsite was directly north of the triple peak formation, and about a mile from the well-traveled road. The first time that I made my way to the location of the campsite was about a year after finding the triple peaks formation. I parked on the side of the main road and hiked to the general area of the campsite. When I was about halfway there, I came across a very faint two-track coming to the area from the southwest, but I did not explore it any further at that time. A couple of years later, I came back to get a GPS reading and take some photos. At that time, I found where the two-track leaves the main road, and was able to drive to a point about a quarter mile from the campsite. It was during this trip that I explored the area to the north of the campsite, looking for the route that the expedition would have used when it left the triple peaks camp.

At about sundown the mules were driven to the water and grass supposed to be 3 miles distant, in two herds.... We have been traveling since yesterday at half-past 2, or for about 30 hours; the weather has been warm, and the mules have had no water. The consequence is that all are fagged out, and we feel that we must reach water soon, or the expedition become demoralized and we fail of getting through to Camp Floyd across the Great Salt Lake Desert by a new return-route, as I had hoped.... Journey from Tyler's Springs 36.9 miles.[17]

The end of this very long day found most of the men resting in this waterless camp, while a few others and almost all of the livestock were somewhere in the mountain to the east, still trying to reach the elusive springs that had been reported by Stevenson. Although Stevenson had indicated that the other springs were only six miles beyond the trifling springs, the actual distance turned out to be closer to twelve miles. Nothing was heard from the men who had been sent to find the springs until the following morning.

Eleven

Triple Peaks to Camp Floyd

Camp 30-E. The campsite was in the foreground. This area is in a large cove about midway along the western base of Keg Mountain. *"Late in the afternoon...we were obliged to halt and encamp for the night in a locality near some triple peaks, where there was neither grass nor water."*

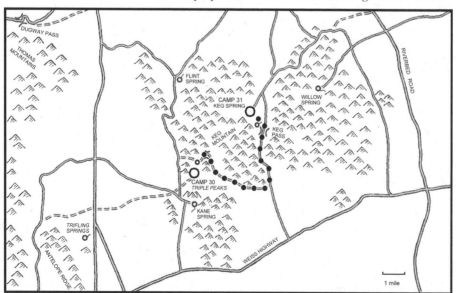

JULY 30, 1859

July 30, Camp No. 30, near Triple Peaks.—We strike our course northeastwardly to one of the springs we hoped to reach yesterday. The animals look sorry enough, and if they do not get water soon, must perish. On our way we were met by Mr. Reese with the remaining animals. He reports he found the other spring through the happy circumstance of meeting a crippled Indian, who showed it to him, just at the time he was despairing of finding it. It is about a mile to the northwest of the first spring. After proceeding in a general northern direction 5.6 miles, or 2.6 miles farther than Stevenson said it would be, we came to one of the springs and encamped.[1]

Previous to setting out that morning, Private Kennedy, at about 9:00 o'clock returned to the camp and reported that the group he had been with had not been able to find the spring they were looking for until after it had gotten light. When they finally found it, they discovered that it was just a small seep, and they would have to do some digging before the animals would be able to get any water from it. The problem was, they did not have anything to dig with. Simpson immediately instructed Sergeant Miller to take some shovels to the spring so that the men who had remained there could dig it out. This apparently did some good, because at about noon the herd that had been at this spring arrived back in camp. Someone in this group reported that the other herd, which included Simpson's own horse, had strayed away during the night. Reese and the other men who had been with that herd were now searching for the missing animals.

Simpson ordered the returning mules to be hitched to the wagons immediately so that they could get moving again. At that time there were not enough animals at the camp to make up teams for all the wagons, so one of the wagons had to be left behind until a team could be sent back for it.

Simpson made some additional comments about the crippled Indian and the efforts the men were making to get water out of the springs. He returned to the subject of the day's journey, and added some further information about the route.

Our route to-day was across a divide about a mile from last camp, and then down a cañon, to within a mile of Sevier Lake Desert on southeast side of these mountains, and then up a ravine across the crest again of the mountain to the north slope of cañon, leading down to Salt Lake Desert, or Sevier Lake Desert, as the dividing rim is scarcely perceptible. Road Good. Journey 5.6 miles.[2]

This proved to be a difficult description to follow. A major part of the difficulty was caused by Simpson's mileage figures. After studying these descriptions at length, plotting various alternate routes on the map, and making a number of trips to the area, I have concluded that the route they followed during this day's travel was as described below.

Upon leaving the camp, they headed in a northerly direction, climbing up the slope through a shallow draw. There is no road or trail in this area today, but I have hiked it a couple times in both directions, and do not believe that this route would have presented any problems for the wagons. After about a quarter of a mile, they rounded the point of a low ridge and made a turn to the northeast. After crossing a low spot on the ridge, they descended its northern slope through another draw. At about six-tenths of a mile from the camp, they reached the bottom of a shallow canyon that runs down the western slope of the mountain. Today, a seldom-used jeep trail follows the almost-always-dry streambed along the bottom of this canyon. When the expedition reached this streambed, they turned to the right and began climbing toward the main ridge of the western half of Keg Mountain. After traveling another half mile, they reached the summit of a low pass that is just slightly over a mile from the campsite. Immediately after crossing this summit, they turned to the southeast. Following a route that went down another shallow canyon, they came to a relatively flat area that forms a large cove in the south side of the mountain. This was the section of the route that Simpson was talking about when he said they went "down a cañon, to within a mile of Sevier Lake Desert on southeast side of these mountains." Here they turned in an easterly direction, keeping as close to the southern base of the rugged foothills as they could. At about four and a quarter miles from camp, they came to the mouth of a narrow canyon that leads northward to Keg Pass. Simpson was referring to this canyon when he said they went up a "ravine." Turning into this canyon, they crossed the summit at Keg Pass and, after descending the northern slope for a short distance, came to a small spring and began to set up a camp.

JUNE 1999

Knowing that my father-in-law had spent a lot of time in this part of the country when he worked as a government trapper, I asked him if he knew of any trails that crossed the western ridge of Keg Mountain. He said that he was aware of only one way to get across this ridge, and he would be happy to show it to me. A few days later, we drove to the west side of Keg Mountain by following a road that comes from the north. When we reached a point about midway along the ridge, we turned eastward into the mountain, following the bottom of a narrow ravine. It was plain to see that during a heavy rainstorm, the ravine would be filled with water, but it was also apparent that it was regularly used as a jeep trail. After about a mile and three-quarters, we crossed the ridge and began to drop down into the large cove on the south side of the mountain. It was quite apparent that the expedition's wagons could have followed this route across Keg Mountain's western ridge. Today's jeep trail does not cross the ridge at the same place that the expedition did, but makes a turn to the north a short distance before reaching the summit, and then goes another two-tenths of a mile before crossing the ridge at a slightly lower spot. This little variation in the route makes a less steep approach to the top of the ridge, but the spot where it crosses the ridge is too far from the campsite. Simpson said the summit was a mile from the camp. The summit that is on the trail that is used today is 1.3 miles from where I believe they camped, while the summit that I believe was crossed by the expedition is slightly less than 1.1 miles.

I am quite certain that this route is the only way that the expedition could have gotten to the interior of Keg Mountain from its western side. But Simpson's distance figures for this section of

the route do not work. In the text of the report, Simpson stated that the distance between the two camps was 5.6 miles. Differing only slightly, the table of distances lists the mileage as 5.7 miles. When I measure it, I get 8.6 miles. Feeling that this discrepancy was too much to simply ignore, I spent a considerable amount of time and effort attempting to find a shorter route through this rugged terrain. I finally had to conclude that there is no other feasible route, and that Simpson's figures for this section of the trail were wrong.

When the expedition reached what Simpson called the ravine, they turned to the north and climbed to the summit of Keg Pass. From there they dropped down the north slope of the ridge for about two-tenths of a mile, and came to the small spring where the soldiers had been digging. Upon reaching this spot, they immediately went about setting up camp, but it did not take them long to realize that their problems were far from over.

Greatly to our disappointment I found it affording but a very small quantity of water; scarcely enough for cooking purposes. Every effort was made, however, by cleaning out the cavity, to collect the water with the greatest possible economy; but after all we could do we could only water the animals by successive bucketfuls, and that at intervals of several minutes. At this rate it was evident that the animals would die before we could satisfy them.[3]

During my many visits to this area over the past few years, I have never found any surface water at the spot where this spring must have been. However, it must be kept in mind that all of these visits have taken place during a period of fairly serious drought. Even though I have never seen any water here, I have observed a good growth of a type of bunch grass that is usually found where there is some subsurface moisture.

I then visited, with Lieutenants Putnam and Murry, the other spring, about a mile to the northwest, and found scarcely a pint of water in it. Notice, bearing magnetically N. 20 E., probably 12 miles off, in the Champlin Mountains [Simpson Mountains], what appears to be a creek [Death Canyon Creek] and plenty of grass.[4]

The first sentence of the above comment makes it very clear there were two different springs in this area. The first one was the slow seep just below the Keg Pass summit. The second, which Simpson at first referred to as the "other spring," was located about a mile to the northwest, and it was the one that the crippled Indian had shown to Reese. There can be little doubt that this second spring was today's Keg Spring, and it is the one that Simpson named Good Indian Spring in honor of Quah-not, the crippled Indian, who lived near it.

At first glance, Simpson seems to contradict himself regarding the location of the camp. First, he states that immediately after reaching the first spring they set up camp: "After proceeding in a general northern direction…we came to one of the springs *and encamped*" (emphasis added). But on his map, in the table of distances, and in two separate places in the text, he indicates that the camp was at Good Indian Spring, which was the second spring that he came to. After wondering about this apparent contradiction for quite some time, it finally occurred to me that they could have camped at both places. Since neither of the springs provided much water, it would make sense for the expedition to have used both of them. Perhaps some of the men stayed at the first spring, while others moved on to Keg Spring. Although it is doubtful that the exact circumstances will ever be known for certain, I think it is quite likely that the main camp was at Keg Spring.

Now to get back to the events that occurred after the expedition arrived at the first spring. When Simpson realized that this small spring was never going to provide enough water for their needs, he took Lieutenants Putnam and Murry and went to Keg Spring. Although they found very little water, their trip was not completely fruitless. When they reached the spring, they could look across the valley to the east and see the Simpson Mountains and a stream flowing down its southwestern slope. They were looking at Death Canyon, which is in clear view from the ridge just above Keg Spring, but out of sight behind the eastern ridge of Keg Mountain from the first spring. An unlimited source of water was now within sight. The next thing to do was to get the animals to the water. The three officers immediately returned to the first spring, where the main body of the expedition was waiting.

As soon as possible send all the mules except the weakest; which can be watered here, to said creek, under care of four dragoons and eight teamsters, Mr. Reese and the old crippled Indian we have found here going along as guides.… The spring which he showed us, and near which he has his wick-e-up, I call the Good Indian Spring, after this Good Samaritan Indian.… The mountains in which we are encamped I call after Major Irvin McDowell, assistant adjutant-general.… The springs near us are represented by the good Indian as having been made by some horse-thieves (white men) about a year and a half ago.[5]

When Simpson returned to the first spring, he immediately detailed a few of the soldiers and teamsters to take most of the animals to the water at the base of the Simpson Mountains. It was probably at about this time that Simpson decided to move at least a part of the expedition to Keg Spring. Due to the fact that the two springs were providing enough water for the men's needs, the main body of the expedition remained at these camps for an extra day and night. Someone was sent back to retrieve the wagon that had been left behind at the triple peaks campsite. Everyone else settled down to spend some time recovering from the rigors of the past few days. William Lee's journal gives a brief description of this day's events:

Saturday, July 30th. Did not leave camp until afternoon, the mules having stampeded in search of water, not having had any all night. We at last started with a majority of the mules, and having to put in a part of the riding mules, we left one of the wagons behind, and marching five and two-thirds miles, came to camp at a small spring with just enough water for cooking purposes. The mules were driven twelve miles to a spring for water. It seems this place has been used as a hiding place for horse thieves and stolen animals. Some of the men found a fine large stone corralle up in the mountains near here, which Pete, our Indian, thinks was built by Tintic (a Ute Indian) for a large number of stolen horses.[6]

The concept that I had developed relating to the expedition's route through Keg Mountain had been based solely on my own reading of Simpson's report, and my visits to the area. It was not until much later that I learned that someone else also believed that the expedition had traveled into the interior of Keg Mountain. In 2002, I was looking at the index for the *Utah Historical Quarterly*, and noticed a reference to an article about Good Indian Spring. I immediately followed up on this, and learned that in 1984, the *Quarterly* had published an article written by Owen Bennion, in which he concluded that Simpson's Good Indian Spring was the same as today's Keg Spring.[7] Bennion had spent several years living and working on a family ranch in the Old Riverbed area, just east of Keg Mountain, and had traveled into the interior of the mountain on numerous occasions.

Although Bennion and I had both concluded that Good Indian Spring and Keg Spring are one and the same, our theories about how the expedition got to this location are different. The map that accompanies his article shows the trail as following the Weiss Highway from Topaz Mountain to the south side of Keg Mountain, then turning north to go over Keg Pass, instead of crossing the western ridge of the mountain, as I believe it did. (See map for July 28 and 29.) As I see it, the problem with Bennion's theory of the route is that he does not account for the trifling springs loop on Simpson's map, the location of the Triple Peaks camp, the divide that was crossed at one mile from this campsite, and the fact that after crossing the divide, they traveled in a southeasterly direction down a canyon. Bennion's route and my route come together at the point where the expedition started up the ravine that leads to Keg Pass.

Also of interest is a footnote to Bennion's article that relates to the origin of Keg Spring's name:

My father, Glynn S. Bennion (a historian and rancher), once told me that Keg Spring was so named because of a keg, half buried in the mud of the spring, found by the California immigrants who camped there on their way to the gold fields. Keg Mountain got its name from the spring.[8]

It is certainly possible that this local legend has some basis in fact. Although they were not necessarily going to the gold fields, we do know that some emigrants did follow Simpson's route to Keg Spring. In his 1859 journal, Edward Mathews indicated that his small party camped at what he called "Indian Springs" on the night of August 15.[9] A few weeks later, Bolivar Roberts, a Chorpenning employee, reported that he had found an emigrant party camped at "Indian Spring."[10]

AUGUST 1, 1859

AUGUST 1, CAMP NO. 31, GOOD INDIAN SPRING. — *9 A.M. The mules which were sent to water night before last are momentarily expected, but we think it best to get the mules we have with us to the next water as soon as possible, since the spring where we are is so small that, without the use of troughs to collect and economize the water, but few can be watered satisfactorily. The civil portion of my party, with three wagons, therefore, move forward, leaving the balance to follow us as soon as the other mules arrive.*[11]

ON THE MORNING of August 1, even though some of the animals had not yet been brought back to the camp, Simpson decided to start moving again. The men hitched up the teams that were available, and began moving down the north slope of Keg Mountain.

Pass down cañon, in a northwardly direction, through a thick grove of cedars, over a rolling country, skirting McDowell Mountains to our right, and in about seven miles reach a desert valley or plain running southeastwardly from Great Salt Lake Valley into Sevier Valley. In about two miles more, reach west foot of bench of Champlin Mountains, and encamp at half past 2 within about two miles of good and abundant water and grass in cañon of the mountains to which the mules are driven. Journey 9.2 miles.... The spring, creek and canyon near our camp I call after Assistant Surgeon Thomas H. Williams, United States Army.[12]

The expedition was following what is now a fairly well-traveled road down the north slope

Camp 31-E. Keg Spring. This was the second spring and the second place that they set up camp after crossing Keg Pass. *"I then visited, with Lieutenants Putnam and Murry, the other spring about a mile to the northwest. . . . I call [it] Good Indian Spring, after the Good Samaritan Indian."*

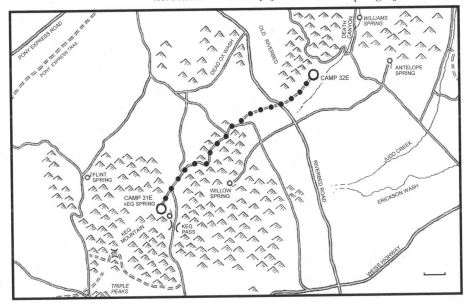

Wagon ruts found by the author and Jim Hall about a tenth of a mile west of Camp 32-E. The cut-downs are difficult to see in the photo but are very distinct when looking at them on-site. Jim stands at the spot where the wagon road crosses the bottom of the gully.

of Keg Mountain. This road soon begins to circle toward the east, and eventually to the south. The expedition left this road when they were 5.6 miles from the camp, just before it makes a bend to the south. After leaving today's road, the expedition's route took them along the north side of a shallow draw until they reached the valley floor. The very bottom of this valley was once the channel of a sizeable northward-flowing stream, and is now known as Old Riverbed. After crossing this area, they began climbing the southwestern slope of the Simpson Mountains. After climbing up the slope for about a mile, they went into camp a short distance to the south of a long and narrow knoll that projects into Old Riverbed, and is aptly named the Snow Plow. This campsite was about two miles southwest of the mouth

of Death Canyon, and about a half mile northwest of the streambed that is now known as Death Canyon Wash. Simpson gave the name of Williams to the creek, the canyon, and a spring. Both Simpson and William Lee mentioned that the camp was about two miles from Williams Spring. In his report relating to his post-expedition work detail, Lt. Smith said the campsite was three miles from Williams Spring.[13] This spring must have been located in Death Canyon Wash, about two miles from the campsite, and about a mile from the mouth of Death Canyon. It is not marked on modern maps, and I have not been able to find it. The nearest spring that can be found in this region today is Antelope Spring, which is up high on the bench, and nearly four miles from the campsite.

SEPTEMBER 2004

I had been examining some aerial photos of the eastern side of Keg Mountain when I observed a faint trail that I had never noticed before. This trace begins at the bend where the expedition's route leaves today's road, and continues down the slope to the bottom of the valley. I had previously believed that the expedition had followed the bottom of the drainage, and I had hiked this route about a year before. The track I now saw on the photo is on the ridge on the north side of the wash. A few days later, Nancy and I drove to this area and, after a little searching, found the almost totally abandoned two-track at the point where it crosses Riverbed Road.

Turning west onto this trail, we headed up the slope toward Keg Mountain. The going was very slow, and on two or three occasions, I had to get out of our SUV and scout ahead to make sure we were still on the trail. We eventually reached today's well-traveled road near the bend. Another section of the trail had been located and traveled.

MARCH 2007

Jim Hall and I made a trip to the southwestern base of the Simpson Mountains to visit the site of Camp 32-E. I had been in this general area several times before, but after some additional study of Google Earth images, I decided that I had placed the campsite too far from the base of the mountain. The purpose of this trip was to make an on-site visit to the new location, to see if it was a place where they could have camped and, if so, to take photographs and GPS readings. Relying on my GPS to take us to the site, we left Riverbed Road and began following a faint two-track in an easterly direction. We were able to drive to a spot that was just a little over a half mile from the new location. Leaving my SUV on the old two-track, we set off on foot in a southeasterly direction and soon arrived at the campsite. We found that it was a smooth and almost level area that would have been a good location for a camp. Looking to the east, we could see a gap in the old lake-level bench, through which the stream coming out of Death Canyon would have flowed. Looking to the west, we could see the old two-track that marks the expedition's trail as it comes down the east slope of Keg Mountain. The trail was heading straight toward us, but it disappeared after crossing the bottom of the valley. Since Simpson's map shows that this section of the trail traveled a straight line, we decided to walk toward the section of the trail that we could see. There were no traces of a trail near the campsite, but we wanted to see if we could find anything farther to the west. It did not take long. After walking for a little over a tenth of a mile, we came to a shallow gully and found clearly visible road cut-downs on both banks. After another hundred yards, we came to a slightly deeper gully, and it also had cut-downs on both banks. Although no trail is visible approaching or leaving either of the gullies, the cut-downs clearly mark the expedition's route as it approached the campsite.

AUGUST 2, 1859

AUGUST 2, CAMP NO. 32, WILLIAM'S SPRING.—*At 5 A.M., after getting breakfast, the whole party moved forward; general course eastwardly, around the southwest base of Champlin Mountains [Simpson Mountains]....At half past 12 we reach a creek [Judd Creek] flowing from the Champlin Mountains, upon which we encamp....I call it after Maj. Henry Prince, paymaster United States Army. The road to-day, in places, stony and rough, and occasionally hilly, on account of ravines....The animals have been scarcely able to get the wagons to camp, so much have they suffered for the past few days on account of the absence of water and incessant traveling.*[14]

THIS WAS ONE of the few times that Simpson failed to mention the distance traveled in the narrative portion of the report. But it is found in the table of distances, and it was 8.7 miles. A straight line between the two camps would measure six and a half miles, but the nature of the terrain forced them to take a route that circled around the southern base of the Simpson Mountains. Although there are several roads crisscrossing this area, except for the last mile and a half, none of them follows the route that the expedition traveled during the first seven miles of this day's journey.

Camp 32-E. Near the southwestern base of Simpson Mountains: *"reach west foot of bench of Champlin Mountains, and encamp. . . within about two miles of good and abundant water and grass."* The animals would have been taken through the gap in the center of the photo.

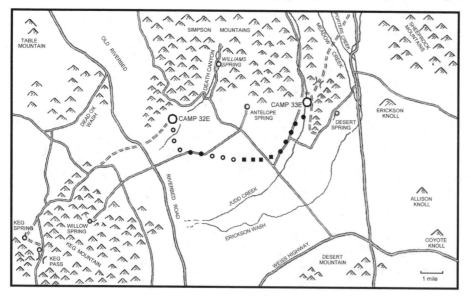

Judd Creek is marked by the band of dark willows in the center of the photo. An old two-track can be seen approaching the crossing.

The stream that Simpson called Prince's Creek is now known as Judd Creek. Several abandoned ranch buildings can be found near the mouth of Judd Canyon, and an occasionally used two-track road comes from the southeast and crosses the stream at this point. Simpson's map indicates that the campsite was on the east bank of the stream. It appears to me that it was about a quarter of a mile downstream from today's crossing, and about the same distance upstream from where traces of a completely abandoned road crossed the creek at one time. Between the two crossings, and for a couple of miles below the abandoned crossing, steep banks make access to the stream difficult, if not impossible. But at the abandoned crossing, the banks on both sides are considerably less steep, and the old road is still visible. After fording the creek, the expedition made its way upstream for about three-tenths of a mile and made camp for the night.

This camp would be Simpson's last. The next day he and Ute Pete would leave the wagons and ride all the way to Camp Floyd without stopping for an overnight camp. The other members of the expedition members would spend two more nights on the trail. Simpson's report does not say anything about the two remaining camps, but their locations are listed in the table of distances.

AUGUST 3, 1859

AUGUST 3, CAMP NO. 33, PRINCE'S CREEK.— *Start at quarter to 6, in advance of party for Camp Floyd, Pete accompanying. Continue up Prince*

Creek for half a mile, and then leave it to left, and pass up a branch cañon, filled with cedars, one-half mile more, to summit of pass, These cañons are of good grade. From summit of pass by pretty good descent, get into a valley, which I call after Maj. Fitz John Porter, assistant adjutant-general.[15]

FROM THE SOUTHEAST CORNER of the Simpson Mountains, a relatively low ridge extends even further southward for about two miles. Judd Creek flows through a shallow canyon that lies between the main part of the mountain and this ridge, and Camp 33-E was located about midway along its length. A two-track road circles around the southern tip of the ridge, and I had traveled on it a number of times before I ever started researching Simpson's trail. When I began studying Simpson's route, I assumed that this road around the south end of the ridge would have been the expedition's route. However, as soon as I started making measurements of the distances, it became apparent that this assumption was wrong. I found that a route around the tip of this ridge would be at least three miles longer than the distance given by Simpson, so I began looking for possible alternatives. As I carefully re-read Simpson's description of the route he traveled that day, I realized that I had overlooked his statement that after leaving the camp, he had traveled upstream. His exact words were "continue *up* Prince Creek for half a mile, and then leave it to left, and pass up a branch cañon" (emphasis added). This statement eliminated the possibility that he had gone around the southern tip of the ridge, because in order to do that he would have had to have traveled downstream from the campsite. So I began looking at the area to the north of the campsite, and soon found a small canyon cutting into the ridge in a northeasterly direction. Taking some measurements along this route, I found that the distance matched Simpson's mileage figures almost exactly.

JULY 2000

During my next trip to the Judd Creek area, I drove past Desert Spring and around the southern tip of the ridge, as I had done many times in the past, but this time I kept to the right instead of crossing the creek near the abandoned ranch buildings. After a short distance, I reached the mouth of the little canyon. To my surprise, I found myself on an old road that was heading into the canyon. Although it was rough and rocky, and I had to keep dodging the juniper trees that overhang the narrow road, I soon found myself at the summit of the ridge. This road appears to have seen a lot of use in the past, but has obviously been abandoned for many years. Just below the summit, on the north side of the slope, an ungated fence has been built across the road, and just beyond that, the road has been completely washed out for several yards. Turning around at the summit, I drove back down the canyon, then back around the southern tip of the ridge, then north again along its eastern base. A little exploring in this area failed to turn up a road that would take me back to the trail, so I parked at Black Spring and began hiking the three and a half miles back to the summit of the little canyon. I headed southwest on an abandoned road that turned out to be the same as the road that crosses the ridge above Judd Creek. Near the center of the valley, I lost the old road for a short distance, but it reappeared as I approached the foothills, and I was able to follow it all the way to the summit. Modern USGS maps show a jeep trail between the summit and Meadow Creek, but the sections of the road that I found between Judd Creek and the summit, and between Meadow Creek and Black Spring, do not appear on the maps.

Simpson referred to the area lying east of the Simpson Mountains and south of Erickson Pass as Porter Valley, naming it after a major in the US Army. Although this name is not in common use today, many of those who are aware of it are under the mistaken impression that it came from Orrin Porter Rockwell, who lived for some time on a ranch that was located about five miles to the north, in the south end of Skull Valley. But Rockwell did not stake out his ranch until several years after Simpson had named the little valley after the officer who was General Johnston's adjutant.[16]

Proceeding northwardly through this valley, in 2.3 miles cross Porter's Creek; 2.7 miles more brings us to the slight rim or divide [Erickson Pass] between

Camp 33-E. On the east bank of Judd Creek. The pass that the expedition used to get into Erickson Valley can be seen in the center of the photo.

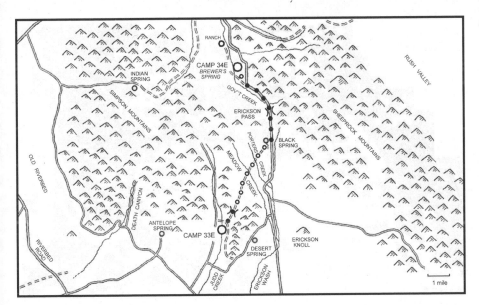

AUGUST 3, 1859

The author believes that this spring in the channel of Government Creek is the one that Simpson named Brewer's Spring.

Skull Valley and Porter Valley, and 3.2 miles more to a spring, which I call after Assistant Surgeon Charles Brewer, United States Army.[17]

In Porter Valley, at about two miles northeast of the summit of the ridge, Simpson's trail crossed a rather sizable streambed that is marked on the maps as Meadow Creek. This was not the creek that he mentioned in the report. After another half mile, he came to the stream that he called Porter's Creek. Meadow Creek is almost always dry, but Porter's Creek is fed by a couple of small springs, and always has at least a small amount of water flowing in it. Perhaps this explains why Simpson did not mention Meadow Creek. After crossing Porter's Creek, Simpson and Ute Pete continued in a northeasterly direction until they reached today's Erickson Pass Road near Black Spring. Turning

directly north here, they crossed Erickson Pass and dropped down the northern slope into the southern end of Skull Valley, where they came to Brewer's Spring. Lee's journal does not mention a name for the spring, but he does say that it was in Tintic Valley, which seems to have been the name for the entire area to the south of Rush Valley at that time.[18]

In the text of his report, Simpson stated that after crossing a rim or divide, which is clearly Erickson Pass, he traveled 3.2 miles and came to a spring, which he named for the assistant surgeon, Charles Brewer. The table gives a different mileage figure, indicating that it was 2.8 miles from the summit to the spring. I have been unable to find a reasonable explanation for this discrepancy, but I am quite certain that I have found Brewer's Spring. At 2.8 miles northwest from Erickson Pass, right in the channel of

Government Creek, there is a spring that produces a constant and fairly substantial flow of water.

Simpson mentioned the spring in his report, but did not say anything about a stream. However, Lt. Smith did mention the existence of a creek in the report of his return trip to the Drum Mountain area. Two weeks following the completion of this assignment, Smith addressed a report to Simpson in which he said that he had followed "Brewer's Creek" while traveling southward on a new trail. This new trail left the expedition's outbound route at the western base of Lookout Pass, and eventually brought Smith to Brewer's Spring, which was where Simpson and the expedition had made an abrupt turn to the east. Smith's report included a description of the route he followed to Brewer's Spring.

On the morning of the 7th I moved west, through Johnston's Pass, to its west foot. Here, as directed by you, I left the beaten road, and turning to the left, moved up a ravine which leads into Johnston's Pass from the south [Little Valley], and furnishes a path thence into the ravine of Brewer's Spring and Creek. The distance by the odometer from the point where I left Johnston's Pass to the point where I struck the ravine of Brewer's Creek is eight miles and four-tenths....From the point where I struck the ravine of Brewer's Creek I moved up that ravine to your recent return trail from California, a distance of three miles.[19]

It appears that Smith's route took him south through Little Valley, then southwest until he struck Government Creek. Following Government Creek upstream for three miles, he came to the expedition's trail at the point where it turned to the east. This was also the place where the expedition camped on the night of August 3, and I am certain that this campsite was near the presently-unnamed spring that I found in the streambed of Government Creek. Although there is an abandoned road that leads from Erickson Pass Road to the area where this spring is located, a locked gate prevents vehicular access.

September 2001

Louis Dunyon and I drove to the Government Creek area in an attempt to find Brewer's Spring.

We had examined a USGS 7.5-minute map of the area, and had found the symbol for a spring in the Government Creek channel, and it appeared that this spring was located at the correct distance from Erickson Pass. When we reached the area, we found a four-wheel-drive trail that took us to the creek at a spot about a quarter mile downstream from the spring. We walked upstream along the east bank of the creek until we came to the general area of the spring. We had a GPS receiver with us, programmed with the approximate coordinates of the spring, but we could not be entirely certain that we ever arrived at the right place. The problem was that on that day, there was a substantial flow of water coming down the creek, and we could not tell whether or not there was a spring in the channel. Three years later, near the end of a very dry summer, I returned to this area again. There was no water in the streambed above the spring, and this time the existence of the spring was obvious. As soon as I saw it, I realized that Lou and I had been at the correct place during our earlier trip. In the very bottom of the streambed, I found a pool of water about six feet in diameter and about three or four feet in depth. Flowing out of the pool was enough water to produce a stream that was nearly a foot deep.

The names Brewer's Spring and Brewer's Creek did not survive for long. By 1864, emigrant journals were mentioning a Government Spring, which I believe was about three miles to the north of Brewer's Spring.[20] Some maps from the mid-1860s show a Government Spring in this general area.[20] It is probably safe to assume that the nearby stream had begun to be called Government Creek at about this same time. What might be a clue to the origin of this name is found in Charles Tuttle's journal. On August 8, 1859, he wrote: "We encamped for noon on a small stream where there was a large herd of cattle kept they are principally cattle which have been brought through by *government* trains and Freight Trains" (emphasis added).[21] The earliest map showing Government Creek that I have seen is an 1873 mining district map that I found in the Hutchings Museum in Lehi, Utah, but it does not show Government Spring.

Camp 34-E. The campsite was in the foreground, on the east bank of Government Creek. Brewer's Spring is in the streambed at the end of the fence that slants across the left side of the photo.

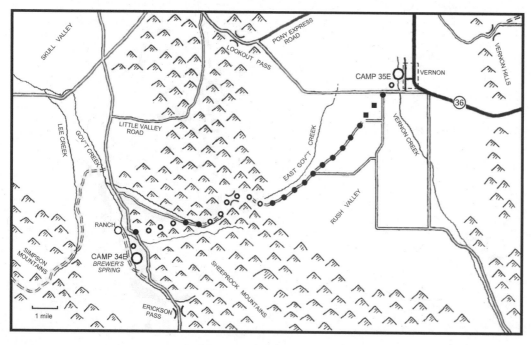

AUGUST 3 AND 4, 1859

ON AUGUST 3, Simpson and Ute Pete passed by Brewer's Spring and climbed over the Sheeprock Mountains to the east. The main body of the expedition traveled this section of the route on August 4, 1859.

Turning northeast, or to the right, in 2.3 miles you reach, by a pretty good ascent, the summit of the Guyot range [Sheeprock Mountains], by what I call Oak Pass [Government Creek Pass], about 5 miles south of General Johnston's Pass [Lookout Pass]. This pass leads, across the Guyot range of mountains, to Rush Valley.... Two miles from summit reach east foot of pass in Rush Valley.[22]

I have been unable to find a name for the summit of this pass on any modern maps, but the 1873 mining district map shows it as "Govt Cañon." It is found on the ridge of the Sheeprock Mountains, between East Government Creek and Government Creek, and very close to six miles south of Lookout Pass. My USGS maps did not indicate a road going over this pass, and after making a couple of trips to the base of the mountain on both sides of the pass, I realized that if I wanted to follow Simpson's trail across this mountain, it would have to be on foot.

SEPTEMBER 1999

I drove part way up the canyon of East Government Creek, and then hiked for about a mile to the summit. A few days later, I drove to the west side of the mountain and part of the way up Government Creek, then hiked about two miles to the summit. On both sides of the pass, I found indications of what appeared to be a long-abandoned road. On the east side, the trail was quite well defined all the way to the summit. On the west side, the traces were very faint, and almost nonexistent in some places. I am certain that this was the route used by the Simpson expedition, and it is almost certain that many other wagons also traveled this trail. The 1873 mining map indicates that it was a usable wagon road. In the summer of 2004, I made another trip up the east side of the mountain to obtain an on-site GPS reading at the summit. I

found that ATV riders have discovered this trail, and what had been a fading track in 1999 has now become a well-worn trail that is channeling run-off water from the slopes above. The old trail is becoming a deep wash. I do not know what is happening on the western slope, but I fear the worst.

AUGUST 3 AND 5, 1859

From east foot of pass strike northeastwardly across Rush Valley for Camp Floyd Pass, in 6.7 miles crossing Meadow Creek, a flowing stream, 4 feet wide and 6 inches deep, and along which are good camping places.[23]

WHEN I FIRST ATTEMPTED to plot the trail across Rush Valley, I had assumed that Simpson had turned to the northeast at the mouth of East Government Canyon and had followed the streambed for some distance. As a result, I initially placed Simpson's crossing of Meadow Creek a little over a mile north of the town of Vernon. The site of this crossing is important, because it is also the place where the main body of the expedition camped that night. Finding that there are no roads that follow, or even come close to, the route that I had plotted, I hiked all the way from the mouth of East Government Creek Canyon to where I thought the crossing and campsite would have been. Three years later, I found that I had been wrong. I was looking at some aerial photos of the area, attempting to make some more precise measurements, when I noticed some faint marks that appeared to be a trail of some sort. I could see that this faint trail leaves today's road at the mouth of East Government Creek Canyon, but instead of following the streambed, it continues in a fairly straight line for some distance. Following these marks on the photos, I found that they gradually turned to the northeast, and then faded out as they approached Vernon. By extending a line from the portion of the trail that is still visible, I found that it comes to Vernon Creek where the stream is the nearest to the center of the town. Taking some measurements on the map, I found that this trail reaches the creek at the distance that was indicated by Simpson.

OCTOBER 2005

A few days after finding the marks on the aerial photos, Jim Hall and I drove to the area southwest of Vernon to see if we could find the trail. He parked his vehicle just south of the town and rode with me to the mouth of East Government Creek Canyon. Heading east on foot, we immediately found the old road and were able to follow it almost all the way to Vernon. We found that in a few short sections, the trail has entirely disappeared, and in one long section, it has become a stream-capture channel that is nearly four feet deep in some places. I am certain that this trail was once a well-traveled wagon road, and because it fits so well with Simpson's mileage figures, I am convinced that it was the route he followed through this area. When I examined the 1873 mining district map from the museum in Lehi, I found that it shows what appears to be a usable road that comes from the Judd Creek area, crosses the Sheeprock Mountains through "Gov't Cañon," passes through Vernon and Five Mile Pass, and ends at Camp Floyd. In other words, the 1873 road follows Simpson's route all the way from the southern base of the Simpson Mountains to Camp Floyd.

In the text of his report, Simpson mentioned that he and Ute Pete crossed Meadow Creek on their way to Camp Floyd, but we have to look in the table of distances to learn that the expedition made an overnight camp on this stream, almost certainly at the point where Simpson crossed it. The name of this stream has changed a couple of times over the years. Before the ranchers of the area began to divert the water for irrigation, the stream flowed in a northerly direction through the entire length of Rush Valley. Simpson called this stream Meadow Creek, and it would seem that this name had been in use for some time. However, a map of western Utah that was published by the US Army Corps of Engineers in 1872 indicates that the name was Faust Creek.[24] The 1873 mining district map shows it as Vernon Creek. This stream begins in the interior of the Sheeprock Mountains, about fifteen miles south of the town of Vernon, and before the water began to be diverted, it sometimes flowed all the way to the northern end of Rush Valley, where it emptied into Stockton Lake. However, even

then, the stream occasionally dried up before reaching the lake. When Simpson was camped on this stream on May 3, during the expedition's outbound trip, he described the stream as follows: "This stream, which is of gentle current, is so narrow that you can jump across it, and is but a few inches in depth. It runs northerly about ten miles and sinks."[25] He knew about the location of the sink because he had traveled through this area the previous October. At that time the sink of Meadow Creek would have been in the vicinity of the now-abandoned community of Center.[26]

Today the stream that has been known as Meadow Creek, Vernon Creek, and Faust Creek has become two different streams. In the southern part of Rush Valley, it is Vernon Creek, and it dries up when it reaches a point just west of the town of Vernon. About four miles north, the second stream, which is now known as Faust Creek, comes to the surface and begins to flow up the valley, where it passes through Atherly Reservoir and dries up within two or three miles to the north. The 1858 expedition made two camps on what they called Meadow Creek. On October 19, during the westbound portion of this trip, they camped on the creek about two and a half miles north of where Pony Express Road intersects with SR 36.[27] Eight days later, while on the way back to Camp Floyd, they camped somewhere near the site of the Faust Pony Express station.[28] The 1859 expedition also made two camps on this stream that they called Meadow Creek. During their outbound journey, they camped on the present-day Faust Creek section. The eastbound camp was about six miles to the south, on the Vernon Creek section.

After crossing Vernon Creek, Simpson cut through the low pass in the Vernon Hills, then followed a straight-line route across the eastern part of Rush Valley and merged with his outbound route at Five Mile Pass. From there he continued to the east, and arrived back at Camp Floyd on the evening of August 3, 1859. The main body of the expedition camped on Vernon Creek on the night of August 4, then traveled to Camp Floyd on August 5.

After I had determined that Camp 35-E was directly west of Vernon, rather than a mile north of town, I had to find a new route through the

Camp 35-E. In southern Rush Valley, near the town of Vernon, on the east bank of Vernon Creek. *"From east foot of pass strike northeastwardly across Rush Valley, crossing Meadow Creek, a flowing stream."*

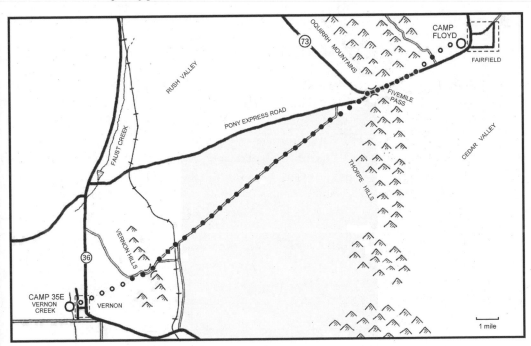

AUGUST 3 AND 5, 1859

area to the east. This turned out to be a surprisingly easy task. Simpson did not mention it in the text of his report, but the table of distances lists a "summit between Meadow Creek and Rush Valley," and lists the distance from the creek to the summit as 3.7 miles. It had always been clear to me that the trail would have crossed the Vernon Hills at some point, but when I had mistakenly placed the camp too far to the north, I had plotted a route that went through a low pass near the northern end of the hills. After moving the campsite to its correct location, I found that this pass was about two miles too far to the north. As I began looking to the east from the new campsite location, it quickly became apparent that the trail would have gone through a low place that lies between the two main peaks of the Vernon Hills, almost directly east of the town. The next step was to plot the route between this summit and Five Mile Pass. The route that I had earlier plotted between the wrong campsite location and Five Mile Pass had not corresponded with any existing road or trail. I had not been very concerned about that because I simply assumed that no one else had ever followed this section of the return route. But when I began looking to the east from the southern summit, I found that a straight line drawn all the way from Vernon to Five Mile Pass would fall directly on top of an existing road. It became apparent that the road between Vernon and Five Mile Pass was another section of Simpson's trail that developed into a well-traveled road. For quite some time, this road must have been used as the main route to Vernon. Later, when the Rush Valley section of Pony Express Road was improved, it became the main road, and this more direct route that went directly from Five Mile Pass to Vernon was almost totally abandoned. Although there is very little traffic on this road today, it is occasionally graded by county road crews, and, with the exception of the first two miles directly east of Vernon,

and about a mile immediately west of Five Mile Pass, this section of the trail can easily be driven in any moderately high-clearance vehicle.

OCTOBER 2005

A few days after I had finally figured out Simpson's actual eastbound route across Rush Valley, Nancy and I drove to this area and got onto the trail near the pass in the Vernon Hills. From there we drove eastward across Rush Valley to Five Mile Pass. This left a two-mile section between the town of Vernon and the Vernon Hills that cannot be driven in any kind of vehicle. Returning to this area a few days later, I hiked eastward from SR 36 toward the Vernon Hills, following this two-mile section of the expedition's route.

In about 18 miles more attaining summit of Camp Floyd Pass [Five Mile Pass] and in about three miles more, at 7.15 P.M., reaching Camp Floyd. Road to-day, except as stated, through Oak Pass [Government Creek Pass], good. Journey 44.5 miles.[29]

Early the next morning Simpson sent Ute Pete back to the main party with a number of hatchets that he thought the men could use to cut their way through the heavy brush in Oak Pass. However, the hatchets went unused because the expedition had gotten through the canyon and across the pass before meeting up with Ute Pete. That night, the expedition made camp on Vernon Creek at the spot where Simpson and Ute Pete had crossed it the previous day. William Lee wrote in his journal; "When we got to camp, we found Pete waiting for us with four days' provisions and several lariats and hatchets."[30] One has to wonder why Ute Pete had stopped at the creek instead of taking the hatchets to where they were needed. The following day, the expedition traveled the rest of the way to Camp Floyd, arriving sometime during the afternoon.

Twelve

After the Return

SIMPSON ARRIVED BACK at Camp Floyd on the evening of August 3, 1859. The following day General Johnston issued a set of orders that included the following:

HEADQUARTERS DEPARTMENT OF UTAH
Camp Floyd, Utah, August 4, 1859

Captain Simpson will dispatch a subaltern of his party over the last 100 miles of his new route, with minute instructions to straighten the portion west of Rush Valley, and establish guide-marks upon it. A detail of one non-commissioned officer and ten dragoons, rationed for twelve days, will escort this officer. This detachment will be immediately prepared, and held ready to march on the arrival of the surveying party.
The depot quartermaster will provide the necessary transportation and material for making stakes, and also for water-troughs at a particular point which Captain Simpson will designate.[1]

There can be little doubt that these orders were issued at Simpson's suggestion. This action makes it apparent that both Simpson and Johnston believed that the return route would make a better wagon road than the outbound trail. Simpson made this clear when he reported the party's arrival at Camp Floyd.

August 5, Camp Floyd.—Topographical party, with escort under Lieutenant Murry, reached this post this afternoon. It seems that Pete was too late in reaching Lieutenant Murry with the hatchets, the party having got through the difficult portion of Oak Pass before they met. The road through the

pass has not been made as practicable for wagons as I had intended, but, in consequence of the General Johnston Pass, 5 miles farther north, being wider and therefore not so liable to obstruction by snow in the winter, and it not lengthening the route a great deal, probably my return route should have come into Rush Valley by this pass. In order to make this connection with my outward route, Lieutenant Smith has received from me, by direction of General Johnston, verbal orders to this effect, and also the following instructions in relation to the shortening the route between Tyler's Springs and William's Spring, and establishing water-troughs at the Marmaduke Spring.[2]

Simpson had already decided to abandon the route that he and the expedition had followed over the Sheeprock Mountains, but he remained determined to establish a road that would follow his "true route" through the center of the Drum Mountains, rather than the route that the expedition had followed through Swasey Bottom, past the southern base of Topaz Mountain and over the western ridge of Keg Mountain. This decision was made in spite of the fact that no one had actually traveled that route. Since the wagons did not arrive at Camp Floyd until sometime during the afternoon of August 5, and since Lieutenant Smith's orders were dated that same day, it appears that he had hardly gotten off his horse when he was handed his orders to head back along the trail. These orders read as follows:

Sir: You will to-morrow proceed to Camp No. 32, near William's Spring, on our return-route from

*Genoa, for the purpose of straightening the road
thence to Tyler's Spring, making the Marmaduke,
or, as it has been called, the Big Horn Spring, a
point of the road.... You will take with you suitable stakes and guide-boards for marking out the
road, as also a number of wooden troughs for the
purpose of collecting and economizing the water of
the Marmaduke Spring for the benefit of emigrants
and other travelers.*[3]

Traveling with two wagons and escorted by
eleven dragoons, Smith left Camp Floyd on the
morning of August 6. The detail followed the
expedition's outbound trail until it reached the
western foot of Lookout Pass. Although it was
not mentioned in the written orders, Smith's
report indicates that Simpson had instructed
him to leave the outbound trail at this point
and turn south "up a ravine which leads into
Johnston's Pass from the south, and furnishes a
path thence into the ravine of Brewer's Spring
and Creek."[4] From where he left the outbound
trail to where he reached Brewer's Spring, Smith
would be opening up a new section of trail that
would replace the section that climbed over the
Sheeprock Mountains. Rejoining the return
trail at Brewer's Spring, Smith followed it to Old
Riverbed, where Camp 32-E had been located.
From that point, Smith's trail becomes much
less certain. One thing that is clear, however,
is that he left the trail that the expedition had
followed out of the interior of Keg Mountain.
In his report he indicated that on the night of
August 8 he had camped near the site of Camp
32-E. After spending most of the following day
in an unsuccessful attempt to find several mules
that had wandered away, he took up his assigned
journey again.

*I followed your trail for about a mile and a half, and
then diverged from it to the right. Our road now lay
through the range of hills in which Indian Spring
is situated, and was necessarily somewhat tortuous, though its general direction was nearly correct.
I halted when the moon set (about midnight), and
continued the march on the morning of the 10th.
We soon emerged from the hills and moved west of
south across the valley west of Good Indian Spring,
reaching Marmaduke Spring about 3 P.M.*[5]

By moving away from the old trail toward the
right, it appears that Smith must have skirted
the northern base of Keg Mountain rather than
following the expedition's trail through its interior. Smith seems to be describing the foothills on the north side of Keg Mountain, and
then the valley that lies between Keg Mountain
and the Thomas Mountains. This route would
have taken him to the area just north of Mount
Laird in the Drum Mountains. Here he found
Marmaduke Spring, and spent some time in an
attempt to develop the springs into a reliable
source of water. His report indicates that he felt
this effort was mostly unsuccessful.

*We found here, by digging, sufficient water for our
immediate wants, but the holes soon ceased to fill
up, and the water gave out entirely before night. It
seemed evident to me, on examination of the locality, that the supposed spring at this point was nothing more than a reservoir of rain-water, retained in
a natural basin of rocks and protected from evapo-
ration by the sand which fills the basin.*[6]

The next morning Smith headed in a westerly direction through the Drum Mountains and
across Whirlwind Valley to Mud Springs. Here
he made some improvements to the spring and
spent the night. On August 12, he started back
toward Camp Floyd but this time he did go into
the interior of Keg Mountain, where he spent
that night and the next at Keg Spring. Here he
left the water troughs that had been intended for
Marmaduke Spring. On August 15, he left Good
Indian Spring and made it all the way back to
Camp Floyd.

Simpson remained at Camp Floyd for only six
days following his return. He must have spent
most of that time getting things in order for his
return trip to Fort Leavenworth, but while still
at Camp Floyd, he learned that a number of
emigrants were planning to travel on his newly
explored route to California. At least some of
them were planning to use his return route.

*August 6, Camp Floyd.—A party of California
emigrants, with seven wagons, take, also, my
return-route. I have furnished them with an
itinerary.*

August 7, Camp Floyd.—An emigrant train of about thirty wagons passed through to-day, taking my more southern route to California. Supplied them with an itinerary.

August 8, Camp Floyd.—Gave Dr. Hobbs, agent of Russell & Co., an itinerary of my inward route. He intends to send immediately over it a thousand head of cattle to California.[7]

Charles Tuttle was traveling with the first group that Simpson mentioned. His journal described what occurred while his party was at Camp Floyd.

Saturday August 6....There had a party just arrived from California. They came a new route which they say is about 250 miles nearer than the old mail route. There was a company of 14 wagons (commanded by Capt Simpson) which had just arrived being the only ones that had come this route. Capt Simpson very kindly offered to let us have an Indian guide to lead us to the right road we gratefully accepted his offer and accordingly he sent one along.[8]

Following the route that Lieutenant Smith had taken, the Tuttle party got onto the return trail at Brewer's Spring, and caught up with Smith where he was camped in Old Riverbed. Traveling just behind Smith, they helped in his efforts to improve the water source at Marmaduke, or Big Horn, Spring, then followed him to Mud Spring. At that point, Smith turned around and the Tuttle party continued westward along the return route.

Another emigrant party, of which Simpson seems to have been unaware, left Camp Floyd on August 14. This was a loosely organized group that included Edward Mathews, who was traveling as a paid passenger in some sort of coach-type wagon that was owned and driven by a Mr. Read of Salt Lake City. The actual number in this group is unknown, but in his journal, Mathews mentions thirty-three other persons. This group followed Simpson's return route all the way to the southwest corner of Carson Lake, then left it to go north to Ragtown, where they got onto the California Trail.[9]

Simpson's return did not go unnoticed by the local press. Probably under the direction of General Johnston, Simpson sent a press release to the *Deseret News* and the *Valley Tan*, newspapers that were being published in Salt Lake City. This release described the route and announced that John Reese was prepared to guide parties of emigrants to Carson Valley.

NOTICE
To California Emigrants and Citizens of Utah Territory

The undersigned is informed that there are many persons at Salt Lake City, destined for California, who are in doubt as to the route they should take. He would inform all such, that by direction of Genl. Johnston, he has within the past three months, explored and surveyed two new routes to California, either of which is about 300 miles shorter than the Old Humboldt, or St. Mary's river route; and from all he can hear and has read, incomparably better in respect to wood, water, and grass. Indeed, by this route the Great Salt Lake desert is entirely avoided, and grass and water may be said to abound, except at few points....

Mr. John Reese, of Genoa, and his son, have just come over the route with me, and will be enabled, and are ready, to conduct any parties of emigrants or herds of animals which may be heading towards California. The young man will doubtless be in the city at the time this notice appears, and Mr. John Reese in the course of about 12 days, as soon as he returns from an expedition under the direction of Lieut. J. L. K. Smith, top'l engineer, who has been charged by General Johnston with the duty of improving the direction of the road within the last one hundred miles, and establishing troughs at a particular spring.

The undersigned is confident that this route will be found from 25 to 50 per cent better than the Old Humboldt River route, and particularly fine for stock driving. It has also the advantage of being a later fall and earlier spring route.

He will, as soon as Lieut. Smith returns, have an itinerary of the route prepared, setting forth the distances between the camping places, and where wood, grass and water con be found, and will send it to the papers of the Territory for publication. This itinerary it would be well for emigrants and others interested in the route to procure and keep.

J. H. Simpson,
Capt. Corps Top'l Engrs.
Camp Floyd, U. T.
August 7th, 1859[10]

A second announcement from Simpson was dated August 7, and published by the *Deseret News* on August 27.

TO CALIFORNIA EMIGRANTS AND THE CITIZENS OF UTAH TERRITORY The undersigned is informed that there are many persons at Salt Lake City destined for California, who are in doubt as to the route they should take. He would inform all such, that by direction of General Johnston, he has within the past three months, explored and surveyed two new routes to California, either of which is about 300 miles shorter than the old Humboldt or St. Mary's River route; and, from all he can hear and has read, is comparably better in respect to wood, water, and grass. Indeed by this route, the Great Salt Lake Desert is entirely avoided, except at a few points. The best route is that from Camp Floyd, through General Johnston's Pass, and thence along the rim between the Great Salt Lake Desert and the General Johnston and Hastings Pass road. J. H. Simpson, Capt. Corps Top'l Eng'rs, Camp Floyd, U. T.[11]

Although George Chorpenning was struggling to keep his mail business going, he was very much aware that Simpson had found a new route between the south foot of the Ruby Mountains and Carson Valley. For the past year, his mail route had turned to the northwest from the foot of the Rubies to join the Humboldt River route at Gravelly Ford. It would have been shortly after Simpson's return to Camp Floyd that Chorpenning began making plans to adopt the new route. By early in 1860, a number of new stations had been built, or were under construction, along this central route, and the switch had been made.[12] However, Chorpenning did not get to make use of this route for long. Within a few months, a new postmaster general had canceled his contract, and the mail route, along with all his assets and facilities, was taken over by Russell, Majors, and Waddell, who began operating the Overland Mail and soon initiated their grand experiment, the Pony Express.

Within a year following the expedition, emigrant traffic on the outbound trail had increased to the point that the army was ordered to begin providing these travelers some protection. In May of 1860, an army patrol, under the command of Lt. Stephen H. Weed, began escorting parties of California-bound emigrants along the central part of the new trail.[13]

Simpson did not linger at Camp Floyd. Just six days following his return, he was on the road again. His immediate objective was to take a quick look at the country to the south of the Uinta Mountains. He traveled up Provo Canyon, turned to the east, and went as far as the present-day town of Duchesne.[14] Turning around at that point, he retraced his steps back to Heber Valley, turned to the north once again, and resumed his trip back to Fort Leavenworth, arriving there on October 15. Spending just four days at Fort Leavenworth, Simpson departed for Washington, DC and began the work of drawing up the final report of his explorations and surveys in the West.

Not everyone was happy to hear about the new wagon route. There were many who, for various reasons, felt that it would be a serious mistake for California-bound emigrants to use this new, and so far unproven, route instead of the well-established Humboldt River route. Perhaps some of the Simpson route detractors may have been thinking about the disaster that had occurred when the Donner-Reed party made their decision to follow the Hastings Road. Others had certain vested interests. One of the most vocal, adamant, and influential opponents of Simpson's route was Frederick W. Lander, the superintendent of the federal government's Pacific Wagon Road Office, and the originator of the Lander Cutoff in western Wyoming and eastern Idaho. Lander had surveyed this cutoff himself, and it had been opened to emigrant traffic the previous year.[15] After getting his cutoff opened, he had been spending most of his time and efforts in promoting it to westbound emigrants. He personally met with many emigrants and potential emigrants, distributing pamphlets that contained road guides featuring his new road. One of his projects was to hire a group of artists to make stereoscopic views of wagon trains, camp scenes, and Indians in full regalia.[16]

Lander was in California when he saw the newspaper accounts of the Simpson expedition. The local papers were heaping praise on Simpson and the new route, claiming that it would soon be carrying all of the traffic between the eastern states and the west coast. This was disturbing news and Lander became even more perturbed when he returned to Washington, DC, and learned that the secretary of war's annual report to Congress claimed that Simpson's road was now the shortest and best route between the Missouri River and the Pacific coast. This was just too much for Lander to ignore. After all, he was the duly-appointed head of a federal agency, and he had spent the last three years locating, surveying, and constructing a perfectly good road that would cut something like five days of travel from the Oregon-California Trail. Now here was this upstart army captain, who had taken a three-month jaunt across the desert, urging all California-bound emigrants to leave the federally-sanctioned wagon route and take a chance on an unproven road. He decided to go on the offensive.

First, he prepared and distributed an extensive briefing paper, which attempted to prove that although the new route might be satisfactory for use by the Overland Mail, and maybe the coming telegraph line, it would be an entirely unsatisfactory, and potentially fatal, route for emigrants traveling by wagon.[17]

In the meantime, Simpson received a letter from Camp Floyd. It was written by Major Fitz J. Porter, at the direction of General Johnston, and it strongly suggested that Simpson curtail his promotion of the new routes.

Since you left this Department many reports have been received tending, if true, to modify in no slight degree, the favorable impression...that your routes to Genoa would be available for the thousands of emigrants and traders with their vast herds who annually traverse this country to California. A few thousand cattle, in herds, have passed over your return route, and have been followed by small parties of emigrants each having

animals in varying numbers from ten to one hundred. Hearing that some of them later were much inconvenienced on account of the scarcity of grass and water (the springs in some places having been exhausted by a small number of animals), and had to make long marches without either. The Commanding General sent an officer of experience whose judgment could be relied upon, to examine the road and report upon its character and the resources of the country for supporting of large trains or herds. A copy of his report is enclosed and also extracts from the letters of persons who have passed over the road. This officer confirms as far as he went the reports which caused his journey and his own impressions of the kind of travel, are confirmed by other reports and by parties which have just passed over your return route. These last say that the cattle have nearly denuded the country of grass and that water is in many places, not abundant.... The Commanding General does not doubt that the routes assessed by you are of real value for military and mail purposes and for the ordinary travel of this country, especially early in the summer and late in the fall—for those who may winter in this country or be late in arriving. They can be advantageously used by parties of emigrants having a small number of animals, and, should the emigration be greatly reduced, these routes will probably be used in preference to, and, perhaps to the exclusion of those generally traveled. Time will prove if they will sustain a large travel; but until the country becomes more opened and its resources prove abundant, the General desires that no efforts be made to turn the main tide of emigration from Lander's road, north of this Territory.[18]

The last sentence seems to be suggesting rather forcefully that Simpson make no more public statements that would lead emigrants to believe that either of the two new routes would be better than the Humboldt River route. I have not found any indication of a direct response to either Porter or Johnston, but Simpson did refer to Porter's letter when he made a public response to comments made by Lander a few weeks later.[19] Although no evidence has been found to support such a speculation, one has to wonder if Lander had anything to do with Johnston's decision to have the letter written.

Lander's next step was to write a lengthy letter to Simpson, asking him if he agreed with a number of recently published statements that described the new route in very complimentary terms. Lander warned Simpson that before he responded, he should consider the fact that "these reports will cause the less experienced emigrants to take your road," then added, "the question is, are you ready to advocate it as suitable for ox-team emigration?"[20]

Simpson responded to Lander's letter with measured diplomacy,

> Be assured that it has been the farthest thing from my mind to do injustice to you, or anyone else, in what I may have reported of the explorations I have recently made between the Rocky Mountains and the Sierra Nevada; and that it shall be my pleasure to set the matter right before the public as soon as practicable.[21]

For some reason, Simpson felt that this statement did not go far enough, and on February 8, 1860, he sent a press release to the editor of the *Washington Constitution*.

> From motives, as I trust, of public good, and desire to do justice to officers of government who have been zealously and efficiently engaged in works of public benefit, I beg leave to make the following statement: It has been made known to the public by the honorable Secretary of War, and the press has given currency to the fact, that during the past year, by authority of the honorable Secretary and the instructions of General Johnston, commanding the Department of Utah, I have opened two new wagon roads from Camp Floyd to California, either of which, in connection with the South Pass or Lieutenant Bryan's road from the Missouri river, forms a highway which is shorter to Sacramento or San Francisco than any other known route.
>
> From data obtained in Utah, it was believed that the difference in favor of my routes was very much greater than is now known to exist; and it was only after I had made a report to the honorable Secretary, on my return to this city, that, the last year's report of Mr. Albert E. Campbell, general superintendent of Pacific wagon roads under the Secretary of the Interior, was placed in my hands.
>
> By this report and the statement of distances which Mr. Campbell has furnished me, I find that very considerable improvements have been made in the old route between the South Pass and the City of Rocks by Mr. F. W. Lander, in the location and construction of a new road, which avoids the Artemisia barrens of the Green River basin with its deleterious waters; the rugged defiles of Wahsatch mountains leading to Salt Lake City, and the circuitous route by the valley of the Bear river.
>
> As these are very important advantages to the heavy ox-migration trains which annually pass over the plains, and which can only accrue on my route after reaching Fort Bridger, and then are intermitted to a degree at the outset of my routes from Camp Floyd, and then again near Carson Lake, albeit between these points there is an abundance of grass and water, it is very possible that emigrants desiring to travel through to California without passing through Great Salt Lake City or Camp Floyd, for purposes of replenishing supplies, or other reasons, would do best to take the Lander cut-off at the South Pass and keep the old road along the Humboldt river.
>
> In thus speaking, however, I do not wish it to be understood that I am in any degree disparaging my routes from Camp Floyd, for it was the decided opinion of the two guides I had with me, and who had been over the Humboldt river road—one of them, Colonel Reese, having several times driven stock over it—and who were, therefore, competent to make a comparison, that my routes were, in respect to wood, water, and grass, very much superior to the old route; and others who have since passed over the routes have reported the same thing. But still there have been reports to the effect that, in consequence of the deficiency of water and grass at some points of the routes, they are not calculated for heavy trans and large herds of cattle, and I cannot, therefore, take the responsibility of diverting the thousands who annually pass over the continent with their immense trains and herds of cattle from the old road, improved as it has been by Mr. Lander between the South Pass and the City of Rocks. Time can only settle which is the best route to the traveling public; and to that arbiter do I leave the decision; only feeling desirous that that route which furnishes the greatest facilities may, as it will, be eventually taken.

There is, however, no question, that for emigrants who may find it necessary to pass through Great Salt Lake City or Camp Floyd, or tarry in that country during the winter, my routes will be found to be much the nearest to Sacramento and San Francisco, and probably the best in other respects; and that in consequence of their being the shortest and situated in a lower and milder region in the winter than the old road, they are the best for the transportation of the mail.

J. H. Simpson
Captain Topographical Engineers[22]

Frederick Lander must have been at least somewhat mollified by Simpson's public statement, because it seems that he dropped the matter at this point.

As Simpson worked on the report of the expedition, the events that eventually led to the Civil War were intensifying. At about the same time that the work was finished, the conflict between the North and South had begun, and the report was essentially put aside for the duration. Following the end of the war, there seemed to be little interest in wagon roads. Everyone was now talking about the transcontinental railroad, and publication of the report was again delayed. Finally, in 1876, Congress authorized its publication.

Simpson remained in the Union Army, and saw action in a number of battles. During a skirmish at Gaines' Mill in June 1862, he was taken prisoner and held in Richmond until sometime in August, when he was released as part of a routine prisoner exchange.[23] Shortly after the end of the Civil War, he was awarded the honorary rank of brevet brigadier general and transferred to the Department of Interior, assigned to the position of the department's chief engineer. His responsibilities included oversight of the construction of railroads, and the administration of all government wagon roads.[24] He retired from the army in 1880, and died in 1883.

In a master's thesis written in 1949, Wilbur Sheridan Warrick included the following comment about Simpson and his career.

James Hervey Simpson has never been given a place of particular importance in the history of the United States. He did not have a flare for publicity

and did not have those romantic characteristics of eccentricities that attract attention. He did not become a popular figure like John Charles Frémont of the Topographical Engineers or Benjamin L. E. Bonneville and Randolph B. Marcy of the Infantry. He was, however, an enthusiastic participant in the opening of the West. He thought of his road surveying and wagon road building not just as a job in hand but as a part of a great transcontinental conquering of rocks and deserts and mountains and valleys in the interest of making the states and territories into a united nation. He thought of his work in shortening overland routes to California not only as an engineering achievement but as a part of a program to bring the West closer to the East....He was not only a military engineer. He was also a man of historical vision.[25]

J. L. Kirby Smith and Haldiman S. Putnam served with the Union Army during the Civil War and lost their lives in battle. Smith was killed during the battle of Corinth on October 4, 1862. Putnam received fatal wounds in the assault of Fort Wagner in South Carolina on July 18, 1863.[26] Albert Sidney Johnston became a general in the Confederate Army and was killed on April 6, 1862, while leading a charge during the battle of Shiloh.[27]

During my travels along Simpson's route, and in getting to and from the various sections that I needed to explore, I have driven approximately 30,000 miles. While hiking the sections that I could not get to in my vehicle, I have covered about 140 miles of Simpson's trail on foot. But because of the fact that I usually had to return to where I had started, I ended up walking almost the same number of miles to get back to my vehicle. I am quite certain that I have been either directly on, or within a few yards of, the entire route. I have visited and have taken photographs and GPS readings at what I believe are all of the seventy different campsites. Although it would be foolhardy of me to claim that I have always discovered the exact spots upon which the members of the expedition pitched their tents, I do feel that I have gotten reasonably close. A project that started out as idle curiosity has taken ten years to complete, and has introduced me to many other historical trails that are crying out to be explored.

Appendix:
Geographic Coordinates

THIS TABLE LISTS latitude and longitude readings at what I have concluded to be the probable locations of the campsites and other checkpoints listed in Simpson's report, and other locations that can serve to identify the route. The coordinates shown in italics were obtained from the Google Earth website (http://earth. google.com/). All of the other readings were made on-site with a Garmin GPS12. Locations shown in italics were mentioned in Simpson's report but not listed in the table of distances. Locations enclosed in brackets were not mentioned by Simpson but have been added to help identify the trail.

LOCATION	LATITUDE (N)	LONGITUDE (W)
Camp Floyd	40° 15.516	112° 06.166
enter Five Mile Pass	40° 14.369	112° 09.227
Five Mile Pass	40° 13.904	112° 10.732
leave Five Mile Pass	40° 13.600	112° 11.800
Camp 1W—Faust Creek	40° 10.423	112° 25.154
cross stream	40° 09.723	112° 25.833
pass mail station	40° 09.258	112° 26.281
east foot of Lookout Pass	40° 06.758	112° 32.820
Lookout Pass at summit	40° 06.944	112° 33.923
Camp 2W—Point Lookout	40° 07.183	112° 34.675
Skull Valley	40° 05.119	112° 42.256
Camp 3W—Simpson Springs	40° 02.343	112° 47.083
Salt Lake Desert	39° 56.869	112° 54.767
Dugway Pass	39° 51.138	113° 05.156
Camp 4W	39° 51.561	113° 06.718
turn "southwardly"	39° 52.513	113° 09.566
enter Cedar Valley	39° 51.994	113° 10.558
[trail joins road]	39° 50.158	113° 13.158
emerge from Cedar Valley	39° 49.100	113° 14.633
foot of slope	39° 47.033	113° 17.650
west side of valley	39° 44.750	113° 23.000
Devil's Hole	39° 45.866	113° 23.900
Camp 5W—South Spring	39° 50.035	113° 23.477
pass warm spring	39° 53.405	113° 25.023
double point of mountain	39° 53.960	113° 26.966
[trail leaves road east of Trout Creek]	39° 42.400	113° 46.750
Camp 6W—Trout Creek	39° 41.879	113° 48.222
pass alkaline spring	39° 41.358	113° 49.233
Camp 7W—Mile Pond	39° 40.237	113° 50.474
foot of slope	39° 39.050	113° 54.983
Little Red Cedar Pass	39° 41.316	114° 00.433
reach valley	39° 40.866	114° 02.916
Camp 8W—Pleasant Valley	39° 41.108	114° 03.800
Cedar Pass	39° 45.600	114° 10.066
western foot of slope	39° 46.660	114° 10.500
[trail turns west]	39° 47.082	114° 10.735
ridge east of Antelope Valley	39° 46.547	114° 11.619
Camp 9W—Cedar Springs	39° 46.416	114° 12.850

LOCATION	LATITUDE (N)	LONGITUDE (W)
Antelope Valley	39° 45.650	114° 18.700
Spring Valley Ridge	39° 46.178	114° 30.426
Camp 10W—Stonehouse	39° 46.811	114° 32.475
turn up canyon	39° 49.633	114° 33.158
leave stream	39° 48.803	114° 36.569
Schellbourne Pass	39° 48.352	114° 38.950
Camp 11W—Schellbourne Ranch	39° 47.633	114° 41.076
Steptoe Valley	39° 48.391	114° 48.050
Camp 12W—Egan Canyon	39° 51.766	114° 54.200
Round Valley	39° 51.833	114° 56.533
Overland Summit	39° 53.916	114° 59.300
second summit	39° 54.304	115° 01.542
Butte Valley	39° 54.716	115° 04.750
Camp 13W—Butte Valley	39° 56.075	115° 12.180
Butte Mt[ns]. ridge	39° 57.410	115° 12.954
reach valley	39° 59.416	115° 14.300
Long Valley	40° 00.266	115° 15.666
begin climbing slope	40° 01.000	115° 16.816
summit	40° 01.600	115° 19.982
Camp 14W—Mountain Spring	40° 00.866	115° 20.333
Maverick Springs summit	40° 00.750	115° 20.900
mouth of canyon	40° 01.783	115° 23.866
Ruby Valley	40° 02.100	115° 25.733
Camp 15W—Station Spring	40° 02.897	115° 29.694
foot of pass	40° 01.950	115° 32.150
Overland Pass	40° 01.073	115° 34.917
leave Hasting's Road	40° 00.800	115° 39.983
Huntington Valley	39° 58.426	115° 43.313
reach stream	39° 58.281	115° 43.439
leave stream	39° 57.900	115° 43.800
Camp 16W—Conners Creek	39° 56.416	115° 45.116
cross stream	39° 55.223	115° 46.628
begin climbing	39° 54.718	115° 47.604
Overland Pass	39° 54.570	115° 48.127
Camp 17W—Telegraph Canyon	39° 54.475	115° 51.566
foot of slope	39° 53.900	115° 52.200
Diamond Valley	39° 52.895	115° 55.250
pass large spring	39° 51.699	115° 58.633
Camp 18W—Sulphur Spring	39° 49.981	116° 04.219
begin turning west	39° 48.783	116° 04.200
begin climbing toward pass	39° 48.300	116° 06.416
Mt. Hope summit	39° 46.133	116° 11.150
[trail comes to Garden Pass road]	39° 45.750	116° 13.658
Camp 19W—Roberts Creek	39° 45.033	116° 17.266
come to parallel stream	39° 38.333	116° 19.141
cross stream	39° 35.200	116° 20.150
pass warm spring	39° 33.316	116° 20.983
Camp 20W—Clover Spring	39° 30.833	116° 22.450
[trail turns toward canyon]	39° 29.250	116° 23.867
Twin Springs Hills summit	39° 28.500	116° 25.633
[trail comes to abandoned road/return trail]	39° 28.200	116° 27.666
Camp 21W & 14E—Willow Creek Ranch	39° 27.542	116° 29.233
[trail turns northwest]	39° 27.650	116° 30.716
Monitor Valley	39° 27.957	116° 33.355
cross Kelly Creek	39° 28.122	116° 34.552
[trail crosses US 50]	39° 28.536	116° 37.755
[trail crossed Dry Creek Road]	39° 29.400	116° 42.616
Camp 22W—Clarke's Creek	39° 29.782	116° 44.308

LOCATION	LATITUDE (N)	LONGITUDE (W)
begin turning west	39° 27.183	116° 44.200
Hickison Summit	39° 26.609	116° 44.815
reach valley, turn northwest	39° 23.135	116° 50.992
come to stream	39° 25.516	116° 51.683
cross stream	39° 27.792	116° 53.579
Camp 23W—Simpson Park Canyon	39° 27.930	116° 53.805
Camp 24W—Simpson Park	39° 30.533	116° 57.643
Emigrant Pass	39° 31.200	117° 02.550
Reese Valley	39° 31.066	117° 05.533
return route intersects outbound route	39° 31.350	117° 08.050
Reese River crossing	39° 31.450	117° 09.600
Camp 25W—Reese River	39° 29.966	117° 11.533
Smith Creek summit	39° 23.133	117° 23.116
Smith Creek Valley	39° 22.950	117° 25.533
Camp 26W—Smith Creek	39° 21.033	117° 31.310
Engleman Creek	39° 20.087	117° 32.489
cross second stream	39° 18.497	117° 34.208
Camp 27W—Campbell Creek	39° 14.341	117° 38.616
foot of pass	39° 13.566	117° 40.666
cross first ridge	39° 14.100	117° 41.116
Skull Canyon summit	39° 14.966	117° 43.266
Camp 28W—Road Canyon	39° 14.378	117° 46.684
creek sinks	39° 14.750	117° 48.491
stream reappears	39° 18.150	117° 52.400
Eastgate	39° 18.361	117° 52.728
[Lincoln Highway signpost]	39° 18.867	117° 56.291
cross Eastgate Wash (from eastbound log)	39° 18.322	117° 57.511
Camp 29W—Middlegate	39° 17.644	117° 59.200
Westgate formation	39° 17.439	118° 02.853
Drumm Summit	39° 17.210	118° 08.559
Labou Flat	39° 16.840	118° 15.138
Sand Springs Pass	39° 16.400	118° 21.083
in Alkali Valley	39° 15.882	118° 23.136
Camp 30W—Sand Springs	39° 16.850	118° 25.341
[trail crosses US 50 on ridge]	39° 17.933	118° 28.583
[trail crosses US 50 in 8-mile flat]	39° 20.633	118° 31.950
[trail crosses Salt Wells road]	39° 21.533	118° 34.625
Camp 31W—Carson Lake	39° 23.216	118° 40.550
[trail left previous day's trail, turned south	39° 22.600	118° 38.833
leave lake	39° 16.233	118° 40.266
Lee Hot Spring	39° 12.522	118° 43.423
pass Stinking Spring	39° 10.434	118° 44.242
[trail leaves US 95, turns south on abandoned road]	39° 06.434	118° 46.516
summit of ridge	39° 05.310	118° 46.777
Camp 32W—Weber Reservoir	39° 03.000	118° 52.016
Camp 33W—Walker River	39° 08.230	119° 00.396
Camp 34W—Stanley Ranch	39° 09.176	119° 06.005
springs on left of trail	39° 09.400	119° 12.500
Point of Mountain	39° 09.533	119° 13.433
come to old wagon road	39° 11.858	119° 15.800
enter canyon	39° 12.700	119° 16.000
Churchill Station Spring	39° 15.066	119° 16.933
[trail turns west]	39° 16.266	119° 17.050
Summit of Ugly Hill	39° 16.500	119° 17.516
Camp 35W—Carson River	39° 17.638	119° 20.473
Camp 36W—Millers Station	39° 17.867	119° 29.399
"Chinatown"/Dayton	39° 14.166	119° 35.483
fork leading to Gold Canyon	39° 14.773	119° 36.603

LOCATION	LATITUDE (N)	LONGITUDE (W)
[trail crosses SR 341]	39° 13.566	119° 38.783
pass through cedar grove	39° 13.261	119° 39.640
[trail crosses US 50]	39° 12.638	119° 40.783
Camp 37W—Carson City	39° 09.240	119° 45.891
cross Clear Creek	39° 06.513	119° 45.021
[trail crosses US 395]	39° 04.403	119° 46.769
Camp 38W & 1E—Genoa	39° 00.029	119° 50.778
Camp 2E—Carson City	39° 09.240	119° 45.891
"Chinatown"/Dayton	39° 14.167	119° 35.448
Camp 3E—Carson Plains	39° 16.900	119° 31.333
pass Pleasant Grove	39° 17.731	119° 29.354
[leave Carson River road to cross Ugly Hill]	39° 17.235	119° 18.412
east foot of Ugly Hill	39° 16.266	119° 17.050
[trail crosses summit of second spur]	39° 16.701	119° 16.486
come back to river valley	39° 17.076	119° 15.546
Camp 4E—Carson River	39° 16.983	119° 13.600
leave river	39° 16.750	119° 11.383
begin climbing hills/Hooton Well	39° 16.570	119° 02.719
first Dead Camel ridge	39° 16.685	118° 59.843
second Dead Camel ridge	39° 16.392	118° 57.583
third Dead Camel ridge	39° 15.984	118° 56.339
[trail comes to 3-way fork]	39° 16.166	118° 54.116
Camp 5E—Carson Sink Station site	39° 16.836	118° 47.697
[trail passes Wildcat Station]	39° 16.450	118° 41.816
join outbound route	39° 16.233	118° 40.266
Camp 6E—Carson Lake	39° 19.982	118° 38.319
[visible ruts on ridge]	39° 20.530	118° 38.091
[visible ruts on ridge]	39° 20.505	118° 38.012
cross ridge	39° 20.500	118° 37.962
[trail comes to Salt Wells road]	39° 19.633	118° 35.216
grassy bottom	39° 19.166	118° 35.000
Rock Springs	39° 17.9950	118° 32.683
join outbound route/rest stop	39° 16.400	118° 24.591
foot of Sand Springs Pass	39° 15.854	118° 23.006
Sand Springs Pass	39° 16.410	118° 21.061
Labeau Flat	39° 16.866	118° 14.983
Drumm Summit	39° 17.216	118° 09.006
Middlegate; "base of mountain"	39° 17.644	117° 59.200
cross arroyo	39° 18.322	118° 57.511
riders reach Cold Creek	39° 23.566	117° 49.950
Camp 7E—Cold Springs	39° 23.716	117° 51.116
Cold Springs summit	39° 25.050	117° 50.633
Camp 8E—lower Edwards Creek	39° 28.933	117° 43.791
Camp 9E—upper Edwards Creek	39° 23.452	117° 41.000
Basque Summit	39° 23.133	117° 41.783
come to Smith Creek	39° 22.991	117° 40.369
reach Smith Creek Valley	39° 22.951	117° 36.715
Camp 10E—Smith Creek	39° 21.633	117° 33.866
join outbound route	39° 21.604	117° 29.825
east side of Smith Creek Valley	39° 22.966	117° 25.500
Smith Creek Summit	39° 23.133	117° 23.116
Reese River Valley	39° 23.733	117° 20.616
leave outbound route	39° 28.408	117° 13.966
Camp 11E—Reese River	39° 28.532	117° 13.522
Reese River crossing	39° 29.195	117° 12.742
join outbound route	39° 31.350	117° 08.050
Reese River Valley	39° 31.350	117° 07.516
Emigrant Pass	39° 31.200	117° 02.550

LOCATION	LATITUDE (N)	LONGITUDE (W)
Camp 12E—Simpson Park	39° 30.100	116° 57.166
Camp 13E—Simpson Park Canyon	39° 27.750	116° 53.583
[trail crosses Willow Creek]	39° 25.116	116° 51.983
join outbound route	39° 23.975	116° 51.300
in valley	39° 23.966	116° 51.320
leave outbound route	39° 23.135	116° 50.992
[trail crosses Pete's Well road]	39° 23.750	116° 46.825
Toquima Summit	39° 24.216	116° 43.966
[trail crosses road]	39° 24.816	116° 41.816
cross Reynolds Creek	39° 26.266	116° 36.816
cross Kelly Creek	39° 26.991	116° 33.900
join outbound route	39° 27.650	116° 30.716
Camp 14E—Willow Creek Ranch	39° 27.542	116° 29.233
[road forks]	39° 27.961	116° 28.191
leave outbound route	39° 28.200	116° 27.666
[trail crosses well-traveled road]	39° 28.700	116° 27.116
Twin Springs	39° 31.116	116° 23.500
cross outbound route	39° 31.650	116° 21.833
in valley & Fountain Spring	39° 32.113	116° 20.200
[trail crosses US 50]	39° 32.916	116° 14.958
Camp 15E—Slough Creek	39° 33.325	116° 13.450
Lee Springs/Hay Ranch	39° 34.816	116° 08.016
enter canyon to Devil's Gate	39° 34.650	116° 05.416
enter Diamond Valley	39° 34.450	116° 03.716
come to stream, turn south	39° 34.666	115° 57.016
Camp 16E—Simpson Creek	39° 32.960	115° 56.101
Diamond Mountains summit	39° 29.249	115° 52.125
come to Pinto Creek	39° 28.769	115° 51.383
mouth of canyon	39° 28.533	115° 51.183
Newark Valley	39° 30.500	115° 47.083
Camp 17E—Water Canyon	39° 33.150	115° 46.566
Newark Valley	39° 32.150	115° 44.083
sign site	39° 30.566	115° 40.266
begin to climb hills	39° 31.983	115° 32.983
Dry Mountain Pass	39° 32.150	115° 30.733
east foot of slope	39° 32.333	115° 30.050
Long Valley	39° 33.366	115° 26.483
west foot of slope	39° 34.533	115° 21.316
Butte Mountain summit	39° 32.816	115° 14.016
Camp 18E—Summit Spring	39° 33.071	115° 13.833
pass Pete's Spring	39° 33.333	115° 13.100
mouth of canyon	39° 33.966	115° 12.716
Butte Valley	39° 33.633	115° 06.533
come to stream	39° 32.766	115° 00.866
Egan Range summit	39° 30.132	114° 59.597
Camp 19E—Archie Spring	39° 27.066	114° 58.500
pass Hercules Gap	39° 21.003	114° 54.000
come to Steptoe Valley	39° 19.683	114° 53.316
Camp 20E—Murry Creek	39° 16.433	114° 51.550
join Mormon road	39° 14.233	114° 50.208
cross stream	39° 13.533	114° 49.600
west slope—Steptoe Canyon	39° 11.341	114° 43.422
cross stream/west slope	39° 11.050	114° 42.916
leave stream, turn south	39° 11.483	114° 41.783
Camp 21E—Cave Springs	39° 10.766	114° 39.766
[trail turns toward West Cooper Pass]	39° 10.279	114° 39.166
West Cooper Pass	39° 09.516	114° 39.500
[trail joins four-wheel drive trail]	39° 08.333	114° 39.200

LOCATION	LATITUDE (N)	LONGITUDE (W)
[trail & four-wheel drive trail join main road]	39° 07.688	114° 38.765
Spring Valley	39° 06.063	114° 34.295
[trail leaves utility road, veers to northeast]	39° 06.060	114° 31.521
Camp 22E—Layton Spring	39° 06.421	114° 27.326
[trail comes to US 50 & 6]	39° 09.402	114° 24.690
mouth of canyon	39° 10.578	114° 23.338
Turnley Springs	39° 09.733	114° 21.483
Sacramento Pass	39° 08.550	114° 20.183
Camp 23E—Strawberry Ranch	39° 05.556	114° 13.416
leave Mormon road	39° 04.400	114° 10.600
cross dry streambed	39° 04.933	114° 07.908
Rush Spring	39° 06.027	114° 02.026
rejoin Mormon road	39° 06.800	113° 58.350
Camp 24E—Baker Creek	39° 07.166	113° 58.050
pass "Plympton"/Knoll Springs	39° 14.866	113° 52.566
foot of slope	39° 17.539	113° 46.039
Cowboy Pass	39° 18.943	113° 43.539
Camp 25E—Tule Valley	39° 20.021	113° 32.900
Camp 26E—North Knoll Spring	39° 15.933	113° 51.942
Camp 27E—South Tule Spring	39° 20.010	113° 31.150
foot of canyon	39° 20.750	113° 22.429
Dome Canyon summit	39° 20.856	113° 19.010
met Collamer on road	39° 20.933	113° 17.250
Camp 28E—Chapin's Spring	39° 21.253	113° 17.212
rejoin Mormon road	39° 18.973	113° 15.218
[trail leaves Mormon road]	39° 18.745	113° 14.954
Sevier Valley	39° 19.783	113° 11.333
turn to left up canyon	39° 24.617	113° 15.071
Camp 29E—Mud Spring	39° 24.420	113° 15.220
[trail crosses main valley road]	39° 29.016	113° 13.183
Whirlwind Valley	39° 31.550	113° 12.366
[trail crosses east-west road]	39° 33.916	113° 11.783
[trail crosses north-south road]	39° 36.083	113° 10.966
summit of Thomas Range	39° 36.377	113° 10.858
11:00 P.M. *rest stop*	39° 37.220	113° 10.408
base of Thomas Range	39° 38.064	113° 10.654
summit	39° 39.271	113° 09.015
3:00 A.M. *rest stop*	39° 40.023	113° 06.816
second summit	39° 40.117	113° 04.455
turn toward spring (5 miles in advance of column)	39° 43.889	113° 03.366
trifling spring/in valley	39° 43.095	113° 01.981
Camp 30E—Triple Peaks	39° 45.466	112° 56.416
[trail joins jeep trail]	39° 45.867	112° 56.056
summit of ridge	39° 45.985	112° 55.500
Sevier Valley	39° 44.983	112° 53.508
Keg Pass	39° 47.127	112° 52.836
first spring	39° 47.249	112° 52.828
Camp 31E—Keg Spring	39° 47.766	112° 53.475
[trail leaves road]	39° 50.858	112° 49.560
in valley	39° 51.418	112° 48.309
[trail crosses Riverbed Road]	39° 51.584	112° 47.428
Camp 32E—Death Canyon Wash	39° 51.800	112° 45.883
[trail crosses road to Judd Creek]	39° 51.315	112° 45.267
[trail crosses Judd Creek]	39° 53.125	112° 39.025
Camp 33E—Judd Creek	39° 53.366	112° 38.916
leave stream	39° 53.654	112° 38.646
summit	39° 54.143	112° 38.237
in valley, *cross stream*	39° 55.866	112° 37.283

Location	Latitude (N)	Longitude (W)
[Black Spring—trail joins road]	39° 56.683	112° 36.431
Erickson Pass	39° 57.937	112° 36.406
Camp 34E—Brewer's Spring	39° 59.617	112° 38.260
Government Creek Pass	40° 01.694	112° 33.962
Rush Valley	40° 01.677	112° 31.853
Camp 35E—Vernon	40° 05.733	112° 26.525
Vernon Hills Pass	40° 06.966	112° 22.494
Rush Valley	40° 09.000	112° 19.435
Five-Mile Pass	40° 13.933	112° 10.750
Camp Floyd	40° 15.541	112° 06.150

Notes

Chapter One

1. James Hervey Simpson, *Report of Explorations across the Great Basin of the Territory of Utah for a Direct Wagon Route from Camp Floyd to Genoa, in Carson Valley, in 1859* (1876; repr. Reno: University of Nevada Press, 1983), 24 (hereafter cited as Simpson).

2. Harold Schindler, *Orrin Porter Rockwell: Man of God, Son of Thunder* (Salt Lake City: University of Utah Press, 1966), 214–17; *Deseret News*, December 12, 1854. The Huntington party followed Captain Beckwith's trail as far as Lassen Meadows on the Humboldt River, then turned southwest to Genoa. Rockwell and Bean went only as far west as Redden Spring, which is found on the western edge of the Great Salt Lake Desert, seven miles north of the town of Callao.

3. Howard R. Egan, *Pioneering the West*, ed. Wm. M. Egan (1917; repr. Salt Lake City: Skelton Publishing, [1990s]), 193–94.

4. Simpson, 75.

5. Ibid., 8.

6. Ibid., 43.

7. Marie Irvine, "Soldier Hollow," *Crossroads Newsletter*, vol. 16, no. 4 (2005), 3. Presentation given to the Crossroads Chapter of the Oregon-California Trails Association, and published in their newsletter.

8. William Lee, "Journal of William Lee," [1858–1859], 5, 10, Utah State Historical Society. Copy of privately published transcription of a journal written by a member of the Simpson Expedition (hereafter cited as Lee).

9. Simpson, 6c.

10. Joseph Tingley and Kris Ann Pizarro, *Traveling America's Loneliest Road* (Reno: Nevada Bureau of Mines and Geology, 2004), 4.

11. Simpson, 77.

12. Ibid., 74.

13. Ibid., 64.

Chapter Two

1. George W. Cullum, *Biographical Register of the Officers and Graduates of the U.S. Military Academy* (New York: D. Van Nostrand 1868), 1:405–6.

Cited by Wilbur Sheridan Warrick, "James Hervey Simpson, military wagon road engineer in the trans-Mississippi West," (master's thesis, University of Chicago, 1949), 5.

2. William H. Goetzmann, *Army Exploration in the American West, 1803–1863* (Austin: Texas State Historical Association 1991), 11–12.

3. James Hervey Simpson, *Report and Map of the Route from Fort Smith, Arkansas, to Santa Fe, New Mexico*, 31st Cong., 1st sess., Senate Executive Document 12 (Washington, DC, 1850), 21–22. Cited by William H. Goetzmann, *Exploration and Empire: The Explorer and the Scientist in the Winning of the American West* (Austin: Texas State Historical Association, 1993), 272.

4. James Hervey Simpson, "Appendix A," in *Report of Lieut. Colonel James H. Simpson to Hon. James Harlan, November 23, 1865*, Annual Report of the Department of the Interior (Washington, DC: Government Printing Office, 1865), 27–29. Cited by Warrick, 118–21.

5. Goetzmann, *Exploration and Empire*, 274.

6. Goetzmann, *Army Exploration*, 240–42.

7. 31st Cong., 1st sess., Senate Executive Document 64, (Washington, DC, 1850). Cited by Warrick, 16.

8. James Hervey Simpson, "Coronado's march in search of the Seven Cities of Cobola and discussion of their probable location," in *Annual Report of the Board of Regents of the Smithsonian Institution, 1869* (Washington, DC: Government Printing Office, 1871), 309–40. Cited by Warrick, 20.

9. Cullum, 405–06. Cited by Warrick, 22.

10. Goetzmann, *Army Exploration*, 351; W. Turrentine Jackson, *Wagon Roads West* (Yale Western Americana Series, no. 9. New Haven, CT: Yale University Press, 1965), 53.

11. Cullum, 405–6. Cited by Warrick, 44.

12. Alexander D. Bache, *Report of the Superintendent of the Coast Survey, 1857*, 35th Cong., 2nd sess., House Executive Document 6, No. 35 (Washington, DC, 1858), 81. Cited by Warrick, 74.

13. Donald R. Moorman and Gene Allred Sessions, *Camp Floyd and the Mormons* (Salt Lake City: University of Utah Press, 1992), 50.

14. Letter from Simpson to Col. John J. Abert, cited in *Report of the Chief Topographical Engineer, Nov. 11, 1858*, 35th Cong., 2nd sess., House Executive Documents (Washington, DC, 1858). Cited by Warrick, 74.
15. Lee, 20; Warrick, 75.
16. James H. Simpson, *Report and Map of Wagon Road Routes in Utah Territory*, 35th Cong., 2nd sess., Senate Executive Document 40 (Washington, DC, 1858–1859), 14–23 (hereafter cited as Simpson, *1858 Report*).
17. Simpson, *1858 Report*, 27.
18. Lee, 33.
19. *Deseret News*, August 17, 1859.
20. Simpson, 67.
21. Ibid., 43.
22. Hubert Howe Bancroft, *History of Utah 1540–1886* (1889; repr. Las Vegas: Nevada Publications, 1982), 468. Goetzmann, *Army Exploration*, 285.
23. Norman E. Wright, "Odometers: Distance measurement on Western emigrant trails," *Overland Journal* 13, no. 3 (1995), 21. According to Dennis and Shirley Orr Andrus, the owners of Orr's Ranch in Skull Valley, the Gunnison odometer was found by Harrison Severe and Mathew Orr, who were among the first settlers in Skull Valley. It was passed on to Mathew Orr's son Daniel, then to Shirley and her sister Geraldine Orr Wright. It was kept at the ranch until about 1997, when the Orr sisters donated it to the museum at Brigham Young University.
24. Simpson, 45.
25. Ibid., 59–60.
26. Ibid., 56.
27. Ibid., 9.
28. Moorman and Sessions, following 176.
29. Simpson, 44.
30. Ibid., 44–45.
31. Ibid., 45. Simpson frequently referred to George Chorpenning's company as the "California Mail Company."
32. John M. Townley, "Stalking Horse for the Pony Express: The Chorpenning Mail Contracts between California and Utah, 1851–1860," *Arizona and the West* 24 (Autumn 1982), 244–45; Leroy Reuben Hafen, *The Overland Mail, 1849–1869* (1926; repr. Norman: University of Oklahoma Press, 2004), 112.
33. Simpson, *1858 Report*, 35.

CHAPTER THREE

1. Simpson, 46.
2. *Deseret News*, November 16, 1859. An article written by "Sirius," the newspaper's "Western Correspondent," mentioned that Faust was the station-keeper at Deep Creek.
3. Simpson, 46.
4. Ibid.
5. Ibid., 47.
6. Lee, 33.
7. Simpson, 47.
8. Simpson, *1858 Report*, 30.
9. Sir Richard Francis Burton, *The City of the Saints; Among the Mormons and across the Rocky Mountains to California*, (1861; repr, Santa Barbara, CA: Narrative Press, 2003), 333.
10. Simpson, 49.
11. Simpson, *1858 Report*, 31.
12. Ibid., 32.
13. Ibid.
14. *Acts, Resolutions and Memorials Passed at the Several Annual Sessions of the Legislative Assembly of the Territory of Utah*, (Great Salt Lake City: H. McEwan, 1866), 188–89. Cited by James Vaun Barber, "The history of highways in Utah from 1847 to 1869," (master's thesis, University of Utah, 1949), 39; also cited by John M. Townley, *The Overland Stage* (Reno: Great Basin Studies Center, 1994), 225.
15. Simpson, 50.
16. Ibid.
17. Horace Greeley, *An Overland Journey from New York to San Francisco in the Summer of 1859* (1860; repr. Lincoln: University of Nebraska Press, 1999), 203.
18. Burton, 337.
19. Simpson, 50.
20. Lee, 34.
21. Ibid.
22. Simpson, 50.
23. Gael S. Hoag, *Salt Lake City to Ely, Nevada*, (road guide compiled and distributed in early 1913 under the auspices of the American Automobile Association), copy in the author's possession.
24. Simpson, 51.
25. Ibid.
26. Ibid.
27. David M. Jabusch and Susan Jabusch, *Pathway to Glory; The Pony Express and Stage Stations in Utah* (Salt Lake City: Treasure Press, 1994), 8, 63; and John M. Townley, *The Pony Express Guidebook: Across Nevada* (Reno: Great Basin Studies Center, 1984), 11. The exact date of the change in the route remains elusive, but it was accomplished prior to November 16, 1859; see note 2 above.
28. Simpson, 51.
29. Ibid.

30. Lee, 34.
31. Simpson, 68.
32. Ibid., 72.
33. Ibid., 75.
34. Ibid., 67.
35. Ibid., 57.
36. Ibid., 51.
37. Ibid., 52.
38. Ibid.
39. Greeley, 265.

Chapter Four

1. Simpson, 55.
2. Lee, 35.
3. Simpson, 55.
4. Ibid., 56.
5. Ibid., 57.
6. Schindler, 317.
7. Simpson, 57.
8. Ibid., 59.
9. Ibid.
10. Ibid., 61.
11. Ibid.
12. Burton, 345.
13. Simpson, 62.
14. Ibid.
15. Ibid.
16. Ibid., 63.
17. Ibid.
18. Greeley, 268.
19. Townley, *Pony Express Guidebook,* 45.
20. Simpson, 64.
21. Ibid., 64–65.
22. Victor O. Goodwin, *"The Humboldt—Nevada's desert river and thoroughfare of the American West"*, (paper, U.S. Department of Agriculture, Nevada–Humboldt River Basin survey, 1966), 4–5.
23. Ibid., 4.
24. Simpson, 65.
25. Ibid.
26. Ibid.
27. Lee, 36.
28. Simpson, 67.
29. Lee, 37.
30. Simpson, 68–69.
31. Townley, *Overland Stage,* 244.
32. Lee, 37.
33. Simpson, 71.
34. Ibid.
35. Ibid.
36. Burton, 356.
37. Simpson, 73.

Chapter Five

1. Simpson, 73.
2. Townley, *Pony Express Guidebook,* 44–45.
3. Simpson, 73.
4. Ibid., 74.
5. Ibid., 111.
6. Ibid., 75.
7. Ibid., 111.
8. Ibid., 75.
9. Burton, 357–58.
10. Ibid., 358.
11. Townley, *Pony Express Guidebook,* 11, 39.
12. Robert D. Harter, ed., *Wagon Tracks; George Harter's 1864 Journey to California* (New York: Patrice Press, 2003), 67.
13. Simpson, 76.
14. Ibid.
15. Ibid.
16. Lee, 38.
17. Simpson, 77.
18. Ibid., 78.
19. Ibid.
20. Ibid., 79.
21. Ibid.
22. Ibid.
23. Ibid.
24. Ibid., 80, 81.
25. Ibid., 81.
26. Ibid., 82.
27. Lee, 39.
28. Simpson, 82.
29. Ibid., 106.

Chapter Six

1. Simpson, 83.
2. Ibid., 83–84.
3. Ibid., 84.
4. Ibid.
5. Ibid. This event is made stranger still by the fact that Reese had probably been in this area previously. He had been a member of the 1854 exploring party sent by Col. Steptoe and led by O. B. Huntington.
6. Ibid., 105.
7. Burton, 362–65.
8. Lee, 39.
9. Simpson, 85.
10. Ibid.
11. Ibid., 105.
12. Townley, *Pony Express Guidebook,* 28.
13. Simpson, 85.
14. Lee, 40.
15. Simpson, 86.

16. Ibid., 105.
17. Lee, 40.
18. Simpson, 86.
19. Burton, 363.
20. Simpson, 86.
21. Ibid., 86–87.
22. Ibid., 87.
23. Lee, 41.
24. Simpson, 87.
25. Ibid., 88.
26. Doyce B. Nunis, *The Bidwell-Bartleson Party: 1841 California Emigrant Adventure*, ed. Doyce B. Nunis, Jr. (Santa Cruz, CA: Western Tanager Press, 1991), 48, 174.
27. Simpson, 88.
28. Ibid., 104.
29. Ibid., 88.
30. Ibid., 89.
31. David L. Bigler, ed., *The Gold Discovery Journal of Azariah Smith* (Salt Lake City: University of Utah Press, 1990), 136; Will Bagley, *A Road from El Dorado; The 1848 Trail Journal of Ephriam Green* (Salt Lake City: Prairie Dog Press, 1991), 27. Bigler notes: "Smith's entries, including distances covered each day, indicate the company traveled by the route now known as the Fort Churchill Road, which generally follows the Carson River between today's Dayton, Nev., and Fort Churchill."
32. Townley, *Pony Express Guidebook*, 24.
33. Simpson, 89.
34. Lee, 41.
35. Townley, *Pony Express Guidebook*, 23.
36. Burton, 366.
37. Simpson, 91.
38. Ibid.
39. Ibid.
40. Ibid., 92, 93.
41. Ibid., 93.
42. Ibid., 96–97.
43. Lee, 42.
44. Simpson, 103.

CHAPTER SEVEN

1. Simpson, 103.
2. Ibid., 148.
3. Ibid., 103.
4. Ibid., 104.
5. Ibid.
6. Burton, 364. Burton used the term "cattle" to describe all livestock, including horses and mules.
7. Lee, 43.
8. Simpson, 104.
9. Ibid.

10. Lee, 43.
11. Simpson, 104–5.
12. Ibid., 104.
13. Ibid., 105.
14. Ibid.
15. Edward James Mathews, "Crossing the Plains: Adventures of Edward James Mathews in '59", n.d., 87, Nevada Historical Society, Reno (copy of privately printed work).
16. Simpson, 105.
17. Ibid.
18. Ibid.
19. Ibid.
20. Ibid., 106.
21. Ibid., 106–7.
22. Ibid., 107.
23. Ibid., 108.
24. Ibid., 107.
25. Ibid., 108. Here Simpson uses the term "North Carson Lake" in referring to what is now known as Carson Sink.
26. Ibid.
27. Ibid., 109.
28. Joe Bensen, *The Traveler's Guide to the Pony Express Trail* (Helena, MT: Falcon Press, 1995), 114.
29. Lee, 44.
30. Simpson, 109.

CHAPTER EIGHT

1. Simpson, 109.
2. Ibid., 110.
3. Lee, 45.
4. Townley, *Overland Stage*, 250.
5. Simpson, 111.
6. Ibid., 76.
7. Lee, 45.
8. Simpson, 111.
9. Lincoln Highway Association, *The Complete Official Road Guide of the Lincoln Highway*, 5th ed. (1924; repr. Tucson, AZ: Patrice Press, 1993), 473.
10. Photograph, Special Collections, Hatcher Library, University of Michigan, filing code Nev. 217. The caption with the photo reads "New route avoiding 'Ford's Defeat'; about 25 miles east of Austin, Nevada."
11. Simpson, 111.
12. Ibid., 111–12.
13. Ibid., 112.
14. Ibid.
15. Ibid., 113.
16. Ibid.
17. Ibid.
18. Ibid.
19. Ibid., 114.

20. Ibid.
21. Ibid.
22. Ibid., 115.
23. Charles M. Tuttle, "The emigrant diary of Charles M. Tuttle," *Wisconsin Magazine of History*, 15 (1931), 233.
24. Mathews, 81.
25. Simpson, 115.
26. Ibid.
27. Ibid., 116.
28. Ibid., 117.
29. Ibid.
30. Ibid., 118.
31. Ibid., 118–19.

CHAPTER NINE

1. Simpson, 118.
2. Ibid., 62.
3. Clifford L. Stott, *Search for Sanctuary: Brigham Young and the White Mountain Expedition* (Salt Lake City: University of Utah Press, 1984), 131–36.
4. Ibid., 131–32.
5. Ibid., 217.
6. Simpson, 119.
7. Ibid.
8. Ibid.
9. Ibid.
10. Ibid., 120.
11. Tuttle, 232.
12. Simpson, 120.
13. Lee, 46.
14. Simpson, 120–21.
15. Ibid., 121.
16. Ibid.
17. Ibid.
18. Ibid.
19. Ibid.
20. Ibid., 122.
21. Ibid.
22. Ibid.
23. Ibid.
24. Lee, 47.
25. Simpson, 122–23.
26. Ibid., 123.
27. John W. Van Cott, *Utah Place Names* (Salt Lake City: University of Utah Press, 1990), 112.
28. Simpson, 124.
29. Ibid.
30. Ibid., 125.
31. Ibid.
32. Owen C. Bennion, "Good Indian Spring," *Utah Historical Quarterly*, 52, no. 3 (1984), 257.

33. Simpson, 125.
34. Lee, 47.

CHAPTER TEN

1. Simpson, 126.
2. Ibid.
3. Ibid.
4. Bennion, 257.
5. Simpson, 126.
6. Ibid.
7. Ibid.
8. Ibid.
9. Ibid., 127.
10. Ibid., 142.
11. Tuttle, 231.
12. The Joy mining camp was established by Henry B. Joy in the 1880s. The mines operated for only a few years before being abandoned. Joy purchased and became the president of the Packard Motor Car Company in 1903, and became the first president of the Lincoln Highway Association in 1913. The original route of the Lincoln Highway passed only 23 miles to the northwest of Joy's mining camp.
13. Simpson, 126.
14. Ibid., 127.
15. Ibid.
16. Ibid.
17. Ibid.

CHAPTER ELEVEN

1. Simpson, 128.
2. Ibid., 129.
3. Ibid., 128.
4. Ibid.
5. Ibid.
6. Lee, 48.
7. Bennion, 256.
8. Bennion, 263.
9. Mathews, 75.
10. *Deseret News*, September 14, 1859. It is unclear whether Roberts was instructed to do so, or was simply attempting to satisfy his own curiosity, but he made a trip that followed the expedition's return route from Camp Floyd to Knoll Springs in Snake Valley. He also observed emigrants camped at what Simpson called Tyler's Spring, today's Mud Spring, at the northeast base of Swasey Mountain.
11. Simpson, 130.
12. Ibid.
13. Lee, 48; Simpson, 130, 142.
14. Simpson, 131.

15. Ibid.
16. Schindler, 337. According to Schindler, Rockwell filed on a section of property that was located on Government Creek near the Tooele-Juab county line. He obtained a patent on the property in 1874.
17. Simpson, 131.
18. Lee, 49.
19. Simpson, 142.
20. Harter, 58; George Edwin Bushnell, "A trip across the Plains in 1864" (unpublished emigrant journal), August 6, 1864.
21. Tuttle, 230.
22. Simpson, 131–32.
23. Simpson, 132.
24. "Map of central and western Utah," in *Explorations & Surveys West of the One-Hundredth Meridian: Compiled under the Direction of Brig. Gen. A. A. Humphreys, Chief of Engineers, U.S. Army* (Washington, DC: Government Printing Office, 1875), atlas sheet number 50; copy in the author's possession.
25. Simpson, 46.
26. Simpson, *1858 Report*, 26.
27. Ibid., 25.
28. Ibid., 35.
29. Simpson, 132.
30. Lee, 49.

CHAPTER TWELVE
1. Simpson, 132.
2. Ibid.
3. Ibid., 133.
4. Ibid., 142.
5. Ibid.
6. Ibid.
7. Ibid., 133–34.
8. Tuttle, 230.
9. Mathews, 75–89.
10. *Deseret News*, August 17, 1859; *Valley Tan*, August 17, 1859.
11. *Deseret News*, August 27, 1859.
12. Goodwin, 5.
13. John D. Unruh, Jr., *The Plains Across* (Urbana: University of Illinois Press, 1979), 175.
14. Simpson, 139.
15. Jackson, 194.
16. Ibid., 213.
17. Ibid., 214.
18. Maj. Fitz John Porter to Simpson, 16 November 1859. Part 2, Old Military Records, Department of Utah Letter Book, vol. 2, 393. National Archives.
19. *Washington Constitution*, February 8, 1860.
20. Lander to Simpson, quoted in "Maps and Reports of the Fort Kearney, South Pass, and Honey Lake Wagon Road," 36th Cong., 2nd sess., House Executive Document 64 (Washington, DC, 1861), 12.
21. Simpson to Lander, "Maps and Reports of the Fort Kearney, South Pass, and Honey Lake Wagon Road," 36th Cong., 2nd sess., House Executive Document 64 (Washington, DC, 1861), 13.
22. *Washington Constitution*, February 8, 1860.
23. Warrick, 117, citing Edward D. Neill, "James Hervey Simpson," *Northwest Review* (April 1883), 77–78.
24. Warrick, 116.
25. Ibid., 131–32.
26. James Hervey Simpson, *The Shortest Route to California* (Philadelphia: J. B. Lippincott, 1869), 32.
27. Bruce Catton, *Terrible Swift Sword*, vol. 2, *The Centennial History of the Civil War* (New York: Doubleday, 1963), 223.

Bibliography

Bache, Alexander D. *Report of the Superintendent of the Coast Survey, 1857.* 35th Cong., 2nd Sess., 1858. House Executive Document 6, no. 35

Bagley, Will. *A Road From El Dorado; The 1848 Trail Journal of Ephriam Green,* Salt Lake City: The Prairie Dog Press, 1991.

Bancroft, Hubert Howe. *History of Utah 1540–1886.* 1889. Reprint, Las Vegas: Nevada Publications, 1982.

Barber, James Vaun. "The History of Highways in Utah From 1847 to 1869." Master's Thesis, University of Utah, 1949.

Beeton, Barbara. "James Hervey Simpson in the Great Basin." *Montana, The Magazine of Western History* 28 (January 1978): 28–43.

Bennion, Owen C. "Good Indian Spring." *Utah Historical Quarterly* 52, no. 3 (1984): 256–57.

Bensen, Joe. *The Traveler's Guide to the Pony Express Trail.* Helena, MT: Falcon Press, 1995.

Bigler, David L. *The Gold Discovery Journal of Azariah Smith.* Salt Lake City: Univ. of Utah Press, 1990.

Burton, Sir Richard Francis. *The City of the Saints: Among the Mormons and across the Rocky Mountains to California.* 1861. Reprint, Santa Barbara, CA: The Narrative Press, 2003.

Bushnell, George Edwin. "A Trip Across the Plains in 1864" (unpublished diary, copy in author's possession).

Catton, Bruce. *Terrible Swift Sword.* New York: Doubleday, 1963.

Cullum George W. *Biographical Register of the Officers and Graduates of the U.S. Military Academy.* New York: D. Van Nostrand, 1868.

Egan, Howard R. *Pioneering the West, 1846 to 1878: Major Howard Egan's Diary.* Ed. Wm. M. Egan. Salt Lake City: Skelton Publishing, 1917.

Goetzman, William H. *Army Exploration in the American West, 1803–1963.* 1959. Reprint, Austin: Texas State Historical Association, 1991.

———. *Exploration and Empire: The Explorer and the Scientist in the Winning of the American West.* 1966. Reprint, Austin: Texas State Historical Association, 1993.

Goodwin, Victor O. "The Humboldt: Nevada's Desert River and Thoroughfare of the American West." Paper written for the US Department of Agriculture—Nevada Humboldt River Basin Survey, 1966.

Greeley, Horace. *An Overland Journey from New York to San Francisco in the Summer of 1859.* 1860. Reprint, Lincoln: Univ. of Nebraska Press, 1999.

Hafen, Leroy R. *The Overland Mail, 1819–1869.* 1926. Reprint, Norman: Univ. of Oklahoma Press, 2004.

Harter, Robert D. ed. *Wagon Tracks; George Harter's 1864 Journey to California* Tucson: The Patrice Press, 2003.

Humphreys, Brig. Gen. A. A., comp. Map of central & western Utah: Atlas sheet number 50. In Explorations & Surveys West of the One-Hundredth Meridian: Compiled under the Direction of Brig. Gen. A. A. Humphreys, Chief of Engineers, U.S. Army. Washington, DC: Government Printing Office, 1875.

Irvine, Marie. "Soldier Hollow." *Crossroads Newsletter* 16, no. 4 (2005): 3.

Jabusch, David M. and Susan C. Jabusch. *Pathway to Glory: The Pony Express and Stage Stations in Utah.* Salt Lake City: Treasure Press, 1994.

Jackson, W. Turrentine. *Wagon Roads West: A Study of Federal Road Surveys and Construction in the Trans-Mississippi West, 1846–1869.* Berkeley: Univ. of California Press, 1952.

Lander, Frederick W. Lander to Thompson, March 1, 1860. 36th Cong., 1st sess., 1860. House Executive Document 64.

Lane, D. R. "Linking Coast to Coast." *Motorland* [magazine of the California State Automobile Association], June, July, August, 1930.

Lee, William. *The Journal of William Lee, 1858–1859.* Privately published, n.d.

Lincoln Highway Association. *The Complete Official Road Guide of the Lincoln Highway.* 5th ed. 1924. Reprint, Tucson: The Patrice Press, 1993.

Mathews, Edward James. *Crossing the Plain: Adventures of Edward James Mathews in '59.* Privately published journal, 1859.

Moorman, Donald R., and Gene A. Sessions. *Camp Floyd and the Mormons: The Utah War.* Salt Lake City: Univ. of Utah Press, 1992.

Nunis, Doyce B., Jr., ed. *The Bidwell-Bartleson Party: 1841 California Emigrant Adventure.* Santa Cruz, CA: Western Tanager Press, 1991.

Porter, Maj. Fitz John. Porter to Simpson, 16 November 1859, Part 2. Old Military Records, Department of Utah Letter Book, vol. 2, 369–71. National Archives.

Schindler, Harold. *Orrin Porter Rockwell: Man of God, Son of Thunder.* Salt Lake City: Univ. of Utah Press, 1966.

Simpson, James Hervey. "Coronado's March in Search of the Seven Cities of Cobola and Discussion of Their Probable Location." In Annual Report of the Board of Regents of the Smithsonian Institution, 1869, 309–40. Washington, DC: Government Printing Office, 1871.

———. Journal of a Military Reconnaissance from Santa Fe, New Mexico to the Navajo Country Made with the Troops under Command of Brevet Lieutenant Colonel John M. Washington, Chief of the Ninth Military Department and Governor of New Mexico. 31st Cong., 1st sess., 1850a. Senate Executive Document 64.

———. Report and Map of the Route from Fort Smith, Arkansas, to Santa Fe, New Mexico. 31st Cong., 1st sess. 1850b. Senate Executive Document 12.

———. Report and Map of Wagon Road Routes in Utah Territory. 35th Cong., 2nd sess. 1858–59. Senate Executive Document 40.

———. Report of Explorations across the Great Basin of the Territory of Utah for a Direct Wagon Route from Camp Floyd to Genoa, in Carson Valley, in 1859. 1876. Reprint, Reno: Univ. of Nevada Press, 1983.

———. Report of Lieut. Colonel James H. Simpson, on the Union Pacific Railroad and Branches, Central Pacific Railroad of California, Northern Pacific Railroad, Wagon Roads in the Territories of Idaho, Montana, Dakota, and Nebraska, and Washington Aqueduct, Made to Hon. James Harlan, Secretary of the Interior, November 23, 1865, Appendix A. 27–29. Annual Report of the Department of the Interior. Washington, DC: Government Printing Office, 1865.

———. The Shortest Route to California: Illustrated by a History of Explorations of the Great Basin of Utah with Its Topographical and Geological Character and Some Account of the Indian Tribes. Philadelphia: J. B. Lippincott, 1869.

———. Simpson to Col. John J. Abert, November 11, 1858. In Report of the Chief Topographical Engineer. 35th Cong., 2nd sess., 1858–59. House Executive Document 11.

Stott, Clifford L. *Search for Sanctuary: Brigham Young and the White Mountain Expedition.* Salt Lake City: Univ. of Utah Press, 1984.

Tingley, Joseph, and Kris Ann Pizarro. *Traveling America's Loneliest Road: A Geologic and Natural History Tour through Nevada along Highway 50.* Reno: Nevada Bureau of Mines and Geology, 2000.

Townley, John M., *The Pony Express Guidebook: Across Nevada with the Pony Express and Overland Stage Line.* Reno: Jamison Station Press for the Great Basin Studies Center, 1984.

———. *The Overland Stage: A History and Guide Book.* Reno: Jamison Station Press for the Great Basin Studies Center, 1994.

———. "Stalking Horse for the Pony Express: The Chorpenning Mail Contracts between California and Utah, 1851–1860." *Arizona and the West* 24 (Autumn 1982): 229–52.

Tuttle, Charles M. "The Emigrant Diary of Charles M. Tuttle," *Wisconsin Magazine of History* 15 (1931): 219–33.

Unruh, John D. Jr. *The Plains Across: Overland Emigrants and the Trans-Mississippi West, 1840–60.* Urbana: University of Illinois Press, 1979.

Utah, Territory of. Acts, Resolutions and Memorials Passed at the Several Annual Sessions of the Legislative Assembly of the Territory of Utah. Great Salt Lake City: H. McEwan, 1866.

Van Cott, John. *Utah Place Names: A Comprehensive Guide to the Origins of Geographic Names.* Salt Lake City: Univ. of Utah Press, 1990.

Warrick, William Sheridan. "James Hervey Simpson, Military Wagon Road Engineer In The Tran-Mississippi West; 1849–1867." Master's Diss., University of Chicago, 1949.

Wright, Norman E. "Odometers; Distance Measurement on Western Emigrant Trails." *Overland Journal* 13, no. 3 (1995): 14–21.

INDEX

Death Canyon Wash, 204
Deep Creek, 20, 232n3
Deep Creek Mountains, 31–32, 35, 37, 192
Delta, Utah, 13
Desatoya Mountains, 76, 81, 83, 87–88, 134–35, 138, 141
Deseret News, 11, 219–20
Desert Mountains, 105, 107
Desert Spring, 208
Devil's Gate, 153
Devil's Hole, 27–29, 31
Diamond, Jack, 59
Diamond Mountains, 33, 56, 59, 151, 153, 155–56
Diamond Springs, 59
Diamond Valley, 59, 61, 153
Disappointment Hills, 180
Dodge, Frederick, 117–19, 135, 138
Dodge Valley, 138. *See also* Edwards Creek Valley
Dome Canyon, 181–83, 185
Domínguez and Escalante, 2
Donner-Reed Party, 1, 53, 220
Drum Mountain, 191–92, 211, 217–18
Drumm Summit, 94
Dry Creek, 65, 69, 71, 73
Dry Flat Valley, 94 . *See also* Fairview Valley
Dry Mountain, 158–59
Duchesne, Utah, 220
Duck Creek, 44, 165
Dugway Mountains, 10, 22–23, 25, 27
Dugway Pass, 23, 25, 27, 193
Dugway Station, 23
Dunyon, Louis, 28, 189, 193, 211

E

Eagle Butte, 71, 73
Eagle Valley, 113, 115
East Government Creek, 213–14
Eastgate, 44, 90–92
Eastgate Creek, 90, 94
Eastgate Wash, 90–92, 134
Edwards Creek, 135, 138
Edwards Creek Canyon, 138
Edwards Creek Valley, 140
Egan, Howard, 1–2
Egan Basin, 46, 48
Egan Canyon, 44, 46, 48
Egan Mountains, 44, 48, 159, 161, 163
Egan's Springs, 22. *See also* Simpson Springs
Eightmile Flat, 96, 98, 133
Elko, Nevada, 1, 52, 55
Ely, Nevada, 161, 163, 165–66, 170
Emigrant Pass, 76, 18, 143, 146
Empire, 113
Engelmann, Henry, 4, 11, 83

Engelmann Creek, 83
Erickson Pass, 208, 210–11
Eskdale, Utah, 175, 177–78
Esqueviara, Jim, 62, 65–66
Eureka, Nevada, 56, 153, 155
Eureka County, 63

F

Fairfield, Utah, vii, 15
Fairview Valley, 94
Fallon, 101, 110, 127, 129
Fallon Naval Air Station, 98–99
Faust, Henry "Doc", 16, 19–20, 232n2
Faust Creek 15–16, 19–20, 214
Faust Railroad Station, 10
Faust Ranch, 16
Faust Station, 19, 44, 214
Fillmore, 161, 165, 188
firearms, 33, 117, 163, 161
Fish Springs, 27, 29, 31–32, 42
Fish Springs Flat, 28–29, 191
Fish Springs Mountains, 29, 31
Fish Springs Ranch, 31
Fish Springs Wash, 31
Fish Springs Wildlife Refuge, 29, 31
Five Mile Pass, 15–17, 214, 216
Floating Island, 183
Fool's Cutoff, 73
Ford's Defeat, 148, 234n10
forge, 11
Fort Bridger, vii, 10, 222
Fort Churchill, 111, 124, 127, 129, 135, 234n31
Fort Kearny, 10
Fort Laramie, 121
Fort Leavenworth, 5, 10, 13, 121, 218, 220
Fort Schellbourne, 44
Fort Smith, 8
Forty-Mile Desert, 138
Fountain Spring, 150
Fourmile Flat, 96, 98, 133–34
Frémont, John Charles, viii, 1–2, 55–56, 63, 105, 223

G

Garcés, Father Francisco, 2
Garden Pass, 61
Garden Pass Creek, 61
Gate of Gibraltar, 90. *See also* Eastgate
Gate of Hercules, 5, 161, 16. *See also* Hercules Gap
General Johnston's Pass, 10, 19–20, 22, 211, 213, 218, 220. *See also* Lookout Pass
Genoa, Nevada, vii–viii, 1–2, 5–7, 11, 111, 115, 117–19, 121, 135, 138, 150, 218, 231n2
Gibraltar Canyon, 88. *See also* Road Canyon